GW00703247

ISBN 978-1-330-03203-9
PIBN 10008664

FB &c Ltd, Dalton House, 60 Windsor Avenue, London, SW19 2RR.
Company number 08720141. Registered in England and Wales.

For support please visit www.forgottenbooks.com

EGYPT
AND HOW TO SEE IT

ILLUSTRATED BY A. O. LAMPLOUGH

NEW YORK
DOUBLEDAY, PAGE & CO.
LONDON: BALLANTYNE & CO. LTD.

This work has been written and published under the supervision of the Egyptian State Railways, Cairo. A French edition is published by Hachette et Cie., Paris, and a German edition by Adolf Sponholtz, Hannover and Leipzig

PREFACE

The present book is not designed to supplant the many existing guide-books on Egypt, nor—though every effort has been made to ensure accuracy—does it purport to serve as an infallible book of reference to archæologists. Its object is, rather, to aid the visitors to this country by indicating that which is most worth seeing, where they should go, and how they may economise time, money, and fatigue to the greatest advantage.

Cairo and Alexandria, Upper Egypt, the Fayoum, and Lower Egypt are dealt with chapter by chapter, and their interests, characteristics, and chief features presented.

To the text are added appendices giving detailed and practical information of every kind; these have been made as complete as possible. Time-tables and similar particulars, which vary from time to time, are arranged so as to apply to the coming winter season, *i.e.*, November 1907 to April 1908. In subsequent annual editions, not only will the text be revised, but the appendices will be brought up to date, so as to be correct for the following season.

This guide-book is also published in French and German editions.

Cairo,
October 1, 1907.

CONTENTS

CONTENTS

LIST OF ILLUSTRATIONS

LIST OF ILLUSTRATIONS

THE SKETCHES HAVE BEEN REPRODUCED AND PRINTED IN COLOUR AT THE BALLANTYNE PRESS, LONDON

In the desert, Tel-el-Kebir

CHAPTER I

GENERAL INFORMATION

THE best months for Egypt are from October to May. The weather is delightful all through, save for a very few days. In the worst years, indeed, one may possibly count ten days that are not quite perfect, but a few showers, one or two days of rain, and perhaps one day of rather hot wind and dust in April are all one need expect. The rest is sunshine and warmth such as even the Riviera cannot afford.

Of routes there is a very wide choice: one can go by long sea, which takes from twelve to fifteen days and is certainly cheapest, or one may go from Marseilles, Genoa, Naples, Venice, Trieste, Brindisi, or Constantinople. The shortest route is, of course, *via* Brindisi, and takes four and a half days. Full particulars are given on page 202.

It is as well to secure a passage early, as, especially in the late autumn, the boats may be crowded. One may note here that it is almost always possible to secure a place in the P. & O. Brindisi Mail Express, even at the last moment.

As to clothes and general equipment, no very special measures need be taken. Ordinary English summer clothing is quite adequate, though it is best to take a few thick things as well. Moreover, Cairo is quite as fashionable, from the point of view of dress, as a European capital, and affords plenty of occasions for wearing smart clothes.

Cairo has plenty of shops, and one can procure almost anything necessary. The prices are in some cases a little higher than in Europe. Special outfits, tropical helmets, smoked glasses, green veils, &c., are really never wanted in winter, except once in a way for an excursion in the desert on a very hot day. Sometimes at Luxor or Assouan, or for Sakkara, one requires a little protection against glare and sun, even in the cold weather, but never in Cairo, Alexandria, or in most parts of Egypt for that matter. For such requirements Cairo affords quite as good, if not better, choice than can be found in London.

A luncheon- and tea-basket is useful, and should certainly be brought.

Amateur photographers can procure films at any of the chief tourist resorts at reasonable prices (Cairo, of course, has several photographers' shops), and they can have their photographs developed, or can do this themselves in the dark-rooms provided in most of the hotels.

Those who wish to do any shooting had better not bring cartridges, as most steamship companies put difficulties in the way of the transport of small quantities of ammunition. Cartridges can be obtained in Alexandria and Cairo. For shooting licences and other particulars *see* page 171.

Visitors can, if they wish, hire very good private carriages for the whole or part of their stay, and can almost always find a coachman who knows some English.

Motorists who bring their cars will find good roads in and about Cairo and Alexandria, but that will be about their limit. The country roads are primitive, and in most cases quite impossible for motoring. There are several good garages in Alexandria and Cairo. For particulars as to licence and other information *see* page 170.

From January to the middle of March the hotels are apt to be full, and one should engage rooms beforehand by letter, or there may be trouble on arrival. Full information as to hotels, &c., is given on page 155 *et seq.*, and references will be found in the various articles on Cairo, Alexandria, Luxor, Assouan, &c. &c.

Those who wish to explore the country thoroughly may

be recommended to procure either Baedeker's "Egypt" (price 15*s.*) or Cook's "Egypt and the Soudan" (Professor Wallis Budge, price 10*s.*). These works enter minutely into every possible detail.

Egyptian Money.—The Egyptian pound consists of 100 piastres. A piastre (pt.) is worth about 2½*d.*, 25 centimes, or 5 cents.

English and French gold, particularly the former, are in circulation everywhere. An English sovereign is worth 97½ pt.; a French napoleon is worth 77 pt.

RAILWAY ARRANGEMENTS

Many people are surprised when they come to Egypt to find a railway system which can compare in most particulars with those of Europe and America. There are some 1500 miles of railway, with about 270 stations, under State management, besides a large number of light railways.

The most important trains are composed of large double-bogie corridor carriages of the latest design, lighted by electricity or gas. On all the principal expresses dining- or luncheon-cars are provided, and for the longer journeys sleeping-cars; these are of the well-known type used all over Europe, and are run under an arrangement with the Wagon-Lits Company.

There are three classes of carriages; the thirds, however, are somewhat different from those in England, and it is very unusual to see a European travelling third class. Fares are, on the whole, considerably cheaper than those of English railways. A short journey costs more in proportion than a long one. The second-class fare is half the first-class, and the third half the second.

Return tickets are not issued at present, except on one or two of the suburban lines. No luggage is carried free, except that which is taken by the passenger into the carriage. Special trains, saloons, and the conveyance of carriages or motor-cars can be arranged for at short notice; particulars on these points are given on page 197.

ARRIVAL IN EGYPT

Port Said.—We are told that we are within ten minutes of Port Said; yet we see nothing but water—then, all at once, a collection of houses, and a low-lying line of sand. and the ship is in the channel steaming between buoys De Lesseps' statue dominates the harbour ; one outstretched finger points to his work, the great waterway that joins East to West.

Boats crowd round, full of shouting Arabs, and the moment the ship stops there ensues a rush of frenzied hawkers and minstrels. They sell cigarettes—beware of these—lace, post-cards of more or less dubious interest, Reuter's telegrams, newspapers, anything that may extort piastres. Cook's is a fair remedy if one has much baggage, though a single man of parts and experience may well fight for his own hand, take one of the native boats, and arrive even before Cook's men. The Customs are not exacting as to personal effects ; guns, bicycles, and a few other accessories—one may call them impersonal or commercial—are liable to a duty of 8 per cent. on their value.

Port Said is hardly a place at which to stay. The town is not interesting, and it has few amusements.

One unique phenomenon there is at Port Said, the coaling by night—a hurricane of flying natives, lit up by braziers that flare through the uncanny mist of coal-dust. They fling their boards against the ship, rush up with full baskets, hurl the coal into the bunkers, and rush down again. It is a very inferno of haste and efficiency.

The hotels here are fair as to accommodation. The Savoy, on the sea-front, and the Eastern Exchange, in the centre of the town, are the two best.

If possible, it will be well to take the train at once. There are three trains a day, at 8.10 A.M., 12.30 P.M., and 6.45 P.M. The two latter have dining-cars, and the journey takes from four and a half to five hours. Port Said is 237 kilometres (about 150 miles) from Cairo. The fares are: First class, 95 pt. ; second class, 47½ pt. In the restaurant-car 25 pt. is charged for dinner and 20 pt. for lunch. The full time-table is given on page 175.

Leaving Port Said, the line runs parallel to the Suez Canal and the "Sweetwater" Canal, Port Said's only source of fresh water. On the right is at first the shallow Lake Menzaleh, where one sees, in the winter time, quantities of water-fowl, and now and again pelicans and flamingoes of vivid plumage—rose, scarlet, and flame-coloured. Kantarah, about twenty-five miles from Port Said, is one of the points in the ancient caravan route between Egypt and Syria. It is still used by Bedouins. Pharaohs, Persians, Arabs, even the French under Napoleon, have used that track. It is curious to see ships gliding slowly and silently past, as it

On the banks of the Sweetwater Canal

were, over the sand. One hardly realises that they are on a canal.

From Ismailia to Abou-Hammad is all sand. Tel el-Kebir is in this stretch, and one can still see traces of the British trenches on the right-hand side of the line.

After Zagazig—a large railway and commercial centre—the country is really no more than a vast market garden; almost every yard is under cultivation. Benha, the junction for Alexandria, is the only town of importance after Zagazig; and half an hour after Benha the train enters the suburb of Choubra, and at last steams under the great single arch of Cairo station.

Alexandria.—The arrival at Alexandria is not very impressive; there is a long, low breakwater, a dusty grey line of shore with dusty grey buildings. Inside the breakwater is a forest of masts—"ferry-boats," as the Anglo-Egyptian styles all passenger ships to and from Europe—trading steamers of many lines, colliers near the great active coal-hoists, and little sailing-boats cruising up and down the harbour.

Certain steamship lines have made arrangements with the Railway Administration whereby in winter special trains meet their boats on the quay, and carry passengers direct to Cairo. Passengers by other lines have to fend for themselves. Information on this point can best be obtained from the steamship companies themselves. The Custom House is on the quays, and there are always plenty of cabs. The drive to the station takes about half an hour, first through narrow native streets, then into the wide Place Mohammed Aly and up Rue Cherif Pacha—a fine modern street—thence past the big police station into the railway terminus. The cab fare is 5 pt. For those who wish to pass a few hours, or even a night, in Alexandria there are the Khedivial, Windsor, and Savoy Hotels, all three of which are good. One can go to see Pompey's Pillar, or else drive out to Ramleh in the afternoon. A fuller description of Alexandria is given in Chapter VII.

The journey to Cairo, 130 miles, by express, takes from three to three and a half hours, according to the class of train. The principal trains are·

	A.M.	A.M.	NOON.	P.M.	P.M.	P.M.	P.M.
Alexandria, dep.	7. 0	9. 0	12.0	3.40	4.25	6. 0	11.30
Cairo, arr.	10.25	12.20	3.5	7.10	7.25	9.20	6. 0 A.M.

The 12.0 train has a luncheon-car and the 6.0 P.M. a dining-car. For detailed time-table *see* page 174. The fare, first class, is 87½ pt.; second class, 43½ pt. Sleeping-car supplement on the 11.30 P.M. train, 30 pt.

The journey from Alexandria to Cairo does not possess any great features of interest; the country, once one has left the rather desolate Lake Mariout, is characteristic of the Delta—canals, crops, and camels. Damanhour, standing on a hill, or rather mound—picturesque at a distance—Kafr Zayat, a cotton centre, Tantah, the third largest town in Egypt, but not otherwise of much interest, and Benha, are the only four places worth mentioning on the route.

Tantah, where all the trains stop, has one merit on a warm day, in that boys rush up and down the platform and offer

Near Ramleh

fruit and lemonade, or whisky and soda, and suchlike drinks, often welcome half-way through the journey.

OUTLINE TOURS

Visitors who have only a short time at their disposal may find assistance as to the best way of using it in the three outline tours here given. These tours are not meant to be taken as hard-and-fast schemes, but may be altered and modified to any extent to suit individual requirements.

The Egyptian State Railways do not bind themselves in any way as regards the railway connections shown below.

(1) A Three Weeks' Tour in Egypt

Day.

1. Arrival at Alexandria, or Port Said.
2. (If Alexandria.) Morning: See Pompey's Pillar and the Catacombs. Afternoon: Expedition to Aboukir.
3. Travel up to Cairo.
4. May be devoted to exploring Cairo—Museum, Mosques &c.
5. Visit to Helouan or the Ostrich Farm at Matarieh.
6. In the afternoon visit the Sphinx and Pyramids of Gizeh.
7. Expedition to Sakkara (train from Cairo to Bedrechein, 9.30 A.M.).
8. Spend the morning in Cairo. Visit the barrage in the afternoon.
9. Fayoum and Lake Moeris. Start at 8.30 A.M. from Cairo; change at Wasta; arrive Medinet-el-Fayoum at 11.16. After exploring the town proceed to Abchaway by train at 8.39 P.M., and sleep at the Lake Moeris Hotel.
10. Spend the morning on the lake and return by the train at 4.4 P.M. to Medinet-el-Fayoum.
11. Fayoum to Assiout. Leave Medinet-el-Fayoum at 8.18 A.M., catching the express at Wasta at 9.59 A.M., and arrive at Assiout at 3.45 P.M. If desired, the rock tombs of Beni Hassan can be seen on the way. In this case leave the express at Abou Kerkas at 1.24 P.M., and proceed from Abou Kerkas at 5.15 P.M., reaching Assiout at 8.0 P.M.
12. Expedition to Tel-el-Amarna (lunch should be taken from the hotel). Leave Assiout by the train at 8.59 A.M.; arrive Dair-Moës (for Tel-el-Amarna) at 10.45 A.M.

Leave Dair-Moes at 4.15 P.M.; arrive Assiout 5.59 P.M.

13. Assiout to Luxor, stopping on the way to see either (*a*) the temples of Abydos or (*b*) the temple of Dendera. (Provisions must be taken.) For (*a*) leave Assiout at 8.56 A.M., arriving at Baliana at 12.37 P.M. Leave Baliana at 7.14 P.M., arriving at Luxor at 10.40 P.M. For (*b*) leave Assiout at 5.20 A.M., arriving at Keneh at 11.58 A.M. Leave Keneh at 6.50 P.M.; arrive Luxor at 8.15 P.M.

14.
15.
16. } Luxor. By following the directions given under "Distribution of Time" on page 97 the principal monuments of ancient Thebes can be examined.

17. Luxor to Assouan. The temple of Esneh can be taken on the way. In this case leave Luxor at 6.20 A.M., arriving at Esneh at 8.45 A.M. Leave Esneh by the express (dining-car attached) at 12.16 P.M., and arrive at Assouan at 5.0 P.M. If it is desired to go straight to Assouan, leave Luxor at 10.30 A.M. by the express, arriving at Assouan at the same time.

18. Assouan—the bazaars, Bishareen camp, and ancient quarries.

19. Assouan—Philæ and the Dam. Leave Assouan at 9.0 A.M. or 10.45 A.M. for Shellal (half-hour by train). The return from Shellal can be made by train at 2.50 or 6.0 P.M. A pleasant alternative is to take a boat at the Dam and return by river.

20. Assouan to Luxor and Cairo. If direct, leave Assouan at 10.15 A.M; arrive at Luxor at 4.45 P.M. By leaving Assouan at 5.50 A.M. it is possible to see the temple of Edfou on the way. The train arrives at Edfou at 10.28 A.M. Leave Edfou by the express (dining-car) at 1.38 P.M., arriving at Luxor at 4.45 P.M. Leave Luxor by the *train de luxe* at 6.30 P.M., or by the night mail at 5.30 P.M.

21. Arrive in Cairo at 8.0 A.M., or 7.5 A.M. respectively, and proceed to Alexandria or Port Said.

(2) Fifteen Days' Tour in Egypt

1. Arrival at Alexandria or Port Said. (If Port Said, it will be best to leave the same night and spend an extra day in Cairo.)
2. Travel to Cairo.

On he Mahmoud eh Cana A exandria

3. } See the sights of Cairo.
4. }
5. Fayoum. Leave Cairo 8.30 A.M.; arrive Medinet-el-Fayoum at 11.16 A.M.
6. Fayoum to Assiout. } Details are given in the "Three Weeks' Tour."
7. Expedition to Tel-el-Amarna. }
8. Assiout to Luxor. }
9. } At Luxor. (*See* "Distribution of Time,' page 97.)
10. }
11. Luxor to Assouan. (*See* "Three Weeks' Tour.")
12. } At Assouan.
13. }
14. Assouan to Luxor and Cairo. (*See* "Three Weeks' Tour.")
15. Arrive in Cairo 8.0 A.M. Proceed to Alexandria or Port Said.

(3) Another Arrangement for Fifteen Days

1. Arrival at Alexandria or Port Said, and proceed to Cairo.
2. }
3. } Can be spent in Cairo.
4. }
5. }
6. Fayoum. Leave Cairo for Medinet-el-Fayoum at 8.30 A.M., arriving at 11.16 A.M. Leave Fayoum at 5.34 P.M.; arrive Wasta at 6.30 P.M., and catch the *train de luxe* for Luxor at 8.0 P.M.
7. Arrive at Luxor at 8.35 A.M.
8. } Can be spent at Luxor. (*See* "Distribution of Time," page 97.)
9. }
10. }
11. Luxor to Assouan. (*See* "Three Weeks' Tour.")
12. } At Assouan.
13. }
14. Assouan to Luxor and Cairo. (*See* "Three Weeks' Tour.")
15 Arrival in Cairo 8.0 A.M. Proceed to Alexandria or Port Said.

CHAPTER II

CAIRO

As the train comes to a standstill in Cairo station the visitor is besieged by a crowd of hotel porters, but this need cause no annoyance. If rooms have been engaged previously, all that is necessary is to pick out the representative of the particular hotel chosen. He will take charge of the luggage and lead the way to the hotel omnibus outside.

First to be considered are the hotels. Driving from the station, one reaches "Shepheard's" in a few minutes; then just beyond it is the Continental. Turn to the right and you pass the Angleterre, then, going towards Kasr-el-Nil, the National and the Savoy. On the river-bank, just to the south of the bridge, is the new Semiramis, in Kasr-el-Doubara, a great quarter for the wealthy residents. If you go over the bridge, and to the right hand, you reach Ghezireh Palace and its garden. Here also are the fashionable villas.

There are several other hotels, more economical, but quite comfortable: the Métropole, Eden Palace, New Khedivial, and Bristol. There are, too, plenty of *pensions:* the Imperial, Carlton House, Villa Victoria, Rossmore House, Pension Sima—to mention a few only. It is also possible to hire a furnished flat for the winter; so there is no lack of choice where to stay.

The Savoy is perhaps the premier hotel, situated at the corner of Kasr-el-Nil and Suliman Pasha streets, a very pleasant part of the town. It is a favourite *rendez-vous* of Cairo rank and fashion. The restaurant, for which the hotel is noted, is always crowded with smart diners-out during the winter. The Savoy Saturday night dances are among the most popular events of the Cairo season.

"Shepheard's" is famous all over the world, and hardly needs recommendation; it always maintains its well-deserved popularity. The hotel is situated not far from the station, in the principal street of the town. In front there is a fine

Bulac and Citadel from Ghezireh

terrace, on which a band usually plays in the afternoon during tea. There is a pretty garden at the back, with shady trees and flowers, and also a tennis-court. The interior is decorated in Arab and Egyptian style; the restaurant and lounge in particular are remarkable.

The Continental is a large new hotel facing the Opera Square and the Esbekieh Gardens, and offers many attractions to its patrons. The terrace has a most animated appearance. This hotel has the most central position of any, and is conveniently near the best shops and the bazaars; in fact, it is a good starting-point for all the sights of Cairo.

A smaller and quieter hotel, the Angleterre, in Sharia-el-Magraby—is greatly appreciated by those who desire a quieter life than is possible in the larger establishments; it is, however, first class, and quite as well managed as any of the big hotels.

The new Hotel Semiramis, only opened last season, is one of the best situated in the town, being alongside the Nile, close to the Kasr-el-Nil bridge, and in the fashionable Kasr-el-Doubara quarter. From its terrace visitors may enjoy one of the most extensive and picturesque views of Cairo. The interior arrangements of the hotel are, needless to say, quite up to date and most comfortable from every point of view.

The Ghezireh Palace Hotel is on the island of Ghezireh —a fashionable suburb. The building was once a palace of the Khedive Ismail, and the decorations are in the most gorgeous and lavish style. As a hotel it ranks with the best; it is about two miles out of Cairo, and the dust and noise of the town are avoided. The distance is no drawback, as there is an electric omnibus as well as plenty of carriages ready to convey visitors all over Cairo; there is also a steam ferry across the Nile. The gardens in which the hotel stands are as beautiful as any in or near Cairo; on the east side is the broad smooth stream of the Nile.

These gardens are gay all the winter through with flowers, and have many shady walks where one may escape for a time from the bustle of the town. During the season a band plays every afternoon on the terrace. In the grounds is the Casino. where the fancy-dress dances and many other festivities are held. A small dance is also held every Thursday in the hotel. Close by are the grounds of the Sporting Club, where polo, golf, tennis, and croquet are played, and where the races take place every fortnight during the season.

Mena House Hotel, at the Pyramids, must not be forgotten; it is about eight miles from Cairo, and is connected with it by a good service of electric trams. The hotel is built on the edge of the desert, close to the Great Pyramid—an ideally healthy spot. The management is excellent, and the arrangements as comfortable as at any hotel in Egypt.

For full particulars of the hotels *see* pages 155–158.

Cairo is the successor of Amru's city El-Fostat, founded in 641 A.D. Its foundations were marked out by Gawhar, the commander-in-chief of the Caliph Muizz, in 969 A.D., and it was named El-Kahira "The Victorious," as the moment when the digging was commenced was signified by Mars being in the ascendant. It was a walled city with gates—Bab-el-Nasr, Bab-el-Foutouh, and Bab-el-Zouileh. The Citadel was built by Saladin. We need not dilate here on its history, but we may cite the quaint and delightful description of it by one Richard Johnson, an Elizabethan, who wrote the lives and exploits of "The Seven Champions of Christendom." Really his impression of Cairo is too good to lose. Apparently the chronology is about 500 A.D., though we find a Ptolemy reigning in Egypt contemporary with Coventry's best mediæval period. Another charming anomaly is that the Great Pyramids are in Greece, and not at Gizeh; but of course in those days there were Paladins, fair distressed ladies, dragons, magicians, and fairies galore, and all this may well compensate for a mere chronological or topographical inaccuracy!

"Grand Cairo," says Richard Johnson, "was then under the subjection of the Egyptian monarchy, and the greatest city of the world; for it was in breadth full three score miles, and had by just account within its walls twelve thousand churches, besides abbeys, priories, and houses of religion. When St. George with his stately attendants entered the gates, they were presently entertained with such a joyful sound of bells, trumpets and drums that it seemed like the inspiring music of heavenly angels, and to exceed the royalty of Cæsar in Rome when he returned from the world's conquest: the streets were beautified with stately pageants contrived by scholars of ingenious capacity, the pavement strewed with all manner of odoriferous flowers, and the walls hung with Indian coverlets and curious tapestry."

Well-a-day! Cairo can hardly, even now, attain the gorgeous dimensions and aspect pictured by the writer's genial fancy, but it is a fine city, and of great extent: to the east and south Abbassieh, the Citadel, then Old Cairo, then Ghezireh; then Boulac, once the port of the metropolis; then, going northwards, Choubra—such are its boundaries. It has well over half a million inhabitants, and a very large European community, and is no mean city in appearance. Stand on the ramparts of the Citadel, and you will see the countless houses and mosques, the quiet, broad stream of the Nile, and, far off, the sharp grey forms of the Pyramids. Turn round, and the old dead town is below you, silent, a city of tombs; hard by, they seem close together, tombs and voiceless huts; farther off, where the desert begins, are the domed shrines, more sparse and conspicuous, of the Caliphs and Mamelukes, under the shadow of the Red Mountain and the Mokattams. To the north are the villages on the Matarieh line, a long string of European houses—almost a new city—ranging from Pont de Koubbeh out to Matarieh itself. Beyond is desert, and the low hills that seem to bound it—palest, clearest yellow and white. One far-off native village, Kafr Gamous, stands out like a tiny fishing hamlet. Its minaret might be the lighthouse at a harbour mouth.

Cairo at present has a slightly unfinished aspect, owing to the immense amount of building involved by the extraordinary incursion of people of all sorts and nationalities during recent years. Those who only knew Cairo ten or fifteen years ago cannot recognise it now, with its crowded streets, fine shops, high white houses, huge hotels, and expansion on all sides. Where were almost waste places are now streets; what was native suburb is now a European quarter.

A walk through the main streets is interest enough in itself. You pass "Shepheard's," its balcony crowded with curious and amused tourists. Hawkers of all sorts are yelling, or coaxing possible purchasers, offering postcards, ornamental fly-whisks, walking-sticks, shawls, "antikas," scarabs fresh from the factory. Snake-charmers and boys with tame monkeys are performing their antics on the sidewalk. Carriages and foot-passengers crowd the road and pavements. At the open-air *cafés* are sitting crowds of Egyptians or—in the evening—foreigners of all kinds. The street widens out at the

Opera Square; to the right hand are shops, opposite them the Opera House, and to the left the railed-in Esbekieh Gardens; straight on is the wide Midan Abdin, close to Abdin Palace. Four main streets lead to the right from the square: the Boulac road, just before the Continental Hotel, as yet rather a dingy, tram-haunted street, though it will be fine enough in four or five years' time, when the Boulac-Ghezireh bridge is built; the Sharia-el-Magraby, wherein is the Angleterre Hotel and also the Turf Club—a fine, open street; then the Sharia-el-Manakh, the Bond Street of Cairo; and the Sharia Kasr-el-Nil, which leads to the Savoy Hotel.

One may go to the Kasr-el-Nil Bridge and look up the river. The Semiramis, the British Agency, and other great houses line the bank; down stream are the barracks, followed by the quaint, native buildings of the Boulac quarter, and a mile or so away is the Embabeh railway bridge. The island of Ghezireh consists practically of the Sporting Club grounds, and the quarter where are all the villas, to the north. All the afternoon and evening smart carriages and motor-cars career round it, and strings of polo ponies pass to and from the polo ground. The road straight on from the bridge and then to the left is one long avenue all the way to Gizeh, and thence to Mena House and the Pyramids.

The Kasr-el-Nil bridge, which connects Cairo with Ghezireh, is opened every day from 1.30 P.M. to 3 P.M. to allow the boats to pass up and down. At that hour it is impossible to cross the bridge, and the only way to get to Ghezireh is by ferry (*see* page 199).

The various interests on the Ghezireh side of the river are the Khedivial Sporting Club, the Aquarium and Grotto, the Zoological Gardens, and the Public Works Department plantations. These last are well kept, and have many beautiful trees and shrubs.

KHEDIVIAL SPORTING CLUB

The Khedivial Sporting Club is the great resort of the English, and most of the European colony. It has a twelve-hole golf course, twelve asphalt tennis-courts, several squash racquet courts, polo grounds and croquet lawns, and a race-course (flat and for steeplechasing). There is an excellent grand stand, and paddock with a quantity of stalls. The race-meetings are almost always crowded. The totalisator is in use (*pari mutuel*), and tickets on the horses can be taken for LE1, or by less wealthy backers for 20 pt. As the principle of payment is the division of receipts, less the percentage due to the totalisator (which goes to the funds of the racing club), one's winnings vary. A favourite whom every one supports may not even pay back his full dollar, and outsiders backed by a few only have been known to pay 60 to 1. Visitors can become temporary members if introduced by a member of the club; they should apply to the secretary. For subscription and entrance to the grand stand on race days *see* page 164.

Cab fares to the Sporting Club from Cairo: Single, 5 pt.; return, 15 pt. (waiting one hour). To the grand stand on race days, return, 30 pt. (waiting three hours).

For particulars of other clubs *see* page 164.

THE ZOOLOGICAL GARDENS

The Zoological Gardens, a great resort of fashionable Cairo on Sunday afternoons, are at Gizeh, close to the plantations. The gardens are well laid out and worth seeing, and the collection of animals—about a thousand specimens—is very interesting.

The gardens are open daily from 9 A.M. till sunset. Entrance: Weekdays, ½ pt.; Sundays, 5 pt. (children, 1 pt.). Tea can be had on Sundays. Cabs from Cairo: Single journey, 10 pt.; return, after waiting two hours, 20 pt. It is also possible to go by tram from Kasr-el-Nil bridge.

THE AQUARIUM

The Grotto and Aquarium, on the island of Ghezireh, can just be seen through the trees on the right-hand side of the road past Ghezireh Palace Hotel entrance. In spring it is one large mound ablaze with geraniums of all sorts and hues, a perfect mass of colour through the dark foliage and stems. The Aquarium contains a quantity of different varieties of Nile fish. It is open daily from 8.30 A.M. till 5 P.M. Entrance: Weekdays, ½ pt.; Sundays, 1 pt. Cabs from Cairo, 15 pt. return, including a wait of an hour.

CHURCHES

The principal English Protestant church—All Saints, the parish church of Cairo—is in Boulac Road, nearly opposite the telegraph office and close to the Turf Club. Services are held at 10.30 A.M. and 6 P.M. every Sunday; Holy Communion at 8.30 A.M. on Sundays, Fridays, and Saints' Days; also after the morning service on the first and third Sundays in the month.

St. Andrew's Church (Church of Scotland) is in Sharia Kasr-el-Nil, next door to the British headquarters. Services are held at 10.30 A.M. and 6 P.M. every Sunday.

The American Mission Church (Presbyterian) is in Sharia-el-Miliguy, near Shepheard's Hotel.

St. Joseph's Church (Roman Catholic) is situated in the Ismailia quarter. The services during the winter season are Sundays and Holy Days, first mass 6 A.M.; mass with sermon in English at 11 A.M. Weekdays: Mass at 6, 7 and 8 A.M.

AMUSEMENTS

One need never be dull in the evening. Every night there is sure to be some kind of entertainment at one or the other of the hotels—dances, fancy-dress balls, cotillions, and concerts.

There are regular weekly dances—on Saturday at the Savoy, Thursday at Ghezireh Palace, and Monday at Shepheard's. Mena House and the Helouan hotels give dances from time to time, and also, once or twice in the season, a gymkhana.

MUSIC

As far as music is concerned, a musical society for quartette and chamber music in general is being founded by a large and influential section of the more musical members of the community. Hitherto the Cercle Artistique (Sharia-el-Madabergh) gave almost the only concerts in Cairo, but every one now realises that it is high time to devote more attention to these things.

The Khedivial Opera House is a fine theatre situated in the centre of the town. It is under a committee of management, who engage a company for the whole winter. Many well-known operas are given. It is somewhat difficult, however, to secure seats, as nearly all the boxes and stalls are held for the season by *abonnés*.

The new Abbas Theatre is most enterprising, and has met with well-deserved success since it started a short time ago.

Italian opera, grand, and light and French *opera bouffe* have met with success worthy of the management. It can hold nearly twelve hundred people, and is not uncomfortable. It is, however, more or less of a temporary nature. All Cairo is hoping for a grand new theatre, plans for which are being studied.

There is in the Ezbekieh Gardens a small theatre, where light French plays are from time to time given (though operas have been attempted also). Occasionally these are really amusing and well acted, though they are naturally of the "Capucines" order—vaudevilles and farces.

There is an Arab theatre in the Ezbekieh quarter, where Arabic (and, be it said, rather weird) versions of Shakespeare are given, and there are sundry Arab music-halls, where the more curious can see native dancing and hear native singing.

THE BAZAARS

The native bazaars are a great institution. They are situated in or near the Mousky, which is the original and oldest commercial street in Cairo—narrow, crowded, picturesque, and quite unlike any other thoroughfare in the city. People of all nationalities and in every sort of clothing pass up and down, or in and out of the big wholesale shops.

About half a mile up the Mousky (beyond the tram crossing) there is a turning on the left; in this are the booths of goldsmiths, small native jewellers, and, further down, copper vendors. About a hundred yards along this side-street is a turning on the right called the Khan Khalil; this is the Turkish bazaar—the best of all the bazaars. The Khan Khalil is very narrow, and parts of it are covered in; its devious paths lead past shops of every kind—jewellers, carpet-sellers, shawl-sellers, amber merchants, brass and copper smiths, Indian and Persian vendors of every and any kind of curio or ornament. Of course one can hardly hope to pick up treasures. Far too many keen dealers have exploited Cairo at various times to leave any really precious "finds." But one can—often at quite a reasonable price—buy charming turquoises, peridots, and other stones. There are quantities of fine carpets and praying-mats, swords, spears, *courbags* (Soudanese rhinoceros-hide whips). As all the wares are exposed to the fullest possible view, it is worth passing through the bazaars, if only to see so motley an exhibition.

The shopkeepers are very civil and zealous to engage the attention of all possible buyers. One has to bargain in most cases, but it is a genial process, sweetened by many cups of coffee, Persian tea, sherbet of sundry kinds, Turkish delight, cigarettes, and suchlike delicacies, and if the purchaser knows the value of the objects he is buying he can be certain of procuring them at their proper price.

On the other (right-hand) side of the Mousky there is a street leading off to the right (exactly opposite the one to the left mentioned above); it widens, and eventually, after various turnings, reaches the Bab-el-Zouileh, whence one can reach the town by Mohammed Aly Street. In this street and the turnings off it are the scent bazaars, and various small shops where one can buy the native blue cloth and other attractive stuffs. But the sellers are all natives here, and very few of them understand English. Instead of turning to the right at the Bab-el-Zouileh, one can go almost straight on into a covered street, where are shoes, native saddlery, and various kinds of leather work. An archway on the right-hand side is the entrance to a courtyard off which is a tent-maker's shop—the street, indeed, is called the Market of the Tent-makers (Souk-el-Kheyamieh). In the shop in question is sold the Akmim cloth, a species of tapestry depicting ancient Egyptian figures of all sorts—animals, men, boats—and every sort of design, in gay colouring. There is a sword bazaar up the Mohammed Aly Street, where are all kinds of weapons.

The chief shops in the Mousky bazaar are: Khauchand (Turkish bazaar), Elias Habib (brass bazaar), Joseph Cohen (a very excellent shop for carpet, embroidery, &c., and perhaps the best place for precious stones). Malluk and Hatoun are the names of two big merchants in the Mousky Street. Malluk has a large collection of mushrabiyeh (or lattice) woodwork, inlaid work, &c.

Cabs from the Opera Square to the bazaars, 5 pt.; or return, after waiting, 15 pt.

MOSQUES

The mosques of Cairo represent some of the finest examples of Oriental architecture, though many of the older buildings have been allowed to fall into a sad state of disrepair. A committee has, however, been formed to undertake their preservation, and under its auspices considerable progress has been made towards the restoration of those of greatest interest.

To obtain admission the visitor must be provided with tickets, costing 2 pt. each, and obtainable at the hotels, tourist agencies, Post Office, or at the mosques themselves.

All visitors have to put on large Arab slippers (provided at the mosques) over their boots—a compromise with the Moslem injunction to take off shoes or boots before entering.

For the sake of convenience, we may divide into two groups those mosques which, from their antiquity or other associations connected with them, are most worthy of a visit: (1) those in the neighbourhood of the Citadel, and (2) those situated in or about the Mousky quarter. Those of the first category can be visited in the morning, and the others in the afternoon.

The Sultan Hussan, situated close to the Citadel, is a fourteenth-century mosque of vast dimensions. The massive gateway is 85 ft. high, with a stalactite domed roof. Inside is the vestibule, which, as the mosque is at present undergoing restoration, is used as a place of worship. The work of restoration will be very thorough, and is expected to take two years to complete. The court is 115 ft. long and 105 ft. broad, and has a large fountain in the centre. It is cruciform in shape, the arms of the cross being formed by four large recesses, which were reserved for the four sects of Islam. The arches of these recesses are very fine, especially that towards the east, the span of which is 70 ft. Under this is the *dikkeh*, or reading-desk, and behind that the *kibla*, or praying niche, ornamented with various inlaid marbles. To the right of the *kibla* is the *nimbar*, or pulpit. A door to the left leads to the mausoleum, in the centre of which is the tomb of the founder of the mosque.

To the left, immediately on entering the courtyard, there is a doorway leading into a *madrassah*, or school, containing 365 rooms, formerly occupied by students. The top stone of this doorway is formed of eleven pieces of black and white marble dovetailed together. The south minaret is the highest in Cairo (280 ft.).

The building has at various times served as a fortress, and lodged in the outer walls may be seen cannon-balls which the French fired from the Citadel.

The unfinished mosque opposite is the Rifaiya, containing

the tomb of the Khedive Ismail. It was built during his reign.

The Mohammed Aly Mosque is actually inside the precincts of the Citadel. Its domed cupola and two slender, graceful minarets are more conspicuous than anything else in Cairo. From any and every point of view the mosque stands out, boldly Oriental, against the dull, dead grey-brown of the hills behind it, dominating Cairo. The mosque was built by Mohammed Aly, the founder of the present Khedivial dynasty; the architect was a Greek from Constantinople. In the court is a fountain, and in the tower to the west is a clock presented to Mohammed Aly by Louis Philippe of France. The interior of the mosque is not very imposing, and the large number of hanging lamps has a rather tawdry effect. The columns and walls are of alabaster up to a certain height. To the right is the tomb of Mohammed Aly, enclosed by a railing.

To the east of the Mohammed Aly Mosque is the so-called "Joseph's Well." It is 290 ft. deep, and on it, in former days, the Citadel depended for its water-supply. Round the well-shaft winds a passage, cut through the rock; half-way down is a platform where was formerly the water-wheel, or *sakkieh*, driven by oxen, which raised the water to the surface.

It is said that when the Citadel was built in the twelfth century Saladin Yusuf discovered the well full of sand and caused it to be cleared. It is called after him, and not after the Joseph of Scripture.

The Ibn Touloun Mosque, built in 879 A.D., is the oldest in Cairo. The walls are of brick, coated with stucco.

The Kait Bey Mosque (fifteenth century), near the Ibn Touloun, is small, but has a most graceful minaret. On the pulpit is some fine carving, and the mosaics on the walls and floor are worth notice.

These mosques will probably take up all the morning.

The Mousky Mosques.—El-Azhar Mosque is in the Sharia El-Halwagi, a turning off the Sharia Mousky. It dates from 972 A.D., in which year Gawhar completed it. In 988 A.D. it was converted into a university, the largest to-day in the Mohammedan world. It has students (about eight thousand in all) from every country, and over two hundred professors. The subjects are, first and foremost, the Koran and its commentaries, and then the "profane" subjects studied in the

Middle Ages. All modern learning and knowledge is ignored. The education is entirely free. Four of the nine rows of pillars in the *liwan*, or sanctuary, were contributed by one Abd-el-Rahman, whose tomb is in the building. This *liwan* is the principal hall of instruction (about 3600 sq. yds. in area). The students sit on their heels round their respective professors, and pay a varying degree of attention to his lecture.

The Sharia Sanadikiah leads from El-Azhar to El-Ghouri Mosque, the interior of which is interesting. Close to it is the Mosque El-Moulaiyad (1415 A.D.). Its fine bronze gate was taken from the Sultan Hassan Mosque. The roof is supported by marble columns, and the lower part of the back wall, inlaid here and there with coloured marble, has seven niches. The upper half is illuminated with texts in gold lettering from the Koran. The roof is of dark material, on which are worked gold arabesque patterns. The pulpit is fine. The whole building was recently restored, and appears, in consequence, cleaner and better preserved than other mosques.

The Mosque of El-Hassanein—close to the Sikket-el-Badistan—dedicated to the two grandsons of the prophet Hassan and Hussein, is the scene of the annual festival of the Shi'ite sect of Mussulmans (chiefly Persians). There is a procession through the principal streets at night, led by dervishes, who cut at one another with swords and cover themselves with blood.

The Muristan, or Hospital of Kalaoun, and the Barkuk Mosque (1410 A.D.) are close together in the Sharia El-Nahasseen, or street of the coppersmiths, who occupy the lower parts of the Muristan.

The Mosque of El-Hakim, further on, has two good minarets. It has also the interest of being nearly as old as the Ibn El-Touloun Mosque (990 A.D.). The two gates of Bab-el-Foutouh and Bab-el-Nasr are close at hand. They and this mosque were fortified by the French. From the Bab-el-Nasr one can get a carriage—there are always plenty standing there—and drive back to one's hotel.

THE MUSEUM OF ANTIQUITIES

The Government collection of Egyptian antiquities, by far the most complete of any in the world, is housed in a large new building close to the Nile and near the Kasr-el-Nil bridge. The cupola over the main entrance can be easily seen at a distance. It is about ten minutes' drive from the Opera Square (cabs, 5 pt.).

The museum is open every day, except Fridays and Mohammedan holidays, from 9 A.M. till 4.30 P.M. in winter.

The entrance is 5 pt. Catalogues are on sale in the building—in English 20 pt. and in French 16 pt. There is a "Salle de Vente" where genuine antiquities can be bought at their proper price.

The ground floor contains the heavier monuments, statues, sarcophagi, stelæ, &c., and the upper floor is devoted to mummies and other less bulky objects.

Ground Floor

The Great Gallery.—In the west wing are sarcophagi of the Ancient and Middle Empire, and in the east wing those of Saite and Ptolemaic dynasties.

The Portico.—Two red granite sphinxes and two colossal statues, one of Amenhotep and the other of Rameses II., are the principal features. There are also two large wooden funeral boats from Dahshur.

Rooms A to F.—Monuments of the Ancient Empire, found mostly at Memphis, Gizeh, and Abydos.

Room A.—Two sacrificial tables in alabaster, each of which is supported by lions.

Room B.—In front are two pillars with palm capitals brought from the temple of Unas, fifth dynasty. A fine diorite statue of King Khephren (fourth dynasty), in which he is represented life-size, seated on a throne, supported by lions; a falcon protects the king's head with outstretched wings. On one side of the king is a wooden statue (found at Sakkara); the smiling face and the modelling of the body are very lifelike: it is called the "Sheikh El-Balad" by the Arabs. On the other side is a squatting scribe in coloured limestone writing on a leaf of papyrus. In the corner to the left is a relief showing a large ape biting a man's leg; the pained look of the victim is most amusing.

Rooms C and D contain a collection of memorial statues and stelæ.

Room E.—Here is a most valuable historical inscription which records the exploits of one Una under the three Pharaohs Teti, Pepi, and Merenra.

Room F contains a beautiful lotus-bud pillar of the fifth dynasty. In a glass case are statues of Prince Rahetep and his wife, Princess Nefert; the colouring is remarkably fresh, and they are amongst the most charming things in the museum. The eyes are made of coloured quartz, and the figures have an exceedingly lifelike appearance. There are also two fine limestone statues of Ranafer, priest of Ptah, and a remarkable statue in bronze of Pepi I., found at Kom-el-Ahmar: the face, hands, and feet are cast (*cire perdue*), the body is hammered out.

Rooms G to L contain monuments of the first Theban Empire.

Room G.—Reliefs from tombs; a mutilated sphinx discovered in the ruins of El-Kab. The objects here are mostly of the transition period before the twelfth dynasty.

Room H.—Wooden statue of the thirteenth dynasty, King Horus. Red granite statue of King Sebek-em-Saf, found at Abydos. Alabaster table of offerings of Princess Nefru-Ptah. Limestone statue of King Amenemhet III. Statue, probably of Mentuhetep I., of the eleventh dynasty, in the garb of Osiris.

Room L.—Tomb chamber of Harhotep, brought from Thebes and restored. Ten fine limestone statues of Usertsen I. of admirable workmanship. A stele on which the straight red lines and small squares made by the artist as a guide when cutting out the hieroglyphics are still visible.

Room J.—Colossal bust of a king of the Middle Empire, with the name of King Merenptah afterwards added, and another colossal statue of King Usertsen IV. from Karnak; also the headless statue of a Hyksos king found at Bubastis.

Room K.—Stelæ from the Middle and early New Empires.

Room L.—Statues of the Hyksos or "shepherd kings." Note the Semitic features, denoting their foreign origin.

Room M.—Statues and stelæ of the eighteenth and nineteenth dynasties. A most remarkable figure of the goddess Hathor in the form of a cow, found recently at Deir-el-Bahari; the colouring is wonderfully well preserved. Fine head in black granite, probably of Harmhabi. Memorial stone of the victories of Amenhotep III., and a sacred serpent dedicated by this king to the temple of Harkhont-Khaiti. Triumphal monument of Thothmes III. from Karnak.

Room N.—Several statues of the lion-headed goddess Sekhet in black granite.

Gallery O.—Stelæ from Abydos and Thebes.

The North Portico.—At the top of the staircase leading to the Atrium are two statues of Ptah, god of Memphis, and a very interesting stele bearing an inscription which is the earliest mention of the Israelites—" Israel is wasted and his seed brought to nothing."

Room P.—Antiquities belonging to the eighteenth and nineteenth dynasties, including several cynocephali (the dog-headed ape sacred to Thoth). A sphinx of Rameses II. A group of Tai and his sister Naye ; the resemblance between the two is striking.

Room Q.—Statues, stelæ, and inscriptions of the nineteenth and twentieth dynasties.

Rooms R and S.—Monuments of the Ramesside period.

Room T.—A statue of Apit-Zoueri, the goddess of births, from Karnak ; the body is in the form of a hippopotamus. Remains of a monolithic chapel of King Nectanebo II.

Room U.—Monuments of the Bubastide or twenty-second dynasty, Saite and twenty-sixth dynasty.

Room V.—Saite and Ptolemaic monuments

Room X.—Monuments of the Ethiopian dynasty. Alabaster statue of Queen Amenhartes. Head of Taharku (the Tirhakah of the Bible). Stele of Piankhi, B.C. 760.

Room Y.—Græco-Roman monuments. A Roman lady. A stele inscribed with the celebrated " Decree of Canopus." A trilingual inscription of Cornelius Gallus, extolling his military exploits in Egypt.

Room Z.—Saite and Græco-Roman monuments.

Room A^1.—Stelæ of the Græco-Roman period.

Room B^1.—Relief from Luxor of Isis and Serapis killing a gazelle.

Rooms C^1 and D^1.—Coptic monuments, tombstones, architectural fragments, capitals of various kinds.

Upper Floor

The Great Gallery.—The mummies and coffins of the priests of Amen and their families, discovered in 1891 by M. Grébaut near Deir-el-Bahari, and dating from the twenty-first and twenty-second dynasties. Each body had an outer and an inner coffin of wood, shaped like a mummy and coated with yellow varnish. The arms are crossed upon the breast, the hands of the men being clenched, those of the women open. The women also have ear-rings.

South Room.—A collection of toilet instruments, statuettes, vases, sticks, and ornaments. In case "G" is part of a triumphal chariot found in 1903 in the tomb of Thothmes IV. It is adorned with very fine representations in relief; the surface is of linen and stucco, originally covered with gold. There is also the reproduction of an Egyptian war-chariot of the eighteenth dynasty; the original is in the museum at Florence.

Room A.—A collection of metal mirrors, also musical instruments, children's toys, sandals, and toilet articles.

Room B.—Pottery and bronze articles.

Room C.—Foundation deposits from Deir-el-Bahari, miniature hatchets, awls, chisels, &c.; statuettes of various periods; amulets found with mummies of the Saite, Ptolemaic, and Greek periods.

Room D.—Funerary statuettes, small funeral barks, caskets, &c. In glass case "S" is a unique example of a sailing-boat of the Middle Empire period.

Room E.—Funerary statuettes and Canopic jars or vases, in which were placed the internal organs of the deceased after being embalmed.

Room F.—Mummy coverings, &c.

Room G.—Manuscripts on papyrus and linen.

Room H.—Writing and painting utensils, palettes, colours; writing on wooden tablets, fragments of pottery, &c.

Room I.—Papyri, drawings on stone and papyrus; one, representing the weighing of the soul, is of extremely good workmanship.

Room J.—Furniture and domestic utensils. Beautiful fragment of a painted pavement from the palace of Amenhotep III. at Medinet Habu. A plan of the tomb of Rameses IX. on a slab of limestone.

Room K.—Weights and measures.

Room L.—Stamped bricks, bronze locks, and door fastenings.

Room M.—Græco-Roman and Coptic remains.

Room N.—Terra-cotta of the Græco-Roman period.

Gallery O.—Græco-Roman statuettes, mummy coverings, and masks in coloured plaster.

Northern Hall.—Statues of gods in stone, bronze, and glazed ware.

Room P.—Contains a splendid collection of ancient Egyptian jewellery.

Gallery Q.—Coffins and mummies of Theban princes and princesses of the twenty-first dynasty.

*Rooms R to C*1.—Contain the royal mummies. This is the largest and most interesting collection in the world.

*Room D*1.—Objects from the earliest Egyptian tombs.

Opening off the great gallery are two rooms containing a collection of arrow-heads, flints, and tools of the Stone Age, used for quarrying in prehistoric times ; also several natural history specimens.

KHEDIVIAL LIBRARY

The Khedivial Library is situated in the Sharia Mohammed Ali, on the left-hand side going towards the Citadel, about fifteen minutes' walk from the Post Office. Tramways also pass the door. It was founded by the late Khedive Ismail Pacha, and removed in 1904 from somewhat unsuitable quarters in the Darb-el-Gamamiz to the fine building which it now occupies. It is open in winter every day except Fridays and Mohammedan holidays from 8 A.M. till one hour before sunset.

Admission is free, but to enter the reading-room and newspaper-room a card is required, which is obtained free on application to one of the attendants.

There are over sixty-six thousand volumes in the library Half of these are in European languages and deal with various subjects—history, geography, and the different sciences ; the other half consists of books in Oriental languages. There are more than thirteen thousand Arabic manuscripts.

In a wing of the building especially set apart for them is a very fine exhibition of illuminated Korans, dating for the most part from the fifteenth and sixteenth centuries. This collection numbers seven hundred in all, and is the finest in existence.

Among the other treasures may be mentioned: Papyri from the first century of the Hegira, *i.e.*, 622–719 A.D. ; a copy of the Koran from the Mosque El-Amr, written about 725 A.D. ; two very large copies, one of which belonged to the Sultan Khish Kadam (1461–1467 A.D.) and the other to the Emir Kait Bey (1468–1495 A.D.), the latter measuring 43¾ in. by 35 in. ; some Persian MSS. of the fifteenth century, with old Persian bindings ; and an Indian album containing thirty-four miniatures of great beauty. To these may be added the Kudatku Bilik, the oldest book in the Turkish language, composed about 1110 A.D. and written in Cairo about 1350 A.D.

There is also a collection of over four thousand coins in gold, silver, and bronze, of the Umaïyad and Abbassid Caliphs and the Mameluke, Turkish, and Circassian dynasties, &c., forming the greatest collection of Egyptian coins extant.

THE ARAB MUSEUM

This is in the same building as the Khedivial Library, but the entrance is round the corner to the left from the latter, in the Midan Bab-el-Khalk.

It is open in winter every day except Fridays and Mohammedan holidays from 9 A.M. till 4.30 P.M.

A catalogue is on sale at the price of 20 pt.

The very fine collection of Arab antiquities, brought in many cases from old Cairo mosques, but also from Upper and Lower Egypt, is divided amongst fifteen rooms. The different objects are arranged separately, and as far as possible in chronological order.

Room 1 contains objects in stone and marble, chiefly funerary stones.

Room 2 contains ornamental objects in stone and marble.

Room 3 contains mosaics, casts, &c., and some very fine examples of mushrabieh work, a large chandelier from the Sultan Hassan Mosque, and other interesting objects in marble.

Room 4 contains some very old carvings in wood, leaves of a door from the mosque of Kalaoun, prayer niches and reading-stands for the Koran, &c.

Room 5 contains four massive old doors, two dating from the thirteenth century and two from Turkish times, mushrabieh work, lattices, &c.

Room 6 contains carved-wood ornaments and doors.

Room 7 contains Arabic tables beautifully inlaid with ivory, wooden nimbar stairs and pulpits from mosques, boxes to hold the Koran, &c.

Room 8 contains mushrabieh work, pulpits, and mosaic stone pavement.

Rooms 9 *and* 10 contain metal work, bronze plated doors, Koran boxes in yellow metal inlaid with silver, engraved vases of ancient workmanship.

Room 11 contains earthenware (faience), some samples of native work, very valuable dish in cornelian, picture of the Ka'aba at Mecca, enamelled on earthenware, made in 1726. In glass cases, fragments of pottery of beautiful design.

Room 12 contains decoration in stucco brought from an Arab room behind the church of Abu Sephen in Old Cairo, &c. &c.

Room 13 contains an interesting room from an Arab house in Rosetta.

Room 14 contains a number of beautiful old hanging-lamps, richly enamelled bottles, and vases.

OLD COPTIC CHURCHES

The old Coptic churches of Cairo are difficult to find, hidden away in out-of-the-way corners, unsuspected by the uninitiated. No tapering spires or Gothic towers indicate their presence. They are unpretentious buildings, very old, somewhat neglected-looking. They keep modestly out of sight, as if the persecutions to which the Copts were exposed in bygone days have made them fearful of exposing themselves to the broad light of day. A simple cross over the doorway or on the top of some little belfry alone distinguishes them from the other buildings which crowd upon and almost overwhelm them.

Their interior has little architectural adornment. They are very small, and can only contain a hundred or so of worshippers at most. To make up for this, perhaps, three churches are in some cases found together or only a few yards apart. They are generally divided into three sections by screens, running transversely across the church, and where there is no gallery another screen forms a lateral division which shuts off the women from the men: the sexes are always kept apart.

At the very back, separated from the main body of the church by a screen, is the *nekal*, or sanctuary, where is the altar; access to this is reserved for the priest and his assistants and those about to take Communion. Another curious feature is the fact that there are no chairs or seats of any kind. The few worshippers squat on the floor, or, at certain parts of the service, stand, and as this wearies them in the course of the almost interminable service they provide themselves with crutches upon which to lean.

The service is very primitive, consisting chiefly in long extracts from the Scriptures, according to the ritual for the day, read by the priest in either Coptic or Arabic. The priest is attired in a long black robe, and wears a fez, round which is wound a turban of black cloth. This is a relic of the old days when, according to the laws imposed upon them by their Arab conquerors, the Copts were obliged to wear this dress to distinguish them from the Moslems. They are generally assisted in the service by boys, who form the choir, carry the censer, and help to read the prayers.

The majority of the ancient Coptic churches are to be found in Old Cairo. The best way to reach them is by the tram which goes down the Sharia-el-Ainy, starting originally from the Ataba El-Kadra, near the Post Office (the "Clapham Junction" of all the trams). The road is lined with private houses as far as Kasr-el-Ainy Government Hospital, near which is the Kasr-el-Ainy Mosque, where are the Howling Dervishes. Just before reaching the Aqueduct (built in 1518 A.D.) a road turns off to the left, passes the old English cemetery, and leads to the Convent of St. Menas (Deir Mari Mena), marked off from the other buildings by a small cross on a little belfry. It is surrounded by a wall, in which is a gateway leading to a courtyard. Another doorway opposite opens on to a little court, and thence into the precincts of the church.

Outside the entrance are the boots of the few worshippers attending the service. The walls of the apartment are whitewashed, and on two sides are some old pictures representing the Virgin Mary, the Crucifixion, and other scenes from the New Testament; opposite is a kind of balcony reached by a pair of movable steps. The floor is covered by a well-worn carpet, bordered by rush matting. In the centre is a small well containing water, with which, on the Thursday of Holy Week, the priest performs the ceremony of washing the feet of his congregation; opposite this are a pair of burning tapers in rude candlesticks, and close to them a lectern. From the beams in the roof, suspended by ropes, are glass candelabra of common but no doubt ancient workmanship. Around the walls are pictures of saints. In the centre is a reading-desk, with a large Bible, printed in Coptic characters down the centre, with Arabic translation at the side. On the left hand, separated by a screen, is the sanctuary containing the altar.

There are also two other churches here, close together, but they do not call for any special remark.

One has now to return towards the Aqueduct, and to keep to the east side of the Helouan railway for about a mile. Just past the new Protestant cemetery is a high wall enclosing a garden of palm-trees, and terminating in a small dwelling-house, on the side of which is a plate bearing the name of Chareh Gamehamr. In the corner formed by this building and an old brick wall is a doorway which leads through winding lanes between the houses to the Der Abu Sefen. This comprises three churches, one of which is being restored, and contains a fine old ebony screen inlaid with ivory, an altar casket which dates from the year 1280 A.D., and an altar in marble. It is in a better condition than the church of Deir Mari Mena.

From Abu Sefen the way lies along the Helouan railway line towards the village of Kasr-esh-Shamas, the inhabitants of which are nearly all Copts. At the second level crossing one must turn to the left. Nearly opposite is a short incline leading towards a door in the wall, whence a narrow winding path leads between the dwelling-houses to the church of Abu Sergeh. It is larger than the others, though its size cannot be properly appreciated as it is divided up by screens. On the screen separating the sanctuary from the rest of the church are some very fine old carvings. Underneath the church is a crypt, older than the church itself, reached by a dark flight of steps, where is pointed out an alcove where, according to tradition, the Virgin Mary rested after the flight into Egypt. It also contains an old baptismal font.

A little way further on is a new Greek church, circular in shape. Passing round the side of this a narrow, winding path leads to the beautiful little church of St. Barbara.

Just opposite St. George's railway station a large archway, bearing inscriptions in Arabic, leads into a courtyard; from the other side a broad flight of steps leads towards the church El-Moallaka, much finer than any of the others. Above is a gallery for the women, with mushrabieh windows, through which they can look but remain themselves unseen. The screen dividing off the altar is a beautiful piece of workmanship, being composed of carved ebony and cedar inlaid with ivory. There are some very old pictures of saints and one of the Virgin Mary, which is said to be nine hundred years old. The most interesting object is, however, the pulpit, probably dating from the twelfth century. The church itself was probably built in the sixth century; it is, however, in a remarkably well-preserved condition. In the corner of the right aisle is a cabinet containing caskets in which are said to be preserved the bones of St. Barbara and of other saints.

The return journey may be made from St. George's station by the Helouan railway to Bab-el-Louk station, or by crossing the line and continuing towards the Nile the terminus of the tramway may be reached.

Two churches in the Mousky quarter are worth seeing. They are situated in the Sharia Zuwila, a lane leading out of the Sharia-el-Souren, which is the first turning to the left after passing the tram-line which crosses the Mousky. The churches are built one above the other; the upper one is divided, as in the case of the other churches, by screens, and contains the usual pictures of saints, among which are those of the Virgin, St. Theodore, and St. George, which, according to an inscription, are four hundred years old. The gallery above is occupied bv nuns, who are hidden from sight by a tall screen.

Below the level of this church, and communicating with it by a flight of stairs, is the other, dedicated to the Virgin. It has been recently restored, but great care has been taken to leave it as much as possible in its original state. In an annex is shown a greatly venerated picture of the Virgin Mary and Child; the hands of the Child and the tiara which surrounds His head are of silver.

HELOUAN

Helouan has a certain distinction in that it is, so far, the only modern "desert" town in the north of Egypt. Its chief merits are the fine air and the sulphur baths. Obviously it is more a resort for invalids than for others, yet many prefer it even to Cairo. A group of houses on yellow sand, the range of high, sheer hills to the east, the broad plain down to the river, and, beyond, the Pyramids, Sakhara, Dahshur, and in the far distance Mena—such is Helouan, brilliant, clear-cut, and wind-swept, in keen sunlight. In the evening all is enhanced by the glorious colouring of the sunset: the Pyramids stand out to the last; at first sharp and red, they become dim purple shapes, and then fade with the fading colours. The hills—the Mokattam range—appear as a grim blue-black wall, with intense black depths and profound shadows.

Those who stay at Helouan, if not invalids, will find a fair amount of occupation. There are two or three race meetings and sometimes a gymkhana during the season. Of an evening dances and concerts are held from time to time at the hotels or Casino. The Survey Department Observatory, which is the Greenwich of Egypt, is high up on the hill at the back, and deserves a visit. There are *wadies* or valleys to be explored; purely torrential gullies, full of stones, great and small, carried down by the rush of water from the hills. A few tracks of hare or gazelle appear. A little sparse vegetation—starved, stunted shrubs—shows that moisture now and again exists in these clefts. They give a curious effect of winding desolation.

There is some tennis to be had, and there is also the golf course, with noble hazards. True, the heavy sand here and there and the unduly fast "greens" are occasionally exasperating, but the joy of the three or four difficult "carries," the delight at a fine iron-shot taken clean and full off the difficult surface—these are compensations. It is a real test of good golf.

To give a few practical details: Helouan is about fifteen miles south of Cairo, on the eastern bank of the Nile. The town stands in the desert two hundred feet above the river. Bab-el-Louk is the station for Helouan; it is about five minutes' drive from the Savoy Hotel and eight minutes from the Opera Square. The journey takes about half an hour by the fast trains. The time-table will be found on page 189. Helouan's sunshine average is high—about eight hours per day from November to April—and the average temperature about 60° Fahrenheit. It seldom falls below 60° or rises above 72°. There is scarcely ever any rain.

Helouan is a great place for throat, lung, and digestion troubles; the fine, pure, dry air is about the best remedy possible for these. It has also an excellent bath establishment; the water comes from various thermal springs that rise in the desert. It is stronger than any sulphur-water in Europe, and is known in the medical world for its wonderful curative powers in cases of stiff joints, rheumatoid arthritis, sciatica, chronic gout, and skin affections.

Hotels.—There are several first-class hotels at Helouan, furnished with everything that can ensure the comfort and entertainment of visitors.

The "Grand" is opposite the casino; it has a garden, tennis-courts, and a croquet lawn. The interior arrangements leave nothing to be desired, as the rooms are large and comfortably fitted and the management is excellent. The Helouan Golf Course and Club House belong to the "Grand," and are a great attraction to visitors.

The Tewfik Palace was built as a palace by the Khedive Tewfik Pacha, who greatly appreciated Helouan and often stayed there. The hotel is about ten minutes from the station and close to the racecourse; it also possesses a tennis court.

The Hotel des Bains: this hotel has the advantage of being close to the baths; it is quiet, and the charges are moderate.

El-Hayat—the Sanatorium—high up the hill-side, on the desert, is a comfortable hotel, and is furnished with modern conveniences.

These are the principal hotels, but there are many smaller ones as well as pensions and nursing-homes. A few of these may be mentioned: The Hotel Heltzel, Pension Antonio, Pension Loir, and The Winter Hotel. These can be recommended.

For full particulars of the hotels, *see* pages 158, 159.

There is an English church in Helouan and a resident chaplain. All through the winter there is a resident doctor who is in charge of the baths.

The sports we have already mentioned. The race meetings are held by the Helouan Sporting Club under the rules of the Cairo (Khedivial) Sporting Club. There are bands at the Casino Gardens and at the hotels, and concerts and dances are given from time to time. To the sights which can be visited from Helouan, one may add the Monastery, tombs and caves at Massarah, four miles away and ten minutes by train. The stones for the Pyramids came from these caves, in which are many inscriptions and names. The places of interest at the Cairo end of the line—such as the Aqueduct, Coptic churches, &c.—we mention elsewhere under Cairo; but they can quite easily be reached from Helouan. Further, the Delta Light Railway Company have erected a stand for the ceremony of the Holy Carpet at the Citadel, and the principal hotels sell tickets for train fares and admission thereto.

On the edge of the Palm-grove, Marg

ZEITOUN, MATARIEH AND MARG

Some twenty years ago, beyond Abbassieh, there was nothing but desert, a few tiny hamlets on the cultivated land, the palm-groves of Marg, and then more desert as far as Khanka and Abou Zaabal quarries. Away to the right hand is the bank of the former railway to Suez, and beyond that the watch-towers along the old Suez road.

All this has been changed since the railway line was laid from Pont Limoun (close to Cairo main-line station) to Marg. The villages have become European suburbs, with quantities of flats and villas. Every one is building right and left, and a large proportion of the European colony live there. At Palais de Koubbeh is H.H. the Khedive's palace and his beautiful gardens. At Zeitoun, further on, is a good hotel (The Grand Hotel, *see* page 159). Zeitoun has also a small but flourishing tennis club with two asphalt courts.

Matarieh has its own special interest apart from the other villages in that it occupies the site of ancient Heliopolis, or On, as it was called, the city of the sun god. The priesthood was most powerful here, and at times rivalled even that of Thebes. The city seems to have been in existence in the fourth dynasty, but its great period was the reign of Usertsen I., B.C. 2433, who rebuilt the temple and dedicated it to Horus-Rā—*i.e.*, the rising sun, and Teum, the setting sun, incarnate in the Mnevis Bull. He set up two obelisks before the temple, of which one was thrown down in the thirteenth century. The other still stands—the only visible remnant of that great city. It has on it an inscrpition. Dr. Wallis Budge's translation reads as follows :

"The Horus, the one born of life, King of the South and North, Kheper-Ka-Rā. Lord of the shrine Nekhebet. Lord of the shrine Uatchet, the one form of life, the Son of the Sun. Usertsen of the Spirits of Annu, beloved living for ever, the Golden Horus, the one born of life, the beautiful God, Kheper-Ka-Rā, in the first day of the Set festival truly he made this obelisk, the giver of life for ever."

Joseph, it is said, married the daughter of Potiphar, a priest of the city. In the Ptolemaic period it declined, and its wise men moved to Alexandria. In B.C. 24 it was practically in ruins.

At Matarieh is also the Virgin's Tree, a huge sycamore

under which the Virgin is said to have rested, and the well from which she drew water wherewith to wash the Child's garment. Where she threw it down balsam-plants sprang up, so it is said. The balsam-trees which originated from these were said to grow nowhere else in Egypt, and no Christian was considered to be properly baptized unless a drop of their oil was thrown into the font. The Apocryphal Gospels also state that the idols of On fell down when the Virgin and Child reached the city.

On the desert side of Matarieh is the Ostrich Farm, which is open to visitors. It is an interesting object for an afternoon excursion. The view from the top of the building, round which are the pens of the ostriches, embraces desert and cultivation, Cairo and the Mokattams.

Marg is a thoroughly native mud village in a large grove of palm-trees ; it contrasts strikingly with the European settlements at the other stations.

One can motor out as far as Matarieh, and it is possible that a motor-road may be made shortly as far as Khanka. The trains run every half-hour from Pont Limoun to Marg up to 1.30 at night. The time-table is on page 187.

THE HELIOPOLIS OASIS

The phenomenal extension of Cairo in all directions induced a group of financiers to start the scheme known as the " Heliopolis Oasis " in 1905. Some five thousand acres of high-lying desert land near H.H. the Khedive's Palace at Koubbeh were procured, with the object of building a species of desert pleasure city. The work is at this moment progressing vigorously. A fine road connects Abbassieh with the " Oasis," and a motor service has been organised. An electric railway is also in process of construction, to connect the " Oasis " with Pont Limoun station, and a network of roads has been laid out in the " city " itself. Some fifty villas and shops, a station for the electric railway, a family hotel, a casino in Moorish style, and the Heliopolis Palace Hotel are in course of erection, and a large amount of work has already been achieved.

The Palace Hotel has been conceived on a large scale. It is in the Oriental style of architecture, and will have a fine restaurant on each of its two stories, from whence is obtained a wide view of the desert, the cultivation, and Cairo ;

it will contain four hundred rooms, fitted with every comfort as well as sitting-rooms, reading-rooms, billiard-rooms, concert-rooms, bars, &c. &c. In a word, it is designed to meet every wish and even caprice of the visitor or resident who cares to exchange the heat and dust and rush of Cairo for the quiet and pure air of the desert. Further, the originators of the scheme have laid out a "Sporting Park," as one may call it, for racing, golf, tennis, polo, and other games. The purity of the keen air, the sense of space, the beauty of the surroundings, and the graceful design and arrangement of the whole city lend an unusual charm and distinction thereto.

Another quarter is devoted to the provision of houses and flats for residents whose slender means forbid the high rents exacted in Cairo. There are also various fine villas and mansions being built for the richer residents.

There is a police station, a church, and a mosque in the best Arabic style. In a word, Heliopolis is to be a complete city in the desert, a Cairo *in petto* with its own share of amusements and interests, and without many of the disadvantages that so often weary and annoy the Cairenes. Mr. Edward Dicey, C.B., a well-known writer on Egypt and Egyptian questions, says: "The view of Cairo and of the Pyramids and of the Delta as seen from the Suez desert surrounding the Heliopolis Oasis City is one of the most beautiful I have ever witnessed in any country of the world.'

THE PYRAMIDS AND THE SPHINX

Mena House, the Pyramids, and the Sphinx are as accessible as any one could wish nowadays. There is a really good tramway service between Ghezireh (close to the Kasr-el-Nil Bridge) and Mena.

The fares are: First class, 3 pt.; second class, 1½ pt.

A special late tram leaves Mena House on full-moon nights.

The cab fare from Cairo is 40 pt. single, and 60 pt. return.

The half-hour's run by tram is distinctly attractive. At first the line parallels the left bank of the Nile, and one can watch the river and the Mokattams and Citadel, grey and clear-cut against the sky by day, deep blue and black and studded with yellow lights at night. At Gizeh the line changes its direction, turning almost at right angles towards Mena. After the bridge over the railway is passed, the

The Pyrmaids of Gizeh, from the Desert : Early Morning

whole road is level; on either side is a long plain, in early winter a vast sheet of water as far as the eye can reach, one rose-red expanse at sunset, on which quiver the huge triangular shadows of the Pyramids. Later, the water passes off, and in a month or two all is one wide sea of verdure.

The road is Ismail's creation, built in an incredibly short space of time. It is the finest road in the country. The long avenue of Lebbek trees is crowded with cabs, carriages, motor-cars, native carts, strings of camels, and a few stray cyclists of equally strange nationality and dress. Between the trees, as the tram flies along, one is suddenly aware of those great shapes—sharp, grey-red, rigid above the rough desert cliff. Little black specks move to and fro at their base—people already exploring and sight-seeing.

A crowd of white-robed donkey-boys and dragomans hover round the tram as it arrives. The hotel is a few yards off to the right hand. After seeing the Pyramids and the Sphinx, one may stop and have lunch, or tea on the verandah, before returning to Cairo.

The road curves up the hill to the Pyramids. There is no escape from these great monuments. They stand silent above everything. They appear, faint blue shapes of sharp outline from Galioub as the train approaches Cairo, from Matarieh, from the Ghezireh club grounds above the tree-tops, from any and every point of clear westward view in Cairo.

Their size alone and their form remains. Stripped of their brilliant white smooth casing, once covered with strange carvings and paintings, bereft of the huge precincts and stone gateways, they appear barbarous, rude, rugged, almost meaningless, shapes of forgotten power. And the Sphinx is more wonderful, more mysterious still, Horemku the ancient. No one can tell when the Sphinx came into being. There is a legend that it was in existence at the time when Chephren built his Pyramid. Thothmes IV. cleared away the sand in which it was buried, at the command—given in a dream—of Harmachis, who claimed that it was his statue. Probably a far greater antiquity belongs to it, for Princess Honitsen, daughter of Cheops (builder of the Great Pyramid) speaks, in an inscription on a stele, of a "Temple of the Sphinx" as existing in her day. The following is a translation:

"Horus the everlasting, who overwhelmed his enemies,

the King of Egypt, Khoufou, Giver of Life, hath found the temple of Isis. Queen of the Pyramid. Near to *the temple of the Sphinx* to the north-west of the temple of Osiris, Lord of the Tomb. He hath built his Pyramid hard by the temple of the Goddess, and he hath built the Pyramid of his royal daughter Honitsen near unto this temple. This he hath done to the glory of his mother Isis, Divine Mother, to the glory of Hathor, Lady of the waters which come from the firmament. He hath renewed her glory, and hath rebuilded her sanctuary in stone. He dwelleth with them in his temple."

We see the Sphinx now defaced and mutilated, though Arab writers speak of its once strangely beautiful features. A suggestion this that perhaps it is the sole survivor of a more ancient civilisation still, far beyond our ken; for the Egyptian craftsmen whom we know, did not aim at beauty in itself: tied by convention, the keynote of their work was grandeur—immensity that disdained proportion. And yet, there, close to their most ancient monuments, is that figure perfect in proportion, form, and line, and once in beauty a deeper, more mystical symbol than their most cunning gravings, more real in life than their most immense statues.

The granite temple a short distance south-east of the Sphinx is known as the "Temple of the Sphinx," and is said to have been the sanctuary of Sokaris Osiris: it is of considerable interest. Ancient as they are, the huge slabs of granite of which it is built are so beautifully surfaced and fitted that many of the joints even to-day are hardly perceptible.

But to return to the Pyramids themselves, and such facts as concern them: there are three—the Great Pyramid of Cheops, the second Pyramid of Khephren, and the third, far smaller, of Mycerinus or Menkauru. They are all attributed to the fourth dynasty.

The height of the Great Pyramid is 451 ft. (formerly 482). its sides are 750 ft. long at the base (formerly 768), and it covers an area of about thirteen acres. The second Pyramid is 447 ft. high, and the third only 203 ft.

The Pyramids seem to have been commenced with a nucleus of rock around which were built huge stone steps which were finally filled in with smooth polished stones. The outer casing has been wholly removed at various periods, and only a fragment of it remains on the second Pyramid.

The smooth surface was covered with sculptures and inscriptions.

The chambers and passages inside had their special uses as sepulchres, and were finally closed when the king for whom they were built had been entombed. There used to be a temple close to each Pyramid, devoted to the honour of the monarch.

The Great Pyramid can be climbed: it is an exertion, and though the view is fine, it is quite what one expects from any high point. Ascent by proxy is, however, quite easy and costs a few piastres: the Arab boys are always ready to compete therein.

The Great Pyramid was opened by Caliph El-Mamoun in 820 A.D. on the chance of finding treasure, but the entrance his men made is now blocked up. The present entrance is about 40 ft. from the base. A great vaulted gallery leads down to the subterranean chamber. 90 ft. below the base and 347 ft. from the entrance; it is 11 ft. high and measures 46 by 27 ft. Mariette claimed that this was a false chamber, intended to divert the attention of any one entering from the real tomb. An upward passage leads towards the centre. and is the approach to the "Queen's Chamber" (18 ft. by 17 and 20 ft. high). Mariette considers that here also the passage to the great gallery was closed, so that those who reached this point might suppose they had seen all the Pyramid held. The great gallery is 151 ft. long, 7 ft. wide, and 28 ft. high; it leads to the King's Chamber (34 ft. by 17 and 19 ft. high), in which are the remains of a red granite sarcophagus.

There is much argument about these Pyramids: some even consider that they had some strange metrical and dimensional object. But however their dimensions may have been devised, the consensus of opinion is that they are tombs: for that matter the Pyramid may be a monument to the king's learning as well as a resting-place for his body.

The smallest Pyramid, that of Mycerinus, is said, in one legend, to have been built by one of the princesses on doubtfully acquired resources: another myth assigns it to Rhodopis, but Mycerinus was the real builder. He it is to whom it was revealed by the gods that he had but six years to live, but it is said that he doubled the period by turning day into night.

The following is a translation of an inscription on the

cover of the sarcophagus of King Mycerinus, which was found in the third Pyramid:

"O Osiris, lord of the two lands, Menkauru who livest eternally, child of Heaven, borne on the breast of Nut, begotten of Gabou. Thy mother Nut bendeth over thee from

On the Nile off Sakkara

the vault of Heaven. She maketh thee a god, she bringeth thine enemies to nought. O King Menekauru who livest eternally."

THE TOMBS AND PYRAMIDS OF SAKKARA

This expedition is usually made by train from Cairo to Bedreshein, a journey of about an hour. The best trains are: from Cairo at 7 A.M. and 9.30 A.M.; from Bedreshein at 4.46 P.M. and 8.58 P.M. The fare is: first class, 16½ pt.; second class 8½ pt.. There is a buffet at Bedreshein station where light refreshments can be obtained.

Donkeys with good saddles are waiting at the station, the

price being 10 pt. each for the day; it is a ride of about an hour and a half to Sakkara.

One can visit Sakkara from Helouan; in this case the river has to be crossed by ferry, and altogether it will take about two hours and a half.

The third route is across the desert, about two hours from Mena House by donkey—or better, by sand-cart, a curious but most adequate vehicle with broad tyres for driving on loose sand. This route leads direct to Sakkara. If Memphis and the colossal statues of Rameses are to be seen without making a long detour, the route *via* Bedreshein, which is really the shortest, easiest and most practical, must be taken.

Lunch should be brought from Cairo; here the luncheon-basket is a useful necessity. Lunch can be taken at Mariette's House, close to the principal points of interest, where tables, chairs, &c., are arranged in the shade. Candles or an acetylene bicycle lamp should also be brought, for exploring the underground tombs. If a general Antiquity Pass (*see* page 171) has not been purchased, tickets for Sakkara alone can be obtained at Mariette's House, the Museum in Cairo, or of Messrs. Cook and Son, at 5 pt. per head.

The ruins of Bedreshein and Sakkara are the relics of that great city Memphis, one of the most famous of all ancient cities.

The village of Bedreshein stands on the site of the old town, and as this was situated in the valley which is covered each year by the inundation, little indeed remains of its former greatness; the colossi of Rameses, the foundations of a temple of Ptah, and a few scattered mounds are all that is left. Above, on the edge of the desert, was the necropolis of Memphis, and here there are many well-preserved monuments of the earliest times.

Memphis, it is said, was founded by Menes, first mortal king of Egypt. During the third, fourth, and fifth dynasties it was the capital of all Egypt, the Royal city. Its kings built palaces and temples of unrivalled magnificence, and provided vast tombs to immortalise their greatness.

Throughout the history of Egypt Memphis was of the greatest importance, though only for short periods the capital, and even in Ptolemaic times it was a large and thriving city. The triad, Ptah, Sekhet, and Bast were the principal deities; they resemble the Theban triad Amen, Mut, and Khons.

Ptah was incarnate in the Apis bulls, who were first worshipped, then drowned in the sacred lake, embalmed, and finally buried in the magnificent granite sarcophagi of the Apis Tombs.

The first objects of interest after leaving the station are the Colossi of Rameses II.: these formerly marked the entrance to a temple. The first, made of granite, lies prostrate; its length with the crown, which has fallen off, is over 30 ft. The second colossus is of limestone, 42 ft. high; it stands in an enclosure (4 pt. is charged to enter, unless one has a general pass). The foundations of the temple of Ptah can be seen a little to the north.

From this point it is about an hour's ride to the Step Pyramid. This is the tomb of King Zoser (third dynasty), older than the Gizeh Pyramids; unlike them, it is built in six stages or steps. It is about 200 ft. high. A little to the south-west is the Pyramid of Unas, a king of the fifth dynasty. The walls of the tomb chamber are covered with coloured hieroglyphics which are among the oldest that have been found.

After this, lunch may be taken at Mariette's House, Mariette was the famous French Egyptologist who discovered the Apis Tombs in 1851, and afterwards became Director of Antiquities to the Egyptian Government (1857–1881).

A few minutes distant are the tombs of the Apis bulls or Serapeum; there are nearly four hundred yards of vaulted subterranean passages with niches at intervals in which are the granite sarcophagi of the bulls. Twenty-four of these are still in position; they are cut from a single block of granite, and weigh sixty or seventy tons. The following extract from Mariette's report on his discovery may be interesting:

"I confess that when I penetrated for the first time, on November 12, 1851, into the Apis vaults, I was so profoundly struck with astonishment that the feeling is still fresh in my mind, although five years have elapsed since then. Owing to some chance which it is difficult to account for, a chamber which had been walled up in the thirtieth year of the reign of Rameses II. had escaped the notice of the plunderers of the vaults, and I was so fortunate as to find it untouched. Although 3700 years had elapsed since it was closed, everything in the chamber seemed to be precisely in its original condition. The finger-marks of the Egyptian who had inserted the last stone in the wall built to conceal the doorway were still recognisable on the lime. There were also the marks of naked feet imprinted on the sand which lay in one corner of the tomb chamber. Everything was in its original condition in this tomb, where the embalmed remains of the bull had lain undisturbed for thirty-seven centuries."

Besides the Pyramids, of which there are remains of some twenty or thirty—many still of a considerable height—there are countless tombs and mastabas of the great ones of Memphis. The most interesting of the latter are, perhaps, the Mastabas of Ptahhotep and Ti and the tomb of Mereruka.

The Mastaba of Ptahhotep is between the Step Pyramid and Mariette's house. Ptahhotep was a high official in the time of the fifth dynasty.

The Mastaba of Ti is to the north-east of Mariette's house; it is also of the fifth dynasty. The reliefs on the walls of this and the last-mentioned tomb are of extraordinary excellence, and although they date from about four thousand years before Christ, many of the pictures are wonderfully clear and lifelike; in fact, the work is far better than anything that was produced during the later dynasties.

The Tomb of Mereruka is of considerable size, and contains over thirty rooms. These are divided into three parts: the tomb of Mereruka himself; his wife, Hert-Watet-Khet; and their son, Meri-Teti. They date from the sixth dynasty, and are covered with reliefs, many of which are worth examining.

THE BARRAGE

A visit to the Delta Barrage is undoubtedly one of the pleasantest excursions from Cairo. The expedition can be made most quickly and comfortably by railway; there are plenty of trains from Cairo (main-line station), and the journey takes about half an hour. The most convenient times are:

Cairo, depart—10.45 A.M. and 3.40, 5.25 and 7.55 P.M.
Barrage, depart—2.50, 4.40, 6.20, and 9.30 P.M.

Fares:				
	1st class, single,	6 pt.;	return,	$8\frac{1}{2}$ pt.
	2nd ,, ,,	4 ,,	,,	$5\frac{1}{2}$,,

The Tramway Company also run a service of steamers,

The Barrage

these are, however, frequently crowded with excursionists. A very pleasant private picnic can be arranged by chartering for the day a motor-launch from Messrs. E. P. Blattner and Co. Telephone No. 443 Cairo. The charge is LE4 per day, and the boat holds twelve people comfortably. The river trip takes about two hours.

From the Barrage station there is a trolley line which goes through all the gardens and to all the weirs. This is a novel and pleasing method of progression: the trolleys hold four people (more comfortably two), and are pushed by two Arab boys. The fares are:

	Pt.
From the station to the central canal and back with one or two passengers	3
For each additional passenger . . .	1½
From the station over both Barrages to the Rayah Behera, to both weirs and back (without stopping), one or two passengers	8
For each additional passenger	3

If a stop of any duration is made the fare is reckoned by time.

		1hr.	3hrs.	Whole Day.
Fares by time:	One or two passengers .	10	25	40
	Three passengers	13	30	50
	Four ,,	15	33	60

The Nile, which formerly entered the sea through seven mouths, has now but two—the Damietta and Rosetta branches; these diverge north-east and north-west respectively, from a point a short distance north of Cairo. Just below the point of divergence the barrage is built across both branches; its object is to hold up the level of the water in the Nile so as to allow it to enter three great canals—the Rayah (canal) Tewfikieh, Rayah Menufieh, and Rayah Behira, which commence at this point. They provide water for, and allow of navigation to, almost all parts of the Delta.

The Barrage was one of the great experiments of Mohammed Aly. The plans were drawn up by Mougel Bey in 1835; it took twenty years to build and cost £800,000. On completion, however, it was found that the foundations would not hold owing to the shifting nature of the soil. The works remained—a costly failure—until in 1885 strengthening operations were undertaken by Sir Colin Scott Moncrieff, which were completed in 1890 at a further cost of £460,000, and have been entirely successful.

The various works are built of a reddish yellow sandstone of pleasing colour, and are in Norman style with castellated towers at intervals. These, though unusual enough in such surroundings, have in the distance a most attractive appearance against the trees. The triangle of ground formed by the two branches of the Nile was once fortified, but has since been laid out in gardens.

The trees and the gardens are the great feature of the Barrage: perfect lawns, trees, shrubs, flowers of all kinds, a delightful narrow pond passing beneath a wooden bridge and covered with water-lilies—all is a most attractive contrast to the usual Egyptian scenery. One may well wander all day and never tire of it; and the ordinary Egyptian scenes are all the more appreciated for the very contrast. An afternoon, a whole day, or a long evening can be spent there, as one pleases. Only provisions should be taken; a luncheon- *plus* tea-basket is here, as everywhere in Egypt, the real solution of the question. One may choose some charming spot in the gardens, under trees, on the open lawn; or in one of the Norman towers, where a room exists for such purposes, chairs and tables and an attendant who supplies water for the tea, washes up the things, and generally makes himself useful—all these things are provided.

One thing should be remembered—the gardens are far cooler than Cairo (perhaps their chief attraction is the absence of heat, dust, and glare), and it is apt to be distinctly chilly at night. Wraps and coats should be taken, the more so as the Barrage is almost at its best after sunset.

CHAPTER III

THE FAYOUM

The province of Fayoum lies to the west of the Nile Valley and about fifty miles south of Cairo. It is a most interesting province, and a visit will be found well worth the trouble.

Fast and frequent trains run from Cairo to Wasta in an hour and a half; from Wasta a branch line leads to the capital of the province, Medinet-el-Fayoum. The following are the best trains·

	A.M.	P.M.		A M.	P.M.
Cairo, dep.	8.30	5.15	Abouxah, dep..	6.20	3.40
Wasta, arr.	9.51	6.36	Abchaway, dep.	6.44	4. 4
Wasta, dep.	10.20	7.20	Fayoum, arr. .	7.34	4.54
Fayoum, arr. .	11.16	8.16	Fayoum, dep. .	8.18	5.34
Fayoum, dep. .	11.41	8.39	Wasta, arr.	9.15	6.30
Abchaway, dep.	12.35	9.30	Wasta, dep.	9.30	7.14
Abouxah, arr. .	12.45	9.40	Cairo, arr.	11. 5	8.45

For detailed time-tables, *see* pages 182, 183.

Fares: Cairo-Fayoum, first class, pt. 59½; second class, pt. 30. Other fares, *see* page 195.

After leaving Wasta the branch line crosses a strip of cultivated land, then passes over desert. After a few miles, cultivation again appears. The train traverses one or two gorges; these are peculiar to the Fayoum country, which is even hilly in parts—a curious contrast to the rest of Egypt.

Medinet-el-Fayoum is the capital, twenty-three miles from Wasta. As it is a railway centre, it makes quite the best base from which to explore the country. Two branch lines diverge, one to Abouxah, passing near the Lake Karoun, and the other northwards to Sennourés. Medina is also the centre of a network of light railways which find their way to every part of the province.

The best hotel at Medina is the Karoun Hotel; it is clean and not uncomfortable for a short stay. For particulars, *see* page 162.

On the Bahr-el-Yussuf Canal

The Fayoum is radically different from all the rest of Egypt; it is practically an artificial province—neither more nor less—brought into being by the Bahr-el-Yussuf some four thousand years ago. This "River of Joseph" (probably it existed a thousand years before his day) flows westward from the Nile, and divides into many little canals that water the whole country and ensure its unusual fertility—for it is unusually fertile. Roses, apricots, figs, grapes, olives, corn, cotton, and many another fruit or crop, all are plentiful, and some superior to what we find in the rest of Egypt. Even the sheep and fowls are fat and well-liking.

To the north, east and south are the hills which separate the Fayoum from Egypt and the Libyan Desert. To the north-west is Lake Moeris (Birket-el-Karoun). This was the glory of the province, the home of the sacred crocodiles worshipped by the dwellers in Arsinoë. Arsinoë, like Ombos, had its Tentyris—the city of Heracleopolis whose citizens worshipped the Ichneumon. There was also the Labyrinth, a marvel to Herodotus.

Lake Moeris was probably partly artificial; it was, in fact, a great reservoir that supplied water to all the land lying north of it. King Amenemhet III. (twelfth dynasty) seems to have been the first to put it to this use; he built a regulator and other irrigation works, of which remains are still to be seen at Lahoun. Incidentally it harboured the sacred crocodiles, and also—as nowadays—a quantity of fish.

Arsinoë is a mere heap of *débris*, haunted by the kite and the jackal alone—that great city where Sebek, the crocodile god, was worshipped. Many kinds of fish, too, seem to have been sacred. The priests probably combined this sacred fish culture with practical irrigation, and induced the people on religious grounds to maintain the waterways which were actually to serve the crops. The principle of the widespread utility of Lake Moeris was that the Nile, when high, flowed into it. As the Nile flood receded the surplus water in the lake returned to the river through the various exits and sluices, and repaid its debt.

The modern town of Medinet-el-Fayoum is interesting. The broad Bahr-el-Yussuf flows through it from end to end, bridged here and there, and with streets on either bank. The water-wheels are here (and nowhere else in Egypt) worked by the current itself. Arsinoë is to the north.

THE LABYRINTH AND LAHOUN

The "Labyrinth" and the Pyramid of Hawara are the next objects of attraction, some six or seven miles away. One should procure good donkeys, take a luncheon- and tea-basket—this the hotel can arrange—and start early. The "Labyrinth" is dilapidated enough now, but it must have been a mighty monument in its time, if we may believe Herodotus (and it is singular how often we can), and it must have eclipsed all other Egyptian buildings in size and magnificence. It seems to have been intended as a vast place of assembly for the parliament of ancient Egypt, and, according to Herodotus, it had twelve courts and three thousand chambers, besides many halls, passages, and porticoes. Huge single slabs formed the roofs of the chambers ; it had great red granite or white limestone—as white as Parian marble—monoliths, and many wonderful sculptures describing the history, religion, and interests of the province to which each court was assigned.

The Pyramid of Hawara is half a mile away to the east ; it is the tomb of Amenemhet III., and is attributed to that king and his daughter Ptah-Nefert. Many strange and splendid relics were discovered therein, especially in the vault of Horuta a great noble of the twenty-sixth dynasty. These are now in the Cairo Museum.

Another great monument is the Lahoun Brick Pyramid, an hour and a half distant and close to Lahoun village, with its temple half a mile away ; this was built by Usertsen II., also of the twelfth dynasty. And more interesting still are the traces of an ancient town of the same period, designed and built especially for the men at work on the pyramid and temple, with rows of huts and storehouses. Last of all are the remains of the old dykes and sluices that regulated the exit and entry of the waters of Lake Moeris. One returns by the 4.10 P.M. train from Lahoun, to reach Medinet-el-Fayoum at 5.20 P.M.

For full time-tables of the Fayoum Light Railways, *see* page 188.

SENNOURES

The next excursion of interest is to Sennourés. The Fayoum Light Railway train leaves Medinet-el-Fayoum at

3.40 P.M., and passes through the most fertile and beautiful part of the whole province. One can return by the State Railway train, or by a donkey.

LAKE KAROUN

We have already mentioned Lake Karoun ; but it requires a special visit, even a short stay of a day or two. In the winter there is a hotel open, under management delegated from the Karoun Hotel at Medina ; one should announce one's arrival, by telegraph, the day before.

The station—Abchaway—is under an hour distant from Medina ; a train leaves the latter at 11.41 A.M. and arrives at 12.35 P.M. There are vehicles of sorts in waiting. The drive takes about an hour through a country-side pretty enough in itself, and past picturesque villages, but all is dwarfed by the panorama that reveals a stretch of fertile land, a gradual slope, and then the lake—a turquoise streak, silvery, shimmering, under a pale luminous sky ; beyond, the hills frame it, pale rose and following one another, ramparts between desert and water. The pale green, blue, rose, blend in a perfection of vivid and intense colour.

The hotel is quaintly suited to its surroundings. There is a row of roomy, square tents ranged on a stone platform beside a stream that flows into the lake. The wind whispers and rustles in the reeds that fringe the water. One would expect that a tent on a stone flooring, close to the water-side, would prove a cold sleeping-place ; but it is quite comfortable, and indeed all the arrangements are good. The food is not that of the great hotels, but it is by no means to be despised. There are plenty of boats of various kinds, rowing and sailing, that belong to the hotel.

The lake has still a fine extent of water, some eight miles broad by thirty-five long, and one sees flamingoes and pelicans in the distance, and quantities of duck and other water-fowl, not always easy of approach. On the desert shore are jackals and hyenas, though these are seldom seen. On the far side of the lake are the ruins of Dimâ, apparently a Ptolemaic town of some importance. One may also go to the Kasr Karoun, where are ruins of an Egyptian and of a small Roman temple ; it is some three hours' sail westward from the hotel. But perhaps these ruins will interest few save

At Abchaway

keen Egyptologists. One may surely be forgiven for preferring to spend lazy hours on the lake itself ; its charm and restfulness are a perfect antidote to the fever of the restless pleasure-distraught Cairo life. The return drive to the station is uphill, and one must allow an hour and a half the hotel ponies have been known to jib, and at any rate they are likely to be slow at the ascent. The best available train leaves Abchaway at 4.4 P.M. and reaches Medina at 4.54 ; then goes on to Wasta, arriving there at 6.30 in time for the north- and south-bound expresses.

On the Lake Karoun

Evening on the Nile

CHAPTER IV

UPPER EGYPT

THE name "Upper Egypt" is applied to the country south of Cairo as far as the Soudan frontier—near Wadi-Halfa. Sometimes the name Middle Egypt is used for the stretch between Cairo and Assiout, south of which is Upper Egypt proper.

Above all things, those who visit this country, even if only for a short time, should see Luxor and Assouan—ideally dry, warm and healthy, set in fine rugged hill scenery, the home of monuments as wonderful as any the world possesses; they should be the principal goal of all travellers in the "Land of Khem."

The time-honoured highway is, of course, the Nile. Tourist steamers (for which, *see* page 203) pass up and down frequently; wealthy visitors may hire a private sailing, or, better still, a steam *dahabeah* (or house-boat), but the railway has been so greatly improved lately as to be acknowledged the most comfortable and convenient route. The river journey has, of course, its pleasures and even luxuries, but it can become tedious, and steamers are sometimes overcrowded.

The train is a fast and luxurious substitute. Every night through the season the *trains de luxe* run between Cairo and Luxor; they are made up of dining- and sleeping-cars, and only carry first-class passengers. These trains are really as excellent as any in the world; they do not tear along and shake the life out of the luckless passengers as do the vaunted Riviera "flyers." The cars cannot be surpassed. They have a double roof to preserve an even temperature, double windows that keep out dust and cinders; and, of course, electric fans, ice, and any and everything one can wish for is carried. Their great length and width ensures steady and smooth running, so that one can sleep well all through the journey.

The trains from Cairo and Luxor respectively leave at 6.30 P.M., and dinner (price 25 pt.) is served at 7.30 P.M. At the beginning and end of the season the "Trains de Luxe" do not run, and a sleeping- and dining-car are put on to the 8 P.M. from Cairo and the 5.30 P.M. from Luxor, three times a week, in each direction.

It is as well to secure berths through the Wagons-Lits Company's offices in Cairo and the principal stations, or through the tourist agencies.

Those who wish to get some impression of the country, and who do not mind a long journey by day, can leave Cairo at 8.30 A.M., or Luxor at 7.0 A.M., and they will reach their destination the same evening. They should, however, take a luncheon-basket with them.

The best months are from November to March, before and after which periods the heat is rather too much for many people. But if one cares to brave it, and owing to the purity and dryness of the air it is not really so very trying, one should go south in October; then Egypt presents her greatest wonder, for the "Nile overfloweth all his banks," and the world is one vast sheet of water from the railway to the hills. The sunset fires it to a marvel of flamë that fades to deep red, then rose, at last steely black under the starlight. Here and there a causeway cleaves the flood, a village stands out, a group of palm-trees rise. The desert hills take wonderful colours under the changing light.

People who know no Arabic will probably need a dragoman or guide. It is, perhaps, best to engage one on the spot, and not to take men from Cairo. The local guides know their work and their monuments much better; besides, a strange guide cannot even secure good donkeys, and is often at a disadvantage.

NOTICE

Those who wish to see the monuments and antiquities in Upper Egypt must obtain before starting south an *Antiquity Ticket*, price 120 pt. They can be obtained from the Cairo Museum, the Antiquity Inspector at Luxor, or from Messrs. Cook and Sons.

We would venture to add one word as to the treatment of guides, donkey-boys, and such people in general. They have often an engaging enough manner, and if this is unduly encouraged they are inclined to take far too much liberty, besides which it is most demoralising to themselves. One may show all possible courtesy and consideration to them without thereby exciting the familiarity which is at times rather a deplorable feature of this class.

BAKSHISH: IMPORTANT NOTICE

The following notice has been issued

"The attention of the Egyptian authorities has been frequently drawn, both by visitors and by residents in the country, to the evils resulting from the indiscriminate bestowal of *bakshish* to the inhabitants of the Nile villages and other places visited by tourists during the winter season. The intention of the donors is no doubt kindly, but the practice—more especially in view of the yearly increase of visitors to Egypt—cannot fail to be detrimental to the moral sense and the social well-being of the poorer classes of the community. At the present time many of the poorer inhabitants of those towns on the Nile which are most visited by tourists live almost entirely on what they can obtain by *bakshish* during the winter months. The easy means thus offered of obtaining a small livelihood prevents their adopting any form of labour, and children are brought up to regard the tourist season as the period during which they may, by clamorous begging, enable their parents and themselves to lead a life of idleness for the remainder of the year. The unhealthy tendency of such a system is obvious.

"On the other hand, from the point of view of the Nile travellers themselves, the inconveniences of this universal mendicity are equally obvious, and, as time goes on, cannot fail to increase, unless some means are adopted for checking the practice.

"It would be extremely difficult for the Government to devise an effective remedy for this state of things. The real remedy rests with the travellers themselves. If money were, in future, only bestowed in return for some actual service rendered, or in case of evident and established distress, the present pernicious habit of begging would soon die out, to the advantage both of the people and of the visitors.

"It is with this conviction that we venture to express a hope that our fellow countrymen, when travelling in Egypt, will lend their aid to this important reform by abstaining from the distribution of money in response to mere demands for *bakshish,* bestowing it only when the circumstances appear to them to warrant their generosity.

"Tourists should especially abstain from throwing money from the decks of the steamers to the landing-stages or on to the banks of the Nile for the purpose of witnessing the scramble for the coins; such exhibitions are mischievous as well as degrading.

"(Signed) CROMER, *H.B.M.'s Minister-Plenipotentiary, Agent and Consul-General.*

"RUCKER JENISCH, *Minister-Plenipotentiary, Agent and Consul-General for Germany.*

"J. W. RIDDLE, *Agent and Consul-General for America.*"

The shops in Upper Egypt are, as a rule, primitive, and it is as well to take what one requires from Cairo. There are a few shops—chemists, photograph shops, and suchlike, but very little else in the way of European necessities is to be found. As to clothes, one should take thick things as well as thin; there are occasional cold days, and almost always cold nights. It rains very seldom, but once in a way it does rain, and a waterproof or umbrella may be found most useful, even at Assouan, between November and March. A sun-helmet is really seldom necessary; a straw hat, or at most a *terai* or felt hat, is quite sufficient. The glare in the desert is occasionally trying, and some visitors may find smoked glasses comforting.

The principal trains are as follows:

Cairo, dep., 8.30 A.M., 6.30 P.M., 8.0 P.M.
Luxor, arr.: 10.40 P.M., 8.35 A.M., 9.30 A.M.
Luxor, dep.: 10.30 A.M.
Assouan, arr.: 5 P.M.
Assouan, dep.: 10.15 A M.
Luxor, arr.: 4.45 P.M.
Luxor, dep.: 7.0 A.M., 5.30 P.M., 6.30 P.M.
Cairo, arr.: 8.45 P.M., 7.5 A.M., 8.0 A.M.

The 6.30 P.M. trains from Cairo and Luxor are the *trains de luxe*. Detailed time-tables will be found on page 176 *et seq.*

Fares—1st class: Cairo to Luxor, 206 pt.
2nd „ „ „ 103 „
1st class: Cairo to Assouan, 258½ pt.
2nd „ „ „ 129 „

Train de luxe: 1st class fare plus 100 pt. supplement. Other fares are given on page 195.

CAIRO TO LUXOR BY RAIL

The train passes Embabeh—from whose bridge there is a fine view of the Nile—then Boulac-Dacrour, and Gizeh of the Pyramids. Boulac-Dacrour is a large goods station where all the north- and south-bound trains are sorted. Then Bedrechein, the station for the Sakkarah Pyramids.

Ayat (kilo. 59) is a great resort of snipe and duck. The Pyramid of Lisht is on the right-hand side.

The Pyramid of Meidoun—a monument of some interest—is near Rekkah (kilo. 83).

Wasta (kilo. 92—1 hour 21 minutes from Cairo) is the junction for the Fayoum trains.

The Fayoum may be visited specially from Cairo, or on the way to or from Luxor (*see* page 62). After Wasta the train passes over a long steel bridge that during most of the year seems useless enough, but when the water is passing from the basins its value appears.

Beni-Souef (kilo. 124) is a cotton centre and the capital of the Beni-Souef Moudirieh, but has otherwise no special interest.

For the next 260 kilometres the railway parallels the

Ibrahimieh Canal, whose boats, toiling up or drifting down stream, are picturesque enough.

From Bibeh (kilo. 145) one may visit Deshashah—the ride takes about two and a half hours—and see some interesting fifth-dynasty tombs. After Bibeh the aspect of the country changes, the colours are clearer and richer, and cotton begins to give place to cereals and sugar-cane.

Minieh (kilo. 248) is a large town, but nothing more.

Abou-Kerkas (kilo. 268) is the starting-point for the rock tombs of Beni-Hassan.

TOMBS OF BENI-HASSAN

The journey from Abou-Kerkas station to the rock tombs takes about two hours. The station-master will procure donkeys, but it is as well to give him notice beforehand by telegram. The price for donkeys is from 10 pt. to 15 pt. for the day. The charge on the Nile ferry-boat is ½ pt. each, but a little extra must be given for the donkeys; the donkey-boys will also expect a piastre or two as *bakshish.*

The river, which is crossed in the usual Nile ferry-boat, is about half an hour away, and after leaving the modern Beni-Hassan village one passes along the edge of the desert, striking sharply uphill and arriving at length at a rocky terrace. Cut into the hillside can be seen the entrances to the thirty-nine tombs, a long line of doorways facing the river. These are in varying degrees of preservation. Numbers 2, 3, 15, 17 are in a good enough state, and are of considerable interest. They were probably excavated in the time of the Usertsens of the twelfth dynasty, and they are covered with wall paintings that give, with vivid accuracy, the life of 4500 years ago. There are men and women in all their daily pursuits, fishing, hunting, weaving, and even at dinner—the succession of the common daylight occupations and interests, concessions to the needs of humanity and its amusements. A strange race these Egyptians, who could write their history, their theology, and even their diary on the walls of a catacomb. Their tombs are catalogues of life, and their palaces instinct with the presence and threat of death.

If the visitor has the energy to climb the slope at the back of the tombs—it need not take more than ten minutes—he will see in front the splendid range of Nile and green valley, and behind the arid desert, rolling, limitless.

The Speos Artemidos can be seen on the homeward route; it is known locally as the Stabl-Antar. Antar was a famous pre-Islamic poet and hero, the son of a sheikh and a slave-woman, who by his valour saved his tribe from their enemies, and was in reward given the hand of the tribal chieftain's daughter. The Speos, or cave, was actually

At Abou-Kerkas

excavated by Queen Hachopsonitou, and carried on by Thothmes III. and Seti, father of the great Rameses, but never finished. It is dedicated as a temple to the local cat goddess, Pasht. The graveyard of the sacred cats is close by.

Near Rodah (kilo. 287) are the ruins of Hermopolis and Antinoöpolis, but they are hardly worth visiting. Dair-Moës (kilo. 306) is the station for Tel-el-Amarna, the capital of Amenhotep IV.

TEL-EL-AMARNA

Tel-el-Amarna is about two hours from the station. Donkeys for the excursion can be obtained through the station-master, the charge being about ten to fifteen piastres each per day. The river must be crossed by ferry-boat.

Amenhotep IV. (eighteenth dynasty) made what appears

to have been the only attempt to escape from the influence of the all-powerful Theban priesthood of Amen-Rā. He preferred the worship of a single deity (the sun) to the polytheism of his predecessors, changed his name to Khu-enaten, "The Splendour of the Sun," and obliterated the name of Amen-Rā from the walls of his sanctuaries. The priests appear, however, to have been too powerful for him, and he found it impossible to live at Thebes.

A site for a new capital was chosen at a point half-way between Memphis and Thebes. The famous architect Bek, son of Men, was employed to build a magnificent royal city, adorned with splendid temples, and containing a palace for the king. This city was called Ekhut-Aten—"The Horizon of the Sun."

Besides being a religious reformer, the king appears to have encouraged the advance of art. Under his patronage the enlightened Bek produced some exceedingly fine work, of which an example is preserved in the beautiful stucco pavements which formed part of the king's palace, and which can still be seen.

A number of very interesting cuneiform tablets were found in 1887, being despatches to Amenhotep IV. from the rulers of Mesopotamia and other Asiatic countries. These show that the king's other interests had so monopolised him that he was neglecting the affairs of the empire.

Amenhotep passed the remainder of his life quietly at the new capital with his mother and wife and his seven daughters. Soon after his death his successors returned to Thebes and the thraldom of Amen; the "City of the Sun" was allowed to fall into ruins, and art into its former convention.

Assiout (kilo. 378) is the largest city in Upper Egypt, largely inhabited by Copts.

The trains stop here for five minutes. The station has a good buffet.

ASSIOUT

A town of white minarets, white and grey houses, and many palm-trees, right under a big bluff of scarred, sandy hill, it stands clear and clean against the plain, fortified from the autumn flood by low mud bastions.

There are fairly broad roads past fine houses and gardens, leading then to winding, narrow streets. Many of these are

Street Scene at Assiout

covered in and populous with sellers of Assiout shawls, red slippers, and red and black pottery—vases and cups of rather formal design, animals, monkeys, camels, lizards, quaintly moulded and whimsical of expression.

The barrage is about a mile away—a long, plain, solid succession of arches—and the Nile stretches blue-grey above and below it. Here, too, are gardens, made and in preparation, with delightful weeping-willows. Kingfishers, hoopoes, and water-wagtails hop about and flit to and fro under the brilliant sunlight.

On the Canal, Beni-Korra

Assiout is still rather primitive, perhaps, but it has one small hotel—the New Hotel—close to the station, which is certainly much cleaner than most of its kind. One may well spend two or three days there. There is a certain cleanliness and quiet, too, about the town, an absence of noise or crowd, a distinct picturesque placidity that makes the best of the clear air and the sun.

The country to the south of Assiout is wholly subject to "basin irrigation"; the land is divided up by banks of earth into basins several miles across. In the autumn, when the Nile is in flood, the basins are filled, the water is allowed to stand for a month or six weeks, and then it flows back to the river or into another basin at a lower level.

For this reason it will be noticed that the villages are built on mounds and stand up a few feet above the fields.

Sohag (kilo. 470) is the next place of importance. This is the Mudirieh town, or capital, of Guergueh province. It can claim some attention owing to the proximity of the two great Coptic monasteries, the White and the Red. These once magnificent buildings suffered repeatedly at the hands of the Mamelukes. They are now being slowly and carefully repaired. They are situated on the desert edge.

Sohag itself has only one feature—the river-front. A long line of dwelling-houses faces the Nile, and the road is shaded by lebbek-trees. The soft, peaceful, changing lights on the water, the boats passing lazily up and down, the distant fertile shore, and the hills that bound the view, form a most characteristic picture. In the immediate foreground are the women scrambling up and down the bank, washing clothes, fetching water, and chattering all the time.

Guergueh (kilo. 504) is a large town. There is a very old Roman Catholic convent here, and across the river are the remains of a temple of Rameses the Great.

El-Birbeh, a little to the north of Guergueh, is supposed to be the site of This, or Thinis, the seat of the earliest of all the dynasties—the first and second. In the hills on the left can be seen the rock tombs of the Thinite notables.

Baliana (kilo. 521) is the station for the temples of Abydos. For this expedition donkeys can be engaged at the station; the charge is 10 pt. per day.

ABYDOS

Abydos is some six or seven miles from Baliana station. The route is uninterrupted, over the rich plain, along the high causeway—the one path from river to desert edge when the floods are out. Abydos has one of the most important and interesting of all the temples in Egypt. It was built by Seti I., the father of Rameses the Great, and the bas-reliefs and paintings are as wonderful as any in Egypt, carried out with the greatest skill and exactitude. They are, as in the art of that period, conventional and devoted to elaborate and minute detail, but the thoroughness of the work distinguishes it from almost all that of other epochs.

The important feature of this temple is the Tablet of the Kings. It shows Seti, the king, and Rameses, the prince, offering the sacred fire and reading the hymn; and then follow the cartouches of seventy-six of the most noted kings of Egypt, from Menes to Seti—a great and valuable record for Egyptologists.

The other temple, built by Rameses II., is not in anything like the same state of preservation ; only a part of the outer walls and a few statue-columns remain. There was here a second tablet, copied from that of Seti's temple, and now removed to the British Museum ; but, unlike the original, it is mutilated. Hard by, to the north, is the tomb of Osiris, and a mound of *débris* formed by the countless tombs of ancient Egyptians who sought to be buried near Osiris. So does Abydos represent at once the birth of Egypt and its greatest period ; and, more, it holds the historical record of all the greatest who reigned, from Osiris and Menes even to the days of Seti and Rameses—a great and ancient monument indeed.

Nag-Hamadi (kilo. 556) is the centre of a large sugar district, and the factory is a model of the most modern requirements of that industry.

Just beyond Nag-Hamadi the railway crosses the Nile, and keeps to the east bank from this point onwards. The hills begin to close in towards the river, and culminate near Dabbeh in the huge sheer cliff of Gabel-el-Tarif (left-hand side).

Keneh (kilo. 611) is the home of the potters, the source of the porous jars and bottles of fascinating shapes which one sees all over Egypt. Water in them cools naturally and automatically. It is rather interesting to see the native potter turning the primitive wheel with his foot ; the shapeless clay rises to his touch and takes its appointed form. Many of the houses in the town have their walls built of the spoiled jars, which gives them a curious appearance.

Keneh is the starting-point for the expedition to the temple of Hathor at Dendera.

DENDERA

Dendera is some five miles—about an hour's donkey ride—from Keneh. Its chief feature is its modernity. The Temple is of the late Ptolemaic period. One perceives at once a tendency to depart from the rather grim convention ; the figures on the walls are more lifelike, their faces more expressive, and the great crowning heads of Hathor on the pillars are really beautiful and impressive in themselves. Evidently those who designed the temple and its decorations were thinking of Greek philosophy as well as of Egyptian mythology.

The Nile at Nag-Hamadi

There are many astronomical symbols, and, above all, there is the painted zodiac on the ceiling, and the strange recumbent figure encircling three sides of it.

Sonnini, that same traveller who expatiated on Rosetta, was so struck by Dendera as to give no less than five drawings of different figures. He speaks of undoubted Greek influence—the bundles of plants in the hands of the members of the Hathor procession, unusual in Egyptology, rather suggesting Etruscan vases ; and he is struck by the fleur-de-lis and sceptre or truncheon. The temple is certainly unusual, and happily it is in excellent preservation, though we are told that the fellaheen actually built a village on the top of it, and, further, that some of the Mameluke's troops were in the habit of using the temple at large as a target.

For all the attraction and even beauty of the frescoes and sculpture, one can hardly form a fair impression from inside. Those huge pillars, crowded together, the narrow way between them, the darkness, all give an air of constraint, and not of positive size. It is the roof that reveals the size and height of the temple ; and there, too, is the glorious view over fields and river, and the high sequence of hills behind in whose shadow the House of Hathor dominated the plain.

Tentyris, or Tentyra, an ancient town from which the temple takes its name, was the centre of the crocodile feud. The inhabitants of Tentyra seem to have had a great aversion to crocodiles, and were expert at hunting and killing them ; hence the constant fights with the crocodile worshippers of Ombos, or Kom Ombo.

The cost of the journey is slight enough ; five or six piastres a head usually covers the hire of donkeys and the ferry. Perhaps another piastre or two may be given as *bakshish* if the donkey-boys have been decently helpful and quiet. To do them justice, they are generally well-conducted in these parts.

Near Kous (kilo. 643) there are some fine views of the river on the right-hand side.

In half an hour the train reaches Luxor—673 kilometres (420 miles) from Cairo.

LUXOR

On arrival the trains are met by the porters of the various hotels, and outside, omnibuses and cabs are waiting.

There are several hotels to choose from.

The Winter Palace, a large new hotel which was only opened at the beginning of 1907, is undoubtedly the best. It is most comfortable, and compares very favourably with the best Cairo hotels. It is well designed; the rooms are large, airy, and well furnished; there is electric light, a lift, and many private suites of rooms; the management is

Hills at Dabbeh

excellent. A little way from the village of Luxor, the Winter Palace overlooks the Nile, of which delightful views are obtained from the terrace in front.

The Luxor Hotel is smaller and older, but quite comfortable. It stands in a very pretty garden, with shady walks, and has also a tennis court.

Other hotels are the Karnak, Grand, and Savoy. There is also a *pension* called the Grande Pension de Famille. Full particulars of the hotels will be found on page 162.

The village of Luxor is much like other native villages, and not worth wasting time over. There are several antiquity dealers, whose wares should always be purchased with caution, as the manufacture of antiquities has become a fine art at Luxor. Many shops display photographs of the neighbourhood, and will also develop and print from amateurs' films if desired.

There is an English church in the grounds of the Luxor

At Assirat

Hotel, where services are held regularly by a resident chaplain.

ANCIENT THEBES

Modern Luxor occupies the site of the eastern suburb of ancient Thebes. This city was perhaps the most important of all ancient Egyptian towns. It was built on the right bank of the Nile, but the rocky hills on the western side were used as a necropolis, and the kings and nobles bui t themselves temples there, which became the centres of small towns.

The rise of Thebes appears to date from the eleventh dynasty, when its princes usurped the control of Upper Egypt and increased in power until Amenemhet I. united the upper and lower country under one monarchy and founded the twelfth dynasty. The thirteenth, fourteenth, fifteenth, sixteenth, and part of the seventeenth dynasty apparently only ruled in the north, while the descendants of the old Theban princes continued in power at Thebes.

Ruins at Thebes

During the eighteenth, nineteenth, and twentieth dynasties Thebes was again of the first importance, and its kings devoted much of their energies to building temples and other great works. It was apparently the capital of all Egypt at this time, except during the reign of Amenhotep IV., who started the sun-worship heresy and changed his capital to Tel-el-Amarna. After the twentieth dynasty Thebes gradually declined, although many kings, right down to the time of the Ptolemies, made spasmodic efforts at building.

Monuments and Antiquities of Luxor.—Three days at least are required to see the most interesting of the temples and tombs, but a week or more can be very pleasantly spent here, and many people stay the whole winter, so as to make the most of the warm, dry climate.

It is best to engage a guide for the temples and tombs. There are quite a number of reliable men, and the selection can be made through the hotel. The charge is from 20 pt. to 30 pt. per day; arrangements can be made for longer periods.

There are excellent donkeys for hire. The best course is to select one and keep it throughout one's stay. The charge per day is 10 pt., but the donkey-boy will expect a piastre or two *bakshish*.

Thebes—East Bank.—On the near or east side of the river there are two places of special interest—the temple of Luxor, in the village, two minutes' walk from the hotels, and Karnak, about a mile and a half to the north.

THE TEMPLE OF LUXOR

The temple of Luxor was built by several successive kings at different periods, and dedicated to Amen and his wife and son—Mut and Khons. The principal builders were Amenhotep III. of the eighteenth, and Rameses II. of the nineteenth dynasties. The former built the temple proper, and the latter added the court and pylon on the north. The great colonnade was built under Harmhabi. The original entrance to the temple was through the centre of the north pylon. On either side is a colossal seated statue of Rameses. In front of these were two obelisks of red granite; one of them is still in its place, but the other has been removed and erected in the Place de la Concorde in Paris. On the walls of the pylon are reliefs representing Rameses defeating the Khita (Hittites) at Kadesh.

Beyond the pylon is the great court of Rameses II.; this was surrounded by a double row of columns. In the north-west corner, near the pylon, is a small temple built by Thothmes III., earlier than the great temple inside which it stands. On the south-west wall of this court is a representation of the temple of Luxor as it appeared in its day—a most interesting memorial. To the south is a lofty colonnade of fourteen columns with calyx capitals in two rows. These columns are over forty feet high, and give a most impressive aspect to the whole structure, seen from the river.

Beyond is the hypostyle hall, containing thirty-two papyrus

columns in rows of eight. Many of these are exceedingly well preserved, and on the under sides of the capitals a good deal of the original colouring remains, still brilliant, testifying to the wonderful lasting power of the colours used by the Egyptians, and giving some idea of the gorgeous appearance these old temples must have presented when every inch of column, wall, and ceiling was covered with highly coloured sculptures of gods and kings.

To the south of the hall of columns are several smaller chambers ; and in the centre of these was the sanctuary of the god.

Several of the other rooms are interesting, especialy one called the " Birth Chamber." Its walls bear reliefs depicting the birth of Amenhotep III. Another chamber, adapted apparently by Alexander, son of Alexander the Great, has reliefs of its builder worshipping Amen ; another shows signs of having been used as an early Christian church.

In the days of Thebes' greatness a broad road led from the north pylon of the temple of Luxor to the great temple of Karnak, lined throughout its length—over a mile and a half—on either side with sphinxes. To-day but a few traces of it remain. The scant extent uncovered near Karnak suggests its ancient magnificence.

THE TEMPLES OF KARNAK

There is a good road from Luxor, and carriages can be taken. The excursion may also be made on donkeys (price 5 pt.).

Besides the great temple of Amen, there are at Karnak several smaller temples, of which those of Mut and Khons are the most important. First the immense archway of Euergetes is seen in the distance, and the road passes between rows of sphinxes, and then appears the temple of Khons, fronted by its pylon. This temple was erected by Rameses III. and his successors to the honour of the Theban moon-god Khons, son of Amen and Mut.

It consists of the usual colonnade court, hypostyle hall, and sanctuary. Parts are well preserved, and the inscriptions are interesting. To the left is the small temple of the goddess Apet and of Osiris, which is worth examining.

Two hundred yards to the north is the great temple of

Amen, the "Throne of the World," as it was called—by far the most magnificent of any of the remains of Egypt's former grandeur.

No one builder is responsible for the temple, but almost every king of any note from the twelfth dynasty to the Ptolemies had a hand in its construction.

In front, forming the entrance to the temple, is the great pylon, a gigantic structure nearly 150 ft. high and 350 broad. A magnificent view of all the ruins can be seen from the top, which is easily reached from the left-hand side. In front stretches the great court of the temple, covering an area of over two acres, and once surrounded by columns. In the centre stood a colonnade, now in ruins, but one single perfect column remains, with graceful calyx capital, 70 ft. in height. Beyond the court one gets a glimpse, through the ruined second pylon, of the huge columns of the hypostyle hall. The more distant ruins appear confused; above them towers, a hundred feet into the air, the red-granite obelisk of Queen Hatasu.

There appears to have been a temple at Karnak dating from the Middle Empire, but it remained comparatively insignificant until the eighteenth dynasty. Thothmes I. built two pylons—the fourth and fifth, counting from the west. Queen Hatasu erected two obelisks, one of which has been mentioned; the other lies on the ground, broken. Her brother, Thothmes III., built a separate temple to the east, and surrounded the whole with a wall. The third pylon is attributed to Amenhotep III.

During the nineteenth dynasty Rameses I. built the second pylon, and between this and the third his successors Seti I. and Rameses III. built the great hypostyle hall.

Seti II. and Rameses III. built separate temples to the west of the main building. Nothing more was achieved until the Bubastide kings of the twenty-second dynasty built the great court which joined the temples of Seti II. and Rameses III. to the earlier edifice. Finally the great pylon was added by the Ptolemies. Thus the whole temple must have been over fifteen hundred years in the building. All the kings who had a hand in it left a record of their conquests and other deeds on its walls. Many of these are well preserved and exceedingly interesting.

On the outside of the south wall of the hall of columns is a very interesting relief recording the victories of Shishak, of the twenty-second dynasty, in Palestine. He it was who defeated Rehoboam and spoiled Jerusalem and Solomon's temple. The following is the passage in Scripture (1 Kings xiv. 25–26):

The Archway of Euergetes, Karnak

"And it came to pass in the fifth year of King Rehoboam that Shishak, King of Egypt, came up against Jerusalem. And he took away the treasures of the House of the Lord, and the treasures of the king's house; he even took away all: and he took away all the shields of gold which Solomon had made."

Deciphered from a stele found at Karnak is the following address by the god Amen to King Thothmes III.:

"I come, I grant unto thee to overwhelm the princes of Zahi: I throw them beneath thy feet through all their borders. I show unto them thy majesty, as of the Lord of Light, when thou shinest above their heads even as mine image.

"I come, I grant unto thee to overwhelm the peoples of Asia, to lead into captivity the kings of the Rotonou. I show unto them thy majesty when thou art clad in thine armour, when thou holdest the spear in the chariot.

"I come, I grant unto thee to overwhelm the land of the East: Hafti and Osi shall tremble before thee. I show unto them thy majesty, as it were a young bull, great of heart, horned, whom none can resist.

"I come, I grant unto thee to overwhelm the people who dwell in their harbours: the lands of Mutanou tremble before thee. I show unto them thy majesty, as it were the River Horse, Lord of Fear on the waters, whom none may approach.

"I come, I grant unto thee to overwhelm the peoples who dwell in their islands: they that dwell in the heart of the sea shall hearken to thy shouting. I show unto them thy majesty, as it were an avenger who standeth upon the back of his victim.

"I come, I grant unto thee to overwhelm the Tahounou: the islands of the children of Javan shall bow down to thy thought. I show unto them thy majesty, as it were a raging lion who crouches over the dead in their valleys.

"I come, I grant unto thee to overwhelm the lands on the sea-coast: all the borders of the great circle of the waters are bound to thy hand. I show unto them thy majesty, as it were a hawk whose eye shall see swiftly all that pleaseth him.

"I come, I grant unto thee to overwhelm the peoples that dwell in their marshes, to bind in captivity the lords of the sands. I show unto them thy majesty, as it were the Jackal of the South, Lord of Swiftness, going up and down the two lands.

"I come, I grant unto thee to crush the people of Nubia, even as far as the people of Punt: all is held in thy hand. I show unto them thy majesty, like to the majesty of thy two brethren Horus and Set, whose arm is with mine to assure thy power."

To the south of the great temple of Amen is a pool of water, once the sacred lake; it was lined with stone. There are also the remains of four more pylons, but they are very much dilapidated. From the last pylon an avenue of sphinxes leads to the temple of Mut, built by

Amenhotep III., but bearing the names of many of the later kings.

Most people will consider Karnak well worth a second visit at least ; and, if possible, they should arrange to see it by moonlight—the effect is impressive.

Thebes—West Bank.—On the west side of the Nile there are a great many points of interest which should on no account be missed.

It is best to start at about 10 A.M., to have lunch on the far side, and return to Luxor about 3 or 4 P.M.

Notice should be given to the hotel people, who will arrange for lunch to be sent over to the Rest House erected by Messrs. Cook on the western side.

On the river-front are boats belonging to the various hotels, and on the other side the donkeys are waiting.

THE TEMPLE OF SETI I. AT KURNA

This is about three-quarters of an hour's ride in a north-westerly direction from the landing-stage. It is conspicuous from a distance by the fine columns forming the façade.

The temple, founded in honour of Amen, and partly decorated by Seti I., was completed by his son Rameses the Great, who added many of his own inscriptions. The portion now standing represents only about a third of the original building, as there were at least two pylons, separated from the sanctuary by broad colonnade courts, which have disappeared. The walls bear interesting reliefs of Seti and Rameses before the gods.

THE TOMBS OF THE KINGS AT BIBAN-EL-MULUK

Close to Kurna the desert begins and the spurs of the hills meet the plain. The track enters a rocky valley, which winds, and gradually narrows right into the heart of the hills, arid, rocky, infinitely desolate ; it is well named the "Valley of Death." After half an hour's ride the valley becomes a mere gorge, and ends in two or three rocky clefts. This was the site chosen by the kings for their sepulture.

Cut in the face of the almost perpendicular limestone are a number of small, stone-lined doorways. All the tombs, though of varying size and degree of elaboration, are made on the same plan. A steep, sloping passage, cut downwards, right into the face of the hill, is broken at intervals by recesses, and ends in one or more large chambers supported by pillars of the original rock. In a depression in the floor of the last chamber was laid the massive granite sarcophagus containing the mummy.

The walls of the passage, chambers, and pillars were covered with finely executed and highly coloured reliefs and hieroglyphics. In most cases there are extracts from the two "Books of the Dead," which give directions for the journey of the departed spirit through the under-world. The "Boat of the Sun" also appears frequently.

The following extract from the "Book of the Dead" was found engraved on a sarcophagus. It is a profession of faith and of a righteous life:

"I have committed no fraud against men. I have not tormented the widow. I have not spoken falsely in the tribunal, nor do I know ill-faith. I have done no forbidden thing. I have not exacted of a taskmaster more work than he could do daily. I have not been neglectful. I have not been idle. I have not refused my debts, nor have I wearied in well-doing. I have not done that which is abominable to the Gods. I have not slandered the slave to his master. I have starved none. I have made none weep. I have slain none, nor have I commanded to murder by treachery. I have not stolen the Temple bread. I have not seized the cakes offered to the Gods. I have not taken the food or the fillets of the dead. I have not gained money by fraud. I have not changed the measure of the corn. I have not defrauded the breadth of a finger on the hand. I have not seized land. I have not changed the plates of the balance. I have not falsified the balance. I have not taken the milk from the mouths of the sucklings. I have not hunted the sacred animals in their pastures. I have not taken the divine birds in the net. I have not fished for the sacred fish in their ponds. I have not kept the water back in its season. I have not cut a branch of the water in its passage. I have not quenched the sacred fire at its hour. I have not violated the divine cycle in its chosen offerings. I have not driven the oxen from the sacred pastures. I have not turned aside the God in his procession. I am pure. I am pure. I am pure. I am pure."

In several of the tombs at Biban-el-Muluk the reliefs are

wonderfully perfect, and the colours as fresh as when first put on 3500 years ago. The limestone, too, is of such uniform excellence that in many cases the reliefs are cut in the living rock itself, and their surface is almost like marble.

There are about forty rock tombs in all ; many have been damaged and are not worth seeing, but four or five are of great interest. Nos. 35, 17, and 11 are perhaps the best, and if one can spend more time Nos. 6 and 9 are worth seeing.

The Tomb of Amenhotep II. (No. 35) is of particular interest, as some of the mummies found have been left *in situ.* Besides the mummy of Amenhotep II., which may be seen lying in his sarcophagus, several other kings were also found. Apparently at the time of Thebes' decline the royal tombs were no longer safe from robbers, so that many of the mummies were removed to safer places. This tomb is specially designed to baffle the marauder. The main passage appears to end in a large pit-like chamber, and it was only after considerable trouble that the continuation of it was discovered, as the opening had been bricked up and carefully concealed.

Now that it is opened, a wooden bridge spans the pit, and just beyond is the tomb chamber, with beautifully coloured reliefs. Amongst others the mummies of Seti II., Thothmes IV., and Amenhotep III. were found here, and have been removed to the Cairo Museum.

The Tomb of Seti I. (No. 17) was discovered by Belzoni as early as 1817. The reliefs are considered to be the finest of any in the tombs. They show the king before various gods, also the different stages of the sun-god's passage through the under-world. In the mummy chamber was found only the alabaster sarcophagus ; the mummy was found at Deir-el-Bahari, and is in Cairo.

The Tomb of Rameses III. (No. 11) varies from the others, as on either side of the main passage is a series of small chambers. The most diverse and interesting scenes are depicted on their walls. The mummy of the king was found at Deir-el-Bahari, and is now in the Cairo Museum.

The tombs of Rameses IX. and VI. (Nos. 6 and 9) are also interesting, and should not be missed, unless the visitor is pressed for time

From the Tombs of the Kings a mountain-path leads over the hill. It is about half an hour across to Deir-el-Bahari—a short cut, and not difficult. Near the point where the path emerges into the plain is the Rest House, established by Messrs. Cook and Sons. The usual plan is for the hotel to send lunch here; it can be taken in comfort, and afterwards one can rest for an hour or so in the middle of the day.

This is a favourite pitch for casual antiquity sellers, professional beggars, and *bakshish* hunters. It is best to have nothing to do with them, otherwise life for the rest of the day will be a burden.

TEMPLE OF QUEEN HATASU AT DEIR-EL-BAHARI

A short distance from the Rest House is the temple of Queen Hatasu (eighteenth dynasty, B.C. 1500), rising by broad terraces up the desert slope. The upper court is surrounded on two sides by nearly perpendicular cliffs. The sanctuary and other chambers are cut out of the rock.

It will be noticed at once that the plan of this temple is a complete departure from the usual design adopted by sovereigns of the eighteenth and nineteenth dynasties. In the last year or two much light has been thrown on this point by excavations carried out just south of the temple. The ruins of a temple of Menthuhetep (eleventh dynasty, B.C. 2500), having many points of resemblance to Queen Hatasu's, have been unearthed just alongside the latter.

It seems probable that Queen Hatasu, seeing the older edifice, copied it in some particulars.

The representations of her, though much mutilated by her brother and husband, Thothmes III., who reigned alternately with her, are interesting; as a ruler of Egypt, she is given male attributes, such as a beard and male clothing. Within the upper colonnade is a relief representing her expedition to Punt.

A short distance to the south is the village of Sheikh Abd-el-Kurna, in and around which are a large number of tombs. These belong to grandees and high court officials of the eighteenth dynasty. A few of them are worth a visit, more particularly Nos. 48, 125, and 18.

RAMESSEUM

About fifteen minutes' ride south-east of Sheikh Abd-el-Kurna is the Ramesseum, a large temple dedicated by

Sunset on the Nile, Luxor

Rameses II. to Amen. The entrance is, as usual, through a pylon of colossal dimensions. On the inside are some very realistic representations of the Syrian campaigns; on the south side is the battle of Kadesh, and on the north the Egyptian army encamped.

Very little remains of the first court, except the broken Colossus of Rameses, a statue cut from a single block of red granite. It must have been nearly sixty feet high, and even the fragments that now remain testify to the excellence of the workmanship. The second court is in very fair preservation; it was surrounded by colonnades, and many of the columns (some with statues of Osiris) are still standing. Beyond is the hypostyle hall of forty-eight columns, reached by three flights of steps. The two centre rows have calyx capitals and are higher than the rest, forming a clerestory roof, as at Karnak; part of this roof is still intact. Leading from the great hall are two smaller halls with columns, beyond which was the sanctuary and other rooms. They are, however, in a very ruinous state.

THE TOMBS OF KURNET MURRAI

To the west of the Ramesseum is the hill of Kurnet Murrai, where there are several rock tombs of the eighteenth dynasty. The most interesting is that of Huya, who was governor of Ethiopia under King Tut-enkh-Amen. The wall sculptures are worth examining.

Beyond the hill of Kurnet Murrai is the small temple of Deir-el-Medina, built by Ptolemy IV. and dedicated to Hathor. If time allows, this is worth a visit.

MEDINET HABU

About a mile south of Deir-el-Medina are the temples of Medinet Habu. The principal temple is that of Rameses III.; it very much resembles the Ramesseum in plan, but is in a much better state of preservation. Many of the exploits of Rameses III. are depicted on the walls. The reliefs on the outside walls of the temple are worth notice; both naval and military operations are there depicted.

THE TOMBS OF THE QUEENS

The Tombs of the Queens are about a mile to the north-west of Medinet Habu. That of Queen Titi is the most interesting; it is rëmarkable for the extreme freshness of the colouring.

THE COLOSSI OF MEMNON

These stand in cultivated land about a mile to the north-west of the landing-stage. The two enormous statues represent Amenhotep III. in a sitting position, and are 52 ft. high.

Although much damaged by time and the Nile flood, the Colossi are amongst the most remarkable monuments of ancient Egypt. Their size is all the more apparent on the level plain. Originally they adorned the front of a temple founded by Amenhotep, but of this little or nothing remains.

The northernmost of the two figures excited considerable interest and discussion in Roman times, as at sunrise the statue is said to have emitted a musical note, of which many explanations have been given. Strabo, Pausanias, and Juvenal mention the fact; Strabo, however, was sceptical as to its supernatural origin.

DISTRIBUTION OF TIME

The question of what to see first will depend largely on the amount of time at the disposal of the visitor. In three days one can devote a little time to each point of interest, while some of the most important monuments can be seen in one long day's expedition. In this case both guides and donkey-boys will probably want extra money. The following arrangements are suggested for those with one, two, or three days at their disposal.

One Day

Start from Luxor at 8.30 A.M., and cross the river. Ride to the temple of Seti I. at Kurna, from there to the Tombs of the Kings at Biban-el-Muluk. After exploring two or three of the tombs—say those of Seti I., Rameses III., and Amenhotep III. (Nos. 17, 11, and 35)—ride over the hill to the temple of Queen Hatasu at Deir-el-Bahari and return to the landing-stage, stopping on the way to see the Ramesseum and the Colossi of Memnon. Lunch is taken at Luxor, and the afternoon can be devoted to the temples of Luxor and Karnak.

Two Days

First day.—In the morning the temple of Seti I. and the

Tombs of the Kings can be explored, lunch being taken at the Rest House. In the afternoon ride to the temple of Queen Hatasu; the Ramesseum and Colossi can be seen on the way back.

Second day.—The temples of Medinet Habu, the tombs of Kurnet Murrai, and the temple of Deir-el-Medina may be seen in the morning, returning to lunch at Luxor. The temples of Luxor and Karnak will occupy the afternoon.

Three Days

First day.—In the morning the temple of Seti I. at Kurna and the Tombs of the Kings. Lunch at the Rest House. In the afternoon the Ramesseum and the Colossi.

Second day.—The temple of Medinet Habu, the Tombs of the Queens, and Deir-el-Medina in the morning. Lunch at the Rest House. In the afternoon the temple of Queen Hatasu at Deir-el-Bahari and the tomb of Huya at Kurnet Murrai.

Third day.—The whole day is devoted to the temples of Luxor and Karnak.

LUXOR TO ASSOUAN

At Luxor the line changes to narrow gauge, but the same tradition of comfort is, as far as possible, maintained in the trains; the windows are fitted with smoked glass to counteract the glare, and a luncheon-car is attached to the train.

The journey takes six and a half hours.

At Luxor station there is not only a buffet, but even baths for the dusty.

The best trains leave Luxor at 10.30 A.M. and Assouan at 10.15 A.M. in connection with the *trains de luxe* and night mail from and to Cairo.

The time-tables are given on pages 182, 183.

The fares are:

Luxor-Assouan—1st class, 87½ pt.
2nd „ 44 „

For other fares *see* page 195.

Armant, the first station after Luxor, is unenviably notorious for a breed of dogs whose ferocity renders them useful for watching but rather embarrassing as pets.

Near Maalla are the dazzling white limestone quarries from which comes the stone for the Esneh barrage.

Matâna, the next station, has a big sugar factory.

ESNEH

Esneh is a large native town on the west bank of the Nile. Sir John Aird and Co., the contractors for this as for the Assouan dam, will give permission for those who wish to see the barrage in construction.

The temple of Esneh is quite worth a visit. It is in the centre of the town, and in order to get there from the station

Arab Village near Esneh

the river must be crossed. Donkeys will be found at the station to carry one as far as the river ferry (about ten minutes); the charge is three or four piastres for the return journey. One feature of Esneh is the baskets of parti-coloured straw which can be purchased in the town or at the station.

The temple of Knoumu is one of the latest of all Egyptian monuments, erected in the Ptolemaic period and embellished by various Roman emperors.

The front is 37 m. broad and 15 m. high. At the centre of the architrave is a solar disc, below which are inscriptions in honour of Claudius and Vespasian. Rome is mentioned as the centre of the world. These inscriptions were, of course, far later than the construction of the temple itself.

The capitals of the pillars are richly decorated. On one

of the doors opening on to the sanctuary is a curious fresco, showing Decius sacrificing to Knoumu. Decius is the latest Roman emperor cited in hieroglyphics on Egyptian monuments. On the north wall is a fresco of the hawk-headed Horus netting water-fowl and fish in company with Commodus and Knoumu—a curious trio.

There is a small chapel in the east wall, where are several inscriptions that mention the names of Roman emperors.

Esneh has also a Roman quay wall on the river.

At Mahamid, two stations beyond Esneh, are the ruins of El-Kab, the Nekkab of ancient Egypt and Eileithyiaspolis of the Greeks.

The ruins, about two miles south of the station, are surrounded by an extremely massive wall of mud-brick 37 ft. thick, which, although built during the Middle Empire, is little damaged. There is a very fine view from the north wall.

The small temple of Amenhotep III., to the east, is worth seeing.

There are many other remains. In the hills to the north are rock tombs of the Middle and New Empires and inscriptions by kings of the sixth dynasty; also a small rock temple, reached by a stairway cut in the rock, and built under Euergetes II.

EDFOU

Edfou, the next station, once a great city, is now but a small town. The temple is in the middle of the town on the west bank of the river; it is the most perfect example of an Egyptian temple existing to-day.

The station of Edfou is on the edge of the river, which is crossed by the ferry, and the temple is reached in twenty minutes' walk or ten minutes' donkey-ride.

Horus was the local deity, and to him the temple is dedicated. He was the first "Lord of the Two Lands" in predynastic mythology. The temple, commenced by Ptolemy Euergetes I. and continued by Philopator, was completed by Neos Dionysius, who added the decorative reliefs. Other rulers also added to it. It is a monument to the glory of Horus and the greatness of the Ptolemaic monarchs. The columns are admirably preserved, and richly decorated with fine capitals. The paintings and reliefs on the ceiling of the hall are in good preservation, but have become so black as to be almost invisible.

To right and to left of the entrance are two chapels, one of which was used as a library. The MSS. kept there were

At Kattara

catalogued on the walls. The other was called the room of purification. This rite was similar to Christian baptism, and consisted in aspersions of holy water. There is a picture of the king being purified by Horus and Thoth.

The finest and most delicately conceived relief is that on the north wall of the hall above the door ; it depicts a solar disc and a winged scarabeus in a boat, with two hawk-headed figures of Horus. The hypostyle is supported by twelve pillars with floral capitals and rich decoration.

The walls of the temple are beautifully painted ; everywhere are figures of Horus and Hathor. The most important is the west wall, on which is the textual and pictorial description of the battles of Horus. His foes have crocodile and hippopotamus heads. With Horus are associated the king and Isis. In the first relief the king and Horus are each slaying a hippopotamus with javelins.

A staircase of 242 steps and fourteen stages leads to the platform of the pylon, and one can ascend by a corridor on to the roof of the portico. In the front of the pylon there are four recesses which formerly held the huge flagstaffs which were the feature of every Egyptian temple. An inscription asserts that these were also used as lightning conductors. It is a wonderful temple, in a wonderful state of preservation.

After Edfou for some miles the railway winds round the face of the cliffs, high above the Nile. One of these is crowned by the ruins of El-Sirrag, a Roman fortress. After Kagoug the line crosses the wide plain of Kom Ombo. Only three years ago this was arid desert, but now, through the enterprise of Sir Ernest Cassel, as far as the eye can reach are green crops and evidence of a thriving community.

The next station, Daraw, is a fair-sized town; it is the starting-point of the camel route to Berber and the Sudan. As the train stops one is besieged by native sellers of fans and other articles of Sudanese manufacture.

THE TEMPLE OF KOM OMBO

Donkeys (price 8 pt. to 10 pt.) can be obtained at Daraw for the excursion to the temple of Sebek and Horus. A ride of an hour and a half brings one to the site of the ancient town—of importance in the time of the Ptolemies.

The temple is on the edge of the Nile. Half (the right-hand side) is dedicated to the crocodile-god Sebek, and the left-hand side to Horus. The pylon in front is partly destroyed. Of the columns in the court beyond, only half their height remains, but what is left is finely painted and in good preservation. After the court is the great hypostyle hall. The roof has fallen, but its position is defined by two rows of richly decorated pillars with palm-leaf capitals.

To the right of the north gateway is a finely worked relief of the king, Neos Dionysius, receiving the benediction of a lion-headed Isis and other gods, in the presence of Horus.

The small hypostyle hall has also two rows of pillars; on the shafts are pictures of Euergetes sacrificing to the gods. On the left wall (north-west) is a splendid relief of Horus offering a curious, curved, sickle-shaped sword to Euergetes II. Behind the king are his sister Cleopatra and his wife.

View from the Cataract Hotel, Assouan

There are three rooms to the north-east. In the third is a relief of Ptolemy Philometor, followed by Cleopatra and the two gods of the temple, receiving from Khons the emblem of long life. At this end of the temple are the two sanc-

Temple of Kom Ombo

tuaries, that of Sebek to the right and of Horus to the left. In front of the temple, on the terrace, close to the two sanctuaries, is a small temple devoted to the birth-goddess, but it is mostly in ruins. Last of all is the little unfinished chapel dedicated by Domitian to the glory of Hathor.

Between Daraw and Ghezireh, where the line at times skirts the river, are wonderful views of the sweeping curves of the Nile. Palms on the far bank stand out against the brilliant ochre of the desert hills.

A subtle change seems to have come over the country. It is all of a sudden the Egypt of the picture-books known in one's childhood. The river, sand, and palm-trees are old friends. One looks for a crocodile at the water-side.

After Ghezireh comes the junction for Shellal, and then Assouan.

At Assouan, looking South.

II

ASSOUAN

On arrival the matter of first importance is hotels. There are three large ones. It is hard indeed to choose between the Cataract and the Savoy. Both are first-class and in delightful positions ; both supply all that the visitor can wish. The Cataract Hotel, built high above the Nile, of which there is a splendid view both up and down, is perhaps the most popular. The Savoy is on Elephantine Island, just opposite the town, with gardens and trees. Both hotels have tennis courts. A rather smaller hotel is the Grand, situated in the town facing the Nile ; it has recently been rebuilt, and is very comfortable. Full particulars of the hotels are given on page 163.

There is an English church near the Cataract Hotel, and a resident chaplain holds regular services in winter.

Assouan is not a great centre ; its importance lies principally in its qualities as a winter resort and its archæological interest. It is for all practical purposes the southern boundary of Egypt, and the borderland between races who, for all their relations one with another, have never mingled.

Though a brazen furnace in summer, Assouan can hardly be surpassed as a health resort in winter. Surrounded by desert, the air is dry, yet the usual penalty—dust—is absent. Rain hardly ever falls. The days are warm and brilliantly sunny, but seldom unpleasantly hot during the winter months. The town appears wonderfully clean. There is a refreshing novelty about the scenery—the town lays at the foot of the first cataract, and the river is hedged in by rocks and great rounded boulders of pleasing outline.

Among the places of interest in and near the town, not least are the bazaars—more picturesque than most of their kind. Long-haired, shaggy Bishareen stalk past—often with a lance in their hand; effendis, Greeks, fellaheen, in every kind of dress pass up and down. Many of the shops are worth notice. Sudanese wares, Dervish arms and armour, and different objects of native manufacture make up their varied stock-in-trade.

On the desert above the town is the Bishareen camp. These nomads of the eastern desert, camel and sheep dealers by trade, come into Assouan in winter and pitch their disreputable-looking tents near the town. Many think them worth a visit.

Timber Loading at Shellal

Assouan has, besides its ancient monuments, one great modern achievement—the Dam. This should certainly be visited. It is at the upper end of the cataract, at Shellal, about six miles by rail south of Assouan. This work, completed in 1902, was four years in the building, and has had a tremendous effect on the prosperity of Egypt. The river

Rocks at Shellal

above the dam slopes upwards, but very gently, so that an immense reservoir is formed, stretching south for 120 miles. In winter, when the river is high, some of the water is held back and the reservoir gradually filled. At low Nile, in the spring and summer, when Egypt has hardly enough water to save herself from absolute drought, the sluices are opened and the supply augmented, until, as the river begins to rise for the next flood, the reservoir is empty.

The Dam is 2180 yds. long, 131 ft. high, and at present holds up the water 65 ft. It is built of the red Assouan granite used by the ancients for their most lasting memorials.

The ancient history of Assouan is graven on its rocks. Here are the Syene quarries whence came the huge granite

Philæ

monoliths for many a mighty statue, temple, and obelisk; indeed, wherever the red granite is seen throughout all Egypt every stone had its origin in these quarries, cut laboriously with primitive tools from the rocks of Assouan. shaped and smoothed with consummate skill, then floated down the river on vast rafts, and finally dragged, by the labour of thousands, to their resting-place in some far northern shrine. One huge obelisk, 90 ft. long, can be seen at the quarries, half excavated, with one face still joined to the mother rock.

These quarries, which are to the south of the town, should be visited (donkeys, 5 to 8 pt.).

PHILÆ

The most remarkable monuments are on the island of Philæ, a short distance from the dam. The island has been called the "Pearl of Egypt," and certainly its setting is most beautiful.

The temples, of which there are several, all date from the Ptolemaic period. No doubt there were earlier shrines, but these have disappeared.

The best way to visit Philæ is to take the train from Assouan to Shellal. The journey takes half an hour. The trains are as follows:

From Assouan: 7.0, 9.0, 10.45 A.M., 2.10, 4.0, and 5.10 P.M.
From Shellal: 8.0, 9.40, 10.5 A.M., 12.0, 2.50, and 6.0 P.M.

The fares are: First class, 6 pt.; second class, 3 pt.

At Shellal boats are in waiting.

Since the construction of the Assouan dam the island of Philæ is submerged from about the middle of January till the middle of June. When the water is high the temples must be approached and entered by boat.

After exploring Philæ a visit to the dam can be made, and then one can return to Assouan by boat, down the cataract.

ELEPHANTINE ISLAND

There are the remains of several temples on the south end of the Island of Elephantine, opposite the Cataract Hotel, and also a very old Nilometer, which is worth seeing.

During the winter of 1906–7 some interesting "finds" were

made at this spot; a number of mummied rams in granite sarcophagi were unearthed. Apparently the ram was a sacred animal, and was worshipped in the ancient town of Elephantine.

THE ROCK TOMBS

There are rock tombs of the Ancient and Middle Empires to be seen cut in the hill on the west bank, opposite Elephantine. These are contemporary with the rock tombs of Beni Hassan, and were constructed by the grandees and princes of Elephantine.

CONVENT OF ST. SIMEON

The ancient Coptic convent of St. Simeon is worth a visit. It can be reached in about half an hour from the west bank of the Nile, opposite Elephantine Island.

A Tomb in the Desert

CHAPTER V

THE SUDAN

To a certain proportion of our annual visitors "wintering in Egypt" includes a trip to Khartoum and Omdurman, but these regular travellers to the south can as yet scarcely be called numerous, though their numbers increase annually. Doubtless to many people the word "Sudan" calls up visions of burning deserts, arduous travel, and general conditions remote from civilisation.

Modern enterprise, however, has within a decade brought the ancient capital of the dervishes within a few days' journey of Cairo, and up-to-date means of travel, both by river and rail, combine to render the journey at once comfortable and expeditious.

The following notice has been issued for visitors to the Sudan:

"Travellers, while in the Sudan, are particularly requested to refrain from gaining an easy reputation for generosity by giving money to children, beggars, or other persons who have not earned it.

"At present the population of the Sudan has not been demoralised by indiscriminate almsgiving, but it will not require much of this to make the demand "*Bakshish!*" as importunate and annoying to travellers as in Egypt itself, and to cause a considerable number of natives to forsake the paths of honest industry for the unwholesome existence of preying upon others.

"His Excellency the Governor-General trusts that all travellers will consider this as a personal request from himself, and at the same time would inform them that if they desire to give any money for the benefit of the inhabitants, contributions for hospitals or relief of poverty, assistance to the sick, and relief of deserving cases amongst the poorer classes will be carefully administered by the Governors, and he himself will gratefully receive contributions for what is the Sudan's greatest need, viz., *education.*

"By Order of the Governor-General.

"(Signed) F. J. Nason, Lewa."

There are two routes to the Sudan—the Nile route and the Red Sea route.

THE NILE ROUTE

The first stage, along that reach of the Nile which lies between the great Assouan dam and the second cataract at Wadi-Halfa, is performed by three lines of river steamers—Messrs. Cook and Sons', The Hamburg and Anglo-American Company's, and the Sudan Government steamers.

During the winter season of 1907–8 the Sudan Government steamers will leave Shellal on Fridays and Tuesdays, arriving at Halfa on Sundays and Thursdays. The landing-stage at Halfa is opposite the railway station, and there is an hotel adjacent.

Through express trains, with sleeping- and dining-cars and a limited amount of first-, second-, and third-class accommodation, will leave Halfa at 2.50 P.M. on Sundays and Thursdays, reaching Khartoum North, the present terminus of the railway, shortly before four o'clock the following afternoon.

Down trains from Khartoum North leave at 10.15 P.M. on Sundays and Thursdays, arriving at Halfa at 10.25 P.M. next day, the steamers leaving early next morning for Shellal.

Complete time-tables of Sudan Government Railways trains will be found on pages 191–194 of this guide.

The rolling-stock in use on these express trains has been specially constructed with a view to ensuring the maximum of comfort and freedom from dust. The windows are of tinted glass, and fitted with dust-shields, so that a view can be obtained of the country traversed. The cars are all electrically lighted, while patent cooling and ventilating apparatus has been recently installed.

The fares by express trains from Halfa to Khartoum are as follows (return fares being double the single fares in all cases):

First class and sleeping-car (exclusive of meals)	LE6.750
First class	5.750
Second ,, ...	4.025
Third ,, ...	2.015

Passengers are permitted to take light hand-baggage only into the cars. Ordinary luggage must be registered through and paid for at point of departure. All baggage carried in the baggage-van will be charged for at the rate of 0.07 milliemes per 10 kilogs. per kilometre, which charge includes registration, station, and handling fees, and insures to the value of a sum not exceeding LE10 for each package. The light hand-baggage allowed in cars with passengers is carried at their entire risk.

The Sudan Government Railways will be exempt from all responsibility for loss of or damage to jewellery, money, ornaments, precious stones, and bullion.

Baggage to be registered should be brought to the station at least half an hour before the departure of the train, otherwise it is liable to be refused.

Sleeping-car berths for the journey southwards can be reserved on application to the District Traffic Manager, Sudan Government Railways, Halfa Camp, whose registered telegraphic address is "Rukab, Halfa Camp," also on application to the following tourist agencies at Cairo: Messrs. Thos. Cook and Sons, Ltd., the Hamburg and Anglo-American Nile Co., Messrs. Carl Stangen, Messrs. E. P. Blattner and Co., Agence Lubin.; also the branch offices of the above agencies at Luxor, Assouan, &c.

Seats in the ordinary first-, second-, and third-class carriages cannot be reserved except by special arrangement with the District Traffic Manager, Sudan Government Railways, Halfa Camp. (Telegraphic address: "Rukab, Halfa Camp.")

Cheques are not accepted by the Sudan Government Railways, and the only bank-notes which are accepted are those of the Bank of England and the National Bank of Egypt.

Meals are provided on the sleeping-car trains between Halfa and Khartoum at a fixed tariff as given below, but on ordinary expresses passengers must make their own arrangements.

Tariff in Dining-cars.—The dailv charge for meals is 70 pt., which includes:

Breakfast (8 *a.m.*)

Tea, coffee, eggs, cold meat, bread and butter — 10 pt.

Lunch (1 *p.m.*)

Soup or fish, entrée, joint and vegetables, sweets, cheese, coffee, bread, &c. . — 24 pt.

Afternoon Tea

Tea or coffee, bread and jam, butter, biscuits, cake, &c. . . . . — 6 pt.

Dinner (7.30 *p.m.*)

Hors d'œuvres, soup, fish, entrée, joint and vegetables, sweets, cheese, dessert, coffee, bread, &c. . . . . — 30 pt.

Total per diem . . . . — 70 pt.

Any complaints of service or attendance should be addressed to the District Traffic Manager, Halfa Camp or Khartoum North.

Hot and cold baths are provided at Atbara for the convenience of passengers at a charge of 10 pt.

There are telegraph offices in the railway stations at Halfa Camp, No. 6 Station (Desert Section), Abou Hamed. Berber, Atbara, El-Damer, Shendi, and Khartoum North, Talgwareb, Gebeit, Port Sudan, Sallom, Suakin.

Letters can be posted on the trains.

The attention of passengers is called to the conditions and notices on the reverse side of their railway tickets.

Good hotel accommodation may be obtained at the Grand Hotel, Khartoum.

There is a monthly service of Government steamers south from Khartoum up the White Nile, particulars of which may be obtained from the Agent-General, Sudan Government, War Office, Cairo, or from the Director of Steamers and Boats, Khartoum North.

Distances in Miles from Khartoum

Miles from Halfa.	Stations.	Miles between stations.
—	Halfa	—
126	No. 6 (Desert Station)	126
230	Abou Hamed	104
343	Abidia	113
361	Berber	18
385	Atbara (Junction for Suakin Line)	24
392	El-Damar	7
429	Mutmir	27
471	Shendi	42
496	Wad Ben Naga	25
524	Gebel Gerri	28
547	Wad Ramleh	23
575	Khartoum North	28

	Miles.
Distance from Abou Hamed to Kareima	156
Atbara to Suakin	305
,, to Port Sudan	30[illegible]
Suakin to Khartoum	495

THE RED SEA ROUTE, VIA SUEZ AND PORT SUDAN

Although the new railway which has been built to connect the main line with the Red Sea was primarily intended as a trade route, to facilitate the development of the provinces watered by the Upper Nile and its tributaries, it affords also a comfortable alternative route for visitors to the Sudan.

Passengers intending to use this route travel from Suez to Port Sudan by Khedivial mail steamers, leaving the former port on Wednesday evening, and arriving at the latter on

Friday evening. An express train, conveying sleeping-car, first-, second-, and third-class passengers, and the European mails received *via* Brindisi, leaves Port Sudan at 8 P.M. on Fridays, and runs through to Khartoum, which is reached on Saturday shortly after 6 P.M.

Accommodation on this boat express should, as far as possible, be reserved in advance by letter or telegram addressed to the District Traffic Manager at Suakin, whose telegraphic address is "Rukab, Suakin."

At Atbara Junction, where the boat express passes on to the main line about 10.30 A.M. on Saturday, passengers may enjoy the luxury of a bath for the moderate sum of 10 pt.

The down boat express from Khartoum leaves at 9.15 P.M. on Tuesdays, reaching Port Sudan on Wednesdays shortly after 8 P.M. The steamer leaves at 11 o'clock next morning, so that there is time for travellers to inspect the new town and harbour works. Suez is reached on Saturdav afternoon.

The fares by this route are as follows (return fares being double the single fares)·

First class and sleeping-car (exclusive of meals)	LE5.920
First class	4.920
Second ,, ...	3.445
Third ,, ...	1.720

The charges for meals on the dining-car will be the same as for the Halfa-Khartoum service.

For complete time-tables *see* page 191 *et seq.*

The same regulations are applicable in respect of passengers' baggage, &c., on this service as on the sleeping-car trains between Halfa and Khartoum.

Tickets can be obtained from the various tourist agencies in Cairo available from Halfa to Khartoum and returning *via* Port Sudan, or in the reverse direction—starting from Port Sudan and returning *via* Halfa and Shellal.

The following notice may be of interest to visitors to the Sudan·

"The attention of all travellers is called to Section 10 of the Preservation of Wild Animals Ordinance, published in the *Sudan Gazette*, No. 53, of December 1903, whereby the sale or purchase of hides, horns, flesh, or any trophies of certain animals or birds is absolutely prohibited in the Sudan.

"The animals referred to are: Eland, giraffe, Mrs. Gray's waterbuck, rhinoceros, kudu, wild ass, roan antelope, zebra, white-cared cob, hartebeest, waterbuck, oryx, ibex.

"The birds referred to are: Ostrich, shoebill (*Balœniceps*), ground hornbill (*Bucorax*), secretary bird (*Serpentarius*).

"Any person acting in contravention of this section is liable to a fine not exceeding LE10 or three months' imprisonment, and all such hides, horns, or trophies are liable to confiscation.

"Sportsmen are earnestly invited to co-operate with the Government in enforcing a strict observation of the above law.

"It is clearly in their own interests to discourage the slaughter of animals by natives, who, if they think they will gain a few piastres for a head or skin, will be particular neither as to size, age, nor sex.

"By Order.

"(Signed) J. C. GRAHAME, Bimbashi,

"*For Superintendent Game Preserv. Dept.*"

A Sakkieh

CHAPTER VI

THE DELTA

The shape of Egypt is for all the world exactly like the Eiffel Tower. The shaft is Upper Egypt, and the base is the Delta, formed by the gradual silt of the Nile in its seven—now only two—branches. All the space inside is cultivation ; without is desert. At the junction of the two is Cairo.

Historically Upper Egypt is, of course, far more interesting than the Delta. The ruins of Lower Egypt are few and far between, and seldom in good preservation. It has suffered also at times in its cultivation ; for it depends almost wholly on canals, and therefore on scientific irrigation—now provided by the Delta barrage and supplemented by the new Zifteh barrage.

A wonderful degree of fertility has been attained. Much of the land yields two, and even three, crops in a year.

We give a short description after this article of such towns and places as have any special features, but on the whole there is not very much in the Delta to interest most visitors.

The scenery has none of the grandeur of the Upper Nile Valley, but there is in it a certain peaceful charm. The canals flow under endless avenues of scented mimosa, and here and there below the broad branches of the lebbek-tree the *sakkieh* (the primitive water-wheel so characteristic of Egypt), turned by a slow, plodding "gamoose," drones out its monotonous note.

The villages, their mosque domes and slender white minarets rising from a mass of rich verdure, even the waste and desolate parts, undrained of the salt that has impregnated the land in years of careless watering—in all this there is a certain atmosphere, a quiet clearness, especially in the early morning, and even a variety which Upper Egypt does not afford.

Some of the towns and villages—near Mansourah especially—stand high above the surrounding country. Probably the mounds on which they are built were themselves small towns, Roman, Greek, and Egyptian, the one above the other. At Mehallet-Kebir, a most attractive town, and at Samanoud, near it, quite a number of such things as coins, lamps, small figures, scarabs, &c., are found from time to time.

We cannot suppose that the traveller is likely to devote much time to the Delta, but we can at least show him in the pages following this what are its features and interests, and give him a general impression of them. If he wishes to know Egypt as it really is, he should not forget that Lower Egypt presents it in its most characteristic, and perhaps most charming, aspect. Upper Egypt may be the land of the mighty dead; Lower Egypt is the land of their humbler successors.

A visit can be made to most places in the Delta in a day from Cairo or from Alexandria. Besides the State railways, which serve all the larger places, a network of light railways (worked by the Delta Light Railway Company and the Basse-Egypte - Company) traverse the fields and connect village to village. If one has a day to spare, a trip by the light railway is certainly well worth doing.

BILBEIS

Bilbeis is rather out of the beaten track, and, as it now stands, offers no particularly absorbing sight. It has a slight historical interest as having resisted Ammrath, King of Jerusalem, with great vigour in 1126 A.D. It contained sufficient wealth to occupy his army for three days in pillage.

The town is as uninteresting as most Arab towns, but the surrounding country is pretty—by the Ismailia Canal, for instance, which is the barrier between the cultivated land and the desert. Near the lock is the irrigation rest-house, by itself—a most attractive spot in the evening light. Behind it is a broad track of sand, then a few straggling palms, then the desert, changing rapidly to violet as the shadows lengthen. In the far distance is a line of low hills, of the deepest purple. The canal, luminous in the failing light with soft reflections, stretches straight in either direction. High-masted boats move slowly down the stream.

There are many such attractive places in the Delta—the road from Bilbeis to Abou Hammad, for example. It is about sixteen miles, parallel with the canal bank. The scenery consists of palm-trees, crops of all sorts, and here and there a village. There is many a quaint *sakkieh,* on which a small boy or girl stands, like a charioteer, above the horizontal wheel, yelling now and again and brandishing a stick to prevent the buffalo from going fast asleep.

The whole road is delightful, sunlit and sleepy. Now and again a fat village notable passes on an equally fat donkey, or a splendid dark-faced Bedouin on a fine mare, a true horseman—one would say a centaur but for the flow of robes and the glistening girdle round the head-dress.

Salhieh, again, and Korain, where the French fought, are good places—big palm-groves at the end of all things, on the border of the desert. At Salhieh one walks straight away from civilisation and the railway station on to the sand. Only the line of telegraph posts to Kantarah breaks the monotony. The yellow sand gleams, and the distant mounds here and there fade and seem to take strange shapes in the mirage of the strong sunlight. Now and again one comes on a gipsy-faced woman tending a few goats that nibble the scarce, stunted shrubs. In the distance, perhaps, appears a Bedouin caravan—a long string of camels, laden with a miscellaneous assortment of wares—returning from Syria; for Salhieh is on the old overland route to Asia used since the time of the Pharaohs by just such caravans as one may see to-day.

FACOUS

Facous is a fertile centre of palm-groves that branch off to the East and South above small canals, and villages with quaint winding mud walls, along which the women pass blue-gowned, their great water-jars on their heads. The big canal, Bahr Facous, divides into three or four other canals that range through moderately fertile land and eventually

At Facous

lose themselves in that semi-waste end-of-the-world country so characteristic of certain parts of the Delta. The line past Azazi and Ekiad to Salhieh is a very avenue of palms; the permanent way is the high-road for choice. Salhieh is the end of all things, a palm-grove bounded by desert. whence one can see almost to Kantarah and the Suez Canal.

DAMIETTA

It is rather a far cry to Damietta, but it can be seen in a day, and one need not spend any great length of time there. Besides, the journey itself by Tantah and Mansourah is interesting to any one who really wishes to have an impression of the Delta.

At Damietta

The trains run as follows:

	A.M.	A.M.		P.M.
Cairo	7.45	9.30	Damietta .	4.10
Tantah .	—	11.15	Mansourah .	6. 6
Zagazig .	9.54	—	Zagazig .	—
Mansourah	11.50	12.38	Tantah	7.55
Damietta		P.M. 2.30	Cairo	9.20

Full time-tables are given on pages 184 and 185.

The fares are: 1st class, 85½ pt.; 2nd class, 43 pt..

Tantah and Mansourah are both large and important towns. Tantah has a fine mosque, but its chief fame is that it possesses the tomb of Saïd Ahmed El-Bedawy, a celebrated Moslem saint, in whose honour are festivals in January, April, and August, the last two being the most important. These "Moulids," as they are called, last a week—from Friday to Friday—and are well worth seeing. There is a huge crowd of some 200,000 people, who come in from all the country round. Strange symbolical parades are held of fantastic emblems and curious dances; the uncanny, ceaseless, Arab music and singing is their setting.

After Tantah the train passes Mehallet-Kebir, a charming-old town with many fair minarets and spires. One might be tempted to spend a night there (though this can hardly be recommended unless the traveller does not mind "roughing it," as what inns the town possesses are very primitive). One ought to walk through the town at sunset, up the narrow, covered streets, past the many mosques. Then is heard, startlingly sudden, the magnificent call to prayer breaking out overhead—sonorous, echoing and rolling through the fading night, and dying away in a long wailing note.

Mansourah is a great town for cotton and trade, and has quite a considerable European colony. The chief attraction is the river view, and as a town it is notable as the place where St. Louis was imprisoned in 1250 A.D.

From Mansourah to Damietta the line parallels the river, and passes at first through rich cotton country. None of the small towns are of special interest or importance, though they are characteristic enough of the country.

Damietta itself, like Rosetta, declined as Alexandria rose, but it is still a centre of a small commerce from Greek and Levantine ports, besides the interior of Egypt.

The general impression of Damietta is unique. The river

flows past the curious old houses ; steps descend to the water. Every house has its boat, it is the Venice or Amsterdam of Egypt, and has the charm of all such river-side cities. Behind and above the row of houses at the waterside are minarets, roofs, mosques, a wide extent of buildings ; for Damietta is a town of some size, and has notable bazaars.

Damietta has a history of its own. It was the gate of mediæval Egypt long before it had eclipsed Pelusium and annexed the trade of the eastern delta. It fell before the Byzantines in 860 A.D., but they lost it, and the Sultan El-Metounkel fortified it six years later. Then followed the intrusion of Christian warriors: Roger of Sicily in 1165, others in 1217, St. Louis in 1248. All these attacks were followed by sieges and disasters, and finally rest from such incursions. The Arabs destroyed the ancient city and rebuilt it five miles from its ancient site.

A Street Scene, Damietta

LAKE MENZALEH

Lake Menzaleh, the largest lake in Egypt (165 miles in circumference), is accessible from any station between Kantarah and Port Said —or from Port Said itself, and again on the other side from Matarieh. Matarieh, a fair-sized village which has just suffered severely from a fire (April 1907), is the termination of the "Basse Egypte" Light Railway, which starts from Mansourah.

The lake is shallow, and is largely fed by the Nile. In flood time the whole of what was the Pelusian Plain is under water. The lake is remarkable for the myriads of birds of all sorts that frequent it—geese. swans, pelicans, flamingoes, ducks, and every sort of water-loving fowl.

Sais, a collection of fishermen's huts on the south of the lake, was once an important city, Tanis. It was the capital in the twenty-first dynasty. The numerous obelisks are attributed to Rameses the Great, and a gateway bears his name.

The ruins of the city were uncovered by Mariette, who found huge fallen and broken obelisks and great statues of porphyry and granite. Pillars and stones lie here and there where they fell one by one in the silent ages. Pottery and papyri of great interest have also been found. Amongst them were a table of hieroglyphics and a geographical pamphlet showing the *nomes* or provinces of ancient Egypt.

Tanis is the city written of by Messrs. Rider Haggard and Andrew Lang in "The World's Desire," a really fine book. They present that mighty city in all its glory, the reigning Pharaoh Meneptah, the Hebrews and their exodus, and over all is the glamour of the legend of Helen of Troy and Odysseus, who, in the story, came after many wanderings, and solitary, bereft of wife, child, and home, to find his love and death in the "Land of Khem."

The "Field of Zoan"—mentioned in the Bible—which was one of the most fertile parts of the country, was in the neighbourhood of Tanis. It is now covered by Lake Menzaleh.

Sunset on the Banks of Lake Menzaleh

A Breezy Day at Aboukir

CHAPTER VII

ALEXANDRIA

Alexandria has not the same numerous attractions and interests as Cairo, and visitors to Egypt usually neglect it. Still, it is the second city in Egypt, a great commercial centre, and a really fine town of considerable extent and population.

The weather in spring is very pleasant, being warm and sunny, with little rain. When Cairo has become too hot to be comfortable, one may well go to Alexandria, as it is never unpleasantly hot there.

The suburbs of Alexandria are a special featurë, especially that known as Ramleh, to the east, where are many delightful spring and summer resorts. Splendid bathing, boating, and sailing can be had there. These is also the Sporting Club, which corresponds with that in Cairo. Here one may play golf, tennis, cricket, or football, and race meetings are held from time to time in the spring and summer. The club is situated at "Cæsar's Camp," on the electric tram route from Alexandria to Ramleh.

An exceedingly good service of electric trams connects Alexandria with the suburbs of Ramleh; they run from an early hour in the morning till late at night. The station for

Ramleh on the Cairo-Alexandria line is Sidi-Gaber, about ten minutes from Alexandria terminus ; all trains stop there.

As to amusements, in Alexandria itself there is the Zizinia Theatre, at which the various operatic and dramatic companies perform after or before their stay in Cairo. There are also concerts, and occasionally small dances at the hotels.

There are several clubs—the Khedivial (over the Bourse), the Mohammed Aly, in Rue Rosette, and a recently formed but very comfortable little English club, the Union.

HOTELS

There are many hotels and *pensions* in and around Alexandria, of all classes and suitable to every taste. Of those in the town, the Savoy Palace, Khedivial, Grand Hotel, and Hotel Windsor are the best. These are all first-class, and in any one of them the visitor will find comfortable quarters.

The Savoy Palace is perhaps the most up-to-date, as the hotel was only opened at the beginning of 1907. It possesses everything that makes hotel life pleasant—electric lifts, a French restaurant and American bar, a hair-dressing establishment in the hotel; and there are private suites of rooms provided for the more wealthy visitors.

The Khedivial is situated in the fashionable quarter of the town, and can be recommended.

The Grand Hotel is most conveniently placed in the very centre of the town.

The Hotel Windsor is near the sea. It is rather smaller than the hotels mentioned above, and offers very reasonable terms to its visitors.

At Ramleh the principal hotel is the Grand Casino San Stefano—about ten minutes by electric tram from Sidi-Gaber station. This hotel forms the summer quarters of the Government, and it offers many attractions to its visitors. It is on the sea-shore, and has a splendid terrace facing the sea, on which meals are served in summer and a band plays every afternoon. There are also frequent concerts, an occasional dance, and many other entertainments. Attached to the hotel is a well-equipped bathing establishment, where one may take one's morning bathe in the sea with safety and comfort.

The Hotel Beau Rivage is a minute or two further on by tram. It is smaller and more moderate than the Casino, but, for those who prefer a quieter life, very pleasant. In front is the sea, and behind there is a pretty garden with shady trees and a tennis court.

Other hotels that can be recommended are the New Victoria and the Carlton. They are both close to the tramway and rather nearer the town. Full particulars of the hotels, &c., at Alexandria and Ramleh are given on pages 159–161.

Girl with water-jug.

Villas at Ramleh, surrounded by pretty gardens and near the sea, can be rented for longer or shorter periods. The neighbourhood is charming, and the air fresh and cool. It is a great resort in summer, and a godsend to the jaded officials who cannot escape to England during the heat.

It is necessary to give a note of warning to bathers. Although the bathing is perfectly safe all along the coast, it is not advisable to swim far from the shore without a boat, as there are sometimes powerful currents. There have been several fatalities, and it is not safe for even strong swimmers to venture out too far alone.

For particulars about the churches, *see* page 164.

ALEXANDRIA'S EARLY HISTORY

Historically Alexandria has no very ancient interest. It was founded by Alexander the Great of Macedon and developed by Ptolemy Soter. The latter founded the museum and the great library, among whose keepers are such names as Aristophanes of Byzantium and Eratosthenes of Cyrene. Callimachus the poet arranged and labelled the 400,000 papyri. Ptolemy II. (Philadelphus) built the Pharos, a lighthouse of white marble, once one of the seven wonders of the world. During the reign of the Ptolemies Alexandria must have been a great and magnificent city.

The library and museum were burnt to the ground on Julius Cæsar's entry into Alexandria. In compensation Antony is supposed to have presented Cleopatra and her city with the library of Pergamus, in which were some 200,000 MSS. This second library was destroyed by order of the Caliph Omar about 640 A.D.

The Serapeum was a very wonderful building. Begun by Cæsar and completed by Augustus, it held the statue of Serapis, which was worshipped by both Greeks and Egyptians.

Alexandria was a great centre of Christianity and persecution ; perhaps there was more internecine discord there than in any other city of Christian history. Every one who has read Kingsley's book will remember the fate of Hypatia and the character the author gives to the fierce monks and priests. Arius, Athanasius, Cyril, Nestorius, and many a relentless sectarian contributed their share to Alexandrine discord.

POMPEY'S PILLAR AND THE CATACOMBS

Few relics of Alexandria's former greatness remain ; the most interesting are Pompey's Pillar and the Catacombs. The former consists of a single red-granite shaft about seventy feet high. It was erected by a Roman prefect of Egypt in the reign of Diocletian. It can be easily reached by tram from the Mohammed Aly Square in about ten minutes.

A short distance west of Pompey's Pillar are the Catacombs. Among them are many interesting tombs of the first four centuries A.D. One fine tomb of the Roman period was discovered in 1900, and is well worth a visit. It has most interesting and beautiful reliefs both in Egyptian and Roman style. Professor Wallis Budge in Messrs. Cook's guide-book goes into details fully and with admirable precision.

The two obelisks known as "Cleopatra's Needles" once stood in Alexandria, but they have been removed and are now, one in London and the other in New York.

THE MUSEUM

The Museum is situated in a turning off the Rue Rosette. It is under the care of Dr. Botti, and contains many antiquities, principally of the Græco-Roman period.

MARIOUT RAILWAY

To the west of Alexandria is the terminus of H.H. the Khedive's railway. The line runs south-westwards parallel to the coast for a distance of about 110 miles.

There are many Bedouin settlements on the way, and the country, which a few years ago was waste land and desert, is becoming populated, and now thrives under the influence of the railway.

RUINS OF ST. MENAS

The ruins of the city of St. Menas, the patron saint of Christian Egypt, were, strange to say, only discovered two years ago by the researches of German archæologists. The city is a few hours' ride to the north of Behig, a station on H.H. the Khedive's railway. We owe the information given here to the courtesy of Rowland Snelling, Esq., of Alexandria, who wrote two admirable articles on the discoveries at Mariout in the *Egyptian Gazette* for April 17 and 20, 1907.

" Mariout was a species of Egyptian Lourdes, a city of pilgrimage. The pilgrims used to bear away terra-cotta ampullæ or flasks of the holy water of St. Menas. Some of these flasks are to be found in every museum in Europe. St. Menas was martyred in Phrygia in 296 A.D. His body was brought to Alexandria and placed on a camel, and the beast allowed to wander as he chose. He stopped near Lake Mareotis. A tomb was built there which possessed miraculous powers. Followed a church and then a town. A great basilica was erected in the reign of Arcadius (395–408 A.D.).

" The earliest extant account of it is from an unknown Arab traveller, who visited it probably in the tenth century. The description is contained in a manuscript in the Paris Library, and is as follows: ' Leaving Tarraneh and following the road towards Barca, one comes to Mena, which consists of three abandoned towns in the midst of a sandy desert, with their buildings still standing. The Arabs use it as a place for lying in wait for travellers. There may be seen lofty and well-built palaces with enclosure walls around them. They are for the most part built over vaulted colonnades, and some few serve as dwellings for monks. There are some springs of fresh water, but they are somewhat scanty. Next one comes to the church of St. Menas, a huge building decorated with statues and paintings of the greatest beauty. There tapers burn day and night without ceasing. At one end of the church is a vast tomb with two camels in marble, and upon them the statue of a man carved in marble, who is standing with one foot upon each camel. One of his hands is open and the other closed. This statue is said to represent St. Menas. On the right as you enter the church is a great marble column, in which a shrine is carved containing figures of Jesus, John, and Zacharias. There is also to be seen a statue of the Virgin Mary, hidden by two curtains, and statues of all the prophets. Outside the church are figures representing all kinds of animals and men of all occupations. Among others is a slave merchant holding in his hand a purse upside down. Over the midst of the church is a dome, beneath which are eight figures said to represent angels. Close to the church is a mosque, where the Moslems come to pray. All the surrounding land is planted with fruit trees. The fruit is very good, and used for making syrup. There are also a great many vines from which wine is made.'

"This description proves that for long after the Arab conquest, although the city was uninhabited, yet it was still intact, but the unknown Arab traveller wrote these lines in the tenth century, before the conquest of England by the Normans, and from that time until June 1905 the marble city of the patron saint of Egypt remained lost amidst the wilds of Mariout. The vines and fruit trees have all gone, the springs are dried up, and not a single visitor save the wandering Bedouin has ever passed by the ruined basilicas and monasteries of the Lourdes of Christian Egypt. Although the feast of St. Menas has always been kept up by the Orthodox, Jacobite, and Abyssinian Churches, and the flasks of the holy oil of the saint have been collected in all the museums of Europe, the mystery surrounding the site of the city appeared to be as insoluble as that of the equally recondite Wady-el-Malook in Upper Egypt, until the learned world of Europe was lately apprised of the fact that the city had at last been found by two German savants, the Rev. C. M. Kaufmann and Mr. Edward Falls. After arduous search they arrived, thanks to the chance indications of a Bedouin boy who had discovered a singularly perfect ampulla, at the site of the city.

"On excavating they discovered four basilicas, the crypt of St. Menas, the great baptistery, and many other sacred buildings and baths. The basilica of the emperor must have been a most impressive structure. It was covered with marble and supported by fifty columns. A quantity of beautifully sculptured capitals still remains. There is also a series of sepulchral chambers underground. The tomb and the crypt are also interesting, and must have been beautifully decorated with mosaics. In the holy well, a great cistern eighty-six metres long, have been discovered thousands of ampullæ.

"The Monastery or Koinobion of St. Menas—the most interesting of all the remains—was the finest in the whole of Northern Africa.

"When the city was first discovered the site was covered with a series of low mounds. There was not a wall or trace of a building to be seen. But since this part began to be excavated great progress has been made, in spite of the difficult nature of the work. The pavements of fifty rooms, corridors, and halls have been unearthed at from four to five metres underground. Entering by a portico, which was formerly vaulted, the visitor can inspect a series of rooms. Two courts with large cisterns have been opened up, and a great deal of marble and blocks of fine granite—the latter probably from Taposiris Magna—are to be seen. In this part of the convent some curious little statues of monkeys were found. In the baths of the Koinobion numbers of amphoræ and ampullæ for holy water were discovered, many of them with inscriptions. The Rev. C. M. Kaufmann considers, from the various pottery ovens found here, that all the ampullæ of St. Menas which have been found elsewhere, such as at Kom-el-Shougafa, were made in the factory here, for over eighty different kinds of ampullæ have been found lately in the ruins, and many thousands more are still buried in the earth. Among other noteworthy buildings are the baths connected with the baptistery. They were fitted with waiting-rooms and supplied from large cisterns twenty-two metres deep. A reservoir, forty by seventy metres, has been found close by. In another part of the Koinobion a dining-hall has been discovered. It was probably reserved for distinguished guests. Here was found a magnificent relief in white marble. The roof of this hall was supported by columns, and the walls were covered with marble and porphyry. The Rev. C. M. Kaufmann informs us that, judging from the numerous fine capitals which have of late been found on the west side of the monastery, he hopes to come upon the church of St. Thekla, which is mentioned in the life of the saint. This church was within the Koinobion, and probably some highlv important discoveries will be made there."

ABOUKIR

A very pleasant excursion may be made to Aboukir, a small village about ten miles east of Alexandria, along the coast. It has much historical interest, both ancient and modern. Near it stood the great city of Canopus in Ptolemaic times, and here the Canopic branch of the Nile entered the sea. According to Seneca, Canopus was chiefly remarkable for the luxury and depravity of its inhabitants.

In later times Aboukir is famous as giving its name to Nelson's great battle and victory over the French fleet in 1798. Napoleon defeated the Turkish army in 1799 at Aboukir, and his army was defeated there by Sir Ralph Abercrombie in 1801.

There are frequent trains to Aboukir from Sidi-Gaber (Alexandria-Ramleh Railway Company's station). The journey occupies about thirty-five minutes. The following are the best trains ·

From Sidi Gaber : 10.50 A M , 2.0 and 4.10 P.M.
Aboukir : 1.10, 4.55, 7.0, and 8.35 P M.

The fares are :				
1st class,	single,	4 pt. ;	return,	6 pt.
2nd ,,	,,	3 ,, ;	,,	4 ,,

A good way of making the expedition is to go to Aboukir by railway and on the return to charter donkeys and ride back to San Stefano along the coast. From San Stefano the electric tram takes one to Alexandria in a few minutes.

The sea-shore at Aboukir is of sand, smooth and fine, and it makes a good place for a picnic.

ROSETTA

A visit to Rosetta makes a whole day's expedition from Alexandria.

The trains are as follows :

	A.M.	P.M.		A.M.	P.M.
Alexandria	7.30	3.20	Rosetta	6. 4	3 53
Sidi-Gaber	7.44	3.34	Sidi-Gaber	8.35	6. 2
Rosetta .	9.36	5.50	Alexandria	8.45	6.15

Fares : 1st class, 34½ pt. ; 2nd class, 17½ pt.

The journey itself is interesting. At first are the gardens of Ramleh, then the summer palace of H.H. the Khedive at Montaza is passed. Then the line threads the narrow strip of land between the sea on the left and Lake Edkou on the right. Maadieh and Edkou are resorts of fishers, and their bright-coloured, flat-bottomed boats with high curling prows are seen on the edge of the lake. In winter vast flocks of water-fowl can be seen on the water. Between Boussili and Rosetta is mostly desert, relieved at intervals by tiny villages amid their palms and fruit trees.

Rosetta is a town of considerable size, but its population has dwindled, so that most of the houses appear to be empty. It stands on the western branch of the Nile, near its mouth. For this reason it used to be a port of considerable importance, until, when the Mahmoudieh Canal was cut, the trade of the Delta was diverted to Alexandria. There is still a considerable industry in rice.

The streets are lined with curious, old-world houses, standing aloof, as if Rosetta had long retired from the active race for prosperity.

The town is memorable for one great discovery, the " Rosetta Stone," now in the British Museum. On this stone is engraved a decree which is written in three forms—ancient Egyptian hieroglyphics, Demotic characters, and Greek. It was discovered in 1799, and formed the first key with which the inscriptions of ancient Egypt were deciphered.

Sonnini, who visited Egypt in 1777, is enthusiastic over the " rich, fertile, and beautiful country, the gardens, the odoriferous hedges, encircling bowers still more fragrant. Everything seems to grow by chance ; the orange- and the lemon-tree intertwine their boughs, and the pomegranate hangs by the side of the anone (custard apple)." The writer evidently saw Rosetta in much better case than it is to-day. It is, however, a pleasant place in which to spend a few hours.

In the Oasis of Siwa

CHAPTER VIII

ISMAILIA—SUEZ—THE CANAL—THE PENINSULA OF SINAI AND THE OASES

CAIRO TO ISMAILIA

For two hours one traverses the Delta, swiftly and smoothly, through rich cotton and corn land, bridging canals that flow peacefully between long rows of mimosa-trees. To the right is the pale rose border of low hills that stretch from Marg past Belbeis, along the desert line to Abou-Hammad. There the cultivation ceases. From Abou-Hammad to Tel-el-Kebir is sand—uncompromising sand, and only sand.

The brief halt at Tel-el-Kebir shows the cemetery on the right hand—a green patch, quiet with memories. Again there is sand and waste until Ismailia is reached. There is complete change—a leafy hamlet in the midst of desert. Everywhere is thick foliage of lebbek-trees above carpets of flowers and vegetation, intersected by straight white roads.

At Ismailia

From Ismailia station the road leads straight to the lake, down the avenue that crosses the canal. There one may well pause at the bridge. The bank is a mass of colour—red, orange, white, and blue flowers. Below, the boats lounge past under the trees.

Everything is lazy and peaceful, bathed in warm sunlight. Here and there, down the road, appear neat small houses—bungalows, rather; their verandahs, that tell of easy-going, outdoor life, are gay with many-coloured creepers. Here are no Arab huts, no strenuous shops, nothing but acclimatised quiet.

Then comes the lake—vivid, deep blue. The far-off Asian bank is vivid golden sand, against which stands out the least mark, shrubs or stumps of black wood. Even the steamers, passing up and down, appear black in the keen sunlight. It is all restful, full of calm light and colour.

The trains run as follows :

	A.M.	A.M.	P.M.		A.M.	P.M.	P.M.
Cairo .	7. 0	11. 0	6.15	Ismailia .	9.59	2.1	8.17
Ismailia .	10.16	1.59	9.26	Cairo .	1.25	5.0	11.25

NOTE.—A restaurant-car is attached to the 11.0 A.M. and 6.15 P.M. train from Cairo and the 2.1 P.M. and 8.17 P.M. from Ismailia.

	A.M.	P.M.		A.M.	P.M.
Ismailia	2.15	9.45	Suez Docks	7.30	5.40
Suez Town	4. 3	11.33	Suez Town	7.50	6. 0
Suez Docks	4.20	11.50	Ismailia.	9.38	7.48

NOTE.—A through carriage to Suez is attached to the 11.0 A.M. train from Cairo on Wednesdays, and to Cairo to the 5.40 P.M. from Suez on Saturdays.

Detailed time-tables, page 174.

Fares :				
	Cairo to Suez,	1st class,	96½;	2nd class, 48½.
	,, to Ismailia	,,	70 ;	,, 35.
	Ismailia to Suez	,,	44½;	,, 22.

ISMAILIA TO SUEZ

The journey takes about two hours, through desert land all the way. Bordering the line are stretches of marsh. To the right are the hills, red-brown; to the left the Canal. One can only see the canal momentarily where it appears, blue as the curved blade of a Damascus sword. The only sign of the waterway is the mast or funnel of some ship gliding slowly from station to station.

The wind blows keen, clean, and increasing across the

line. At last come fields, trees, houses, and then Suez (Suez Town)—a dusty old town, stretching in untidy detachments down to the sea.

The train passes through the town and comes out upon a long causeway leading to Suez Docks.

Round the docks is a small town in itself, and the cleanest, pleasantest part of Suez. Here are the Canal Co.'s and other offices, with the houses of the officials facing a shady boulevard. In front passes the ceaseless stream of shipping, entering and leaving the Canal.

Look seaward. The anchorage is bounded on the right by the high red cliffs of Gebel Attakah; on either side the more distant hills tail off, grey-blue, towards the open sea, where runs the road to India and the Far East.

There are two small hotels, the Hôtel Bachet and the Hôtel Bel-Air, but few people stay in Suez unless compelled by the exigencies of travel.

THE SUEZ CANAL

The Canal by day is not profoundly exciting. The progress is slow, the scenery unvaried. One should start in the late afternoon, and take advantage of the night-time. For the night reveals the one feature of the voyage at its best—the Bitter Lakes. After a slow and toilsome journey through the narrow passage, the ship emerges suddenly into the open. The searchlight plays full, brilliant, on the depth of dark sky and water.

Myriad white shapes appear ahead, flitting, dipping, skimming, nearing the boat, then retreating, resting on the water, quitting it, with slow-flapping wings. When they are quite close, under full play of the light, you can see that they are pelicans, with their wide wings, long beak, and pouch beneath. As they pass under the ray they appear as tongues of flame, transparent, mysterious, against the bright darkness of the water.

Here the ships do not stop to exchange courtesies or combat precedence for tying up. A big P. and O., or a long, lean German Lloyd sheers past almost at full speed, ablaze with light. The pilot-boat hangs on for dear life, while the pilot ascends or descends the ladder like a trained acrobat. At length one's own boat makes the entrance, and from the Bitter Lakes the Canal is placid, narrow, and uneventful as far as Port Said.

THE SINAI PENINSULA

A visit to the Sinai Peninsula is an undertaking that requires special preparations, and it is best to apply at once to Messrs. Cook and Son, who are thorough experts in all such matters. They will not only provide all possible and necessary means of transport, but will arrange to charge a fixed price per day. This saves all bargaining and trouble. and is by far the most comfortable and economical process.

The expedition should take about three weeks, which will give plenty of time for seeing the chief objects of interest.

The peninsula itself is a mountainous desert, arid and desolate, but with its own grandeur, and even fascination. It is inhabited by a number of Bedouins, who do a certain amount of rather primitive trading in gum-arabic, charcoal, and manna from the tamarisk trees.

The real interest of the desert is its Biblical and Christian history. One mav see Horeb, Sinai, and many another spot associated with the wanderings of the Chosen People. A visit should be made to the great monasterv of St. Catherine, founded by Justinian in 530 A.D. It is the home of many famous manuscripts—above all, the Sinaitic Codex of the Septuagint, which Tischendorf retrieved after three visits. The monastery is rich in relics and memorials of early saints—St. Helena, Joachim, Simon Stylites of the Pillar, and many another. It is one of the few remaining monuments of the dawn of Christianity.

It is hardly within the scope of this book to enter into a full disquisition on all that others have so admirably described from intimate knowledge and experience. We will but hint at the ancient Church of the Transfiguration, its strange mosaics and medallions, and its great library, in which is the Codex Aureus—twelve hundred years old, written in gold on vellum—the Psalter, and many another treasure of pious craftsmanship. A four days' visit is none too long for the monastery and all that it can show.

Another feature of the Sinai Peninsula is its importance as a field for mining enterprise. There are records of its having been worked as far back as the third dynasty, and the mines bear inscriptions by many of the kings from the thirteenth to the twentieth dynasties. Little further is heard of the peninsula as a whole from B.C. 1200 to the second or third centuries of the Christian era. Turquoises, malachite, and copper were the chief treasures found.

Scarcely any attempts of importance have been made as

yet to reopen these mines, but no one can say what future efforts may not discover in so rich a field.

Sarbut-el-Khâdem is the centre of that long-dead industry, close to Wady-Nasb, where the mines were situated, and here are ruins of columns, and stelæ with inscriptions. There was also a small temple dedicated to Hathor, Lady of Mafkat (or the Turquoise Land), and on its walls were records and reliefs.

The traveller who wishes to study the Sinaitic Peninsula fully will find valuable information in various works. We may quote the Palestine Exploration Fund survey as one of the best, also Professor Hull's "Mount Seir, Sinai" (London, 1885), Dean Stanley's "Sinai and Palestine" and "Ancient History from the Monuments of Sinai," and last, but by no means least in value and interest, Professor Wallis Budge's edition of "Cook's Guide-Book" (1904)

THE OASES

The oases are small patches of fertile land surrounded by desert. Some of them are of considerable extent and have a resident population; others consist of a few palm-trees only, clustered round a single spring. A chain of these oases runs parallel to the valley of the Nile, and from a hundred to two hundred miles from it. It is supposed that they indicate the former course of the river.

In ancient history many of the oases were of considerable importance. Herodotus mentions them as the "Islands of the Blest," and the ancient Egyptian name, "Nabet," signified a place of mummies, in that the legend claimed that the jackal-headed Anubis conducted the spirits of the dead from their tombs in the valley across the mountains and desert to their paradise.

The principal oases, from north to south, are: (1) Siwa, or Jupiter Ammon, which is about twenty days' journey west of Cairo; (2) Bahrieh, opposite Minieh; (3) Farafra, opposite Assiut; (4) Dakhel and (5) Kharga, due west of Esneh, but approached from Farshout; (6) Kurkur, north-west of Kom Ombo; and (7) Selima, south-west of Wadi-Halfa.

It is hardly the province of this book to describe these expeditions and their objects at length. They entail special journeys of several days by camel. They are, of course, highly interesting, but hardly feasible for the majority of visitors.

The Oasis of Siwa, or Jupiter Ammon, is about six miles in length and four or five broad. Herodotus tells us that Cambysis sent a force of 50,000 men to enslave its inhabitants and burn their temple, but a great sandstorm engulfed and destroyed them. Alexander the Great visited this oasis, and was, the legend says, well received by Ammon, the god thereof. It is certain that it was occupied and fortified, probably as far back as the nineteenth dynasty, and many memorials and reliefs are found there to support this. The present population is about 7000. The two principal towns are Siwa and Akermi, which are usually at feud with one another.

It is perhaps as well for those wishing to visit this oasis to apply to the authorities in Cairo, though nowadays there is little likelihood of any difficulty arising to prevent expeditions.

The Oasis of Bahrieh, or Northern Oasis, is four or five days' easy journey from the Fayoum. The population in 1897 was 6000.

The Farafra Oasis is midway between Bahrieh and Dakhel; its population is about 540. It is of very small area, and can never have been very flourishing. There are a certain number of rock tombs to the north, possibly Roman. It can be reached from Minieh in eight days on a good camel.

The Oasis of Dakhel is seven days from Assiut, or four days from the Farafra Oasis. It has over 17,000 inhabitants, 3000 of these living in its chief village, El-Kasr (the fort). There are the ruins of a temple of the Roman period, dedicated to Ameri-Rā or Horus of Behutet by Titus and other emperors (nowadays called Deir-el-Hargar, or the Convent of Stone). The Romans kept a small garrison here, and probably it was frequented by recluses in the third, fourth, and fifth centuries A.D. Its date trade is fairly considerable.

The Oasis of Kharga—the Great Oasis—is about four days' camel-ride from Farshout. Recently the Western Oases Company have started boring operations for artesian wells, with a view to putting a larger area under cultivation. A narrow-gauge railway is also being constructed from the Nile valley (Kharga Junction on the State railways) to Kharga, the capital of the oasis, a distance of about 100 miles. It is hoped that communication will be complete by the winter of 1907–8.

The oasis has a population of about 7000, and there are

about 4500 acres of land under cultivation at present. The principal trade is in dates; there are some 70,000 date-palms, and the fruit is better than that grown anywhere in Egypt.

The principal ancient Egyptian remains are the temple of Hibis (B.C. 521), in which is inscribed an interesting hymn to the sun-god. At Nadara, near the modern capital, are three temples, one of the time of Ptolemy III. (B.C. 240) and the other two of the time of Antoninus Pius (150 A.D.). There are the remains, also, of Roman watch-towers and forts, a circular brick-kiln and tombs, probably of the third and fourth centuries of the Christian era. Near Ein Tabashir are some curious buildings with tiny cubical recesses (eight inches across), which may have been dovecots.

The Oases of Kurkur and Selima are quite small, and of no great interest. Selima, it is true, was an important station on the caravan route for the slave and other trades from East and Central Africa through all the oases to Morocco.

The Wady Natroun, or Natron Valley, is hardly an oasis, as there is little or no cultivation. The valley—about twenty miles long—has several small salt lakes and is remarkable for its alkaline deposits, which furnish salt, sulphate and carbonate of soda, and similar products. The Wady-Natroun has considerable antiquarian interest, and is comparatively easy of access, being but a few hours from Cairo.

There used to be a town in the middle of the valley—a large settlement of Christian monks. St. Macarius, the Egyptian, was the pioneer of these recluses, to the number of some 5000, as well as 600 desert anchorites. He is supposed to be buried in the monastery which bears his name. Ten miles to the west of it is the Monastery of Anaba Bishai, and further on the Syrian Monastery (Deir Suriani), built by John the Dwarf in the time of Constantine. It possessed a fine library, and even now contains three churches, the chief of which is dedicated to the Virgin. There is also the Monastery of Baramus, six or eight miles further west.

The Natron Valley and its monasteries have been visited by many travellers ever since Egidus Lochiensis in 1633. and great stores of manuscripts have been recovered therefrom. They must have been veritable treasuries, especially Deir Suriani. Intending visitors should consult "Visits to Monasteries in the Levant," by the Hon. R. Curzon, who visited the valley in 1837 (fifth edition, 1865).

APPENDIX I

ENGLISH—ARABIC VOCABULARY

As there are many sounds in Arabic not used in English, it is not always possible to express exactly Arabic words with English characters.

If the following rules are observed, however, an approximation to the Arabic sounds will be obtained.

" a " should be pronounced like the French " a."
" ā " " " " a " in " father."
" ū " " " " oo " in " roof."
" oo " " " " oo " in " book."
" kh " " " " ch " in " loch."
" gh " is a guttural combination of " g " and " r."
" r " should always be rolled.

TRAVELLING

Bag	*shanta*
Boat, sailing	*markeb*
,, rowing	*fellūca*
Booking office	*maktab-et-tazaker*
Cab	*arabeeya*
Cab driver	*arbaggy*
Camel	*gamal*
Carriage (railway)	*arabeeya*
Cart (baggage)	*carrox*
Class, first	*daraga breemo*
Class, second	*daraga secūndo*
Custom house	*gūmrook*
Dining-car	*arabeeyat el akel*
Donkey	*hōmār*
Express	*egsbres*
Fare	*oogra*
Ferry	*ma'adeeya*
Guard	*comsāry*
Luggage	*afsh*
Platform	*rasseef*
Porter	*shayyal*
Railway	*sikket hadeed*
Sleeping-car	*arabeeyat en-nōm*
Station	*mahatta*
Station-master	*nāzer el mahatta*
Telegraph office	*maktab et-telegraf*
Telegram	*telegraf*
Ticket	*tazkara*
Train	*babūr, 'attr*
Take my baggage	*khod afshi*
Fetch me a cab	*hat arabeeya*
Are you disengaged ?	*enta fādi*
What is the fare ?	*kam el oogra*
Straight on	*dōghry*
Turn round	*dowar*
Stop	*stanna*
Turn to the right	*yemeenak*
,, ,, left	*shemālak*
Quickly	*'awam, bil agel*
Slowly	*bishwesh*
By the hour	*bil sa'ah*

THE TOWN, SHOPS, &c.

Baker	*farān*
Bootmaker	*gazmaggy*
Bridge	*koobry*
Butcher	*gazzar*
Chemist	*agzaggy*
Church	*kincesa*
The citadel	*el-alla'a*
Hospital	*esbetallia*
Hotel	*locanda*
House	*buyt*, plu. *buy-ūt*

I.

APPENDIX I

THE TOWN, SHOPS, &c.—*continued.*

Jeweller	*gou-a-hir-gy*	School	*madrassa*
Merchant	*tāger*	Shop	*dokān*
Mosque	*gameh'*	Shopkeeper	*sahib-ed-dokān*
The museum	*anteeka-hāna*	Square	*meedān*
Policeman	*shaweesh*	Street	*shareh'*
Police station	*caracol*	Telegraph office	*et-telegraf*
The post office	*el bōsta*	Tram	*tramway*

THE COUNTRY, EGYPT, &c.

Alexandria	*eskandareea*	Mountain	*gabal*
Cairo	*masr*	The Nile	*en neel*
Canal	*teera'a*	River	*el bahr*
Country	*aree-āff*	Road	*sikka*
The desert	*el khalla*	Rock	*hagar*
Earth	*ard*	Sand	*raml*
Egypt	*masr*	The sea	*el bahr*
,, Upper	*el wagh el 'ibly*	Sky	*sama*
,, Lower	*el wagh el bahary*	Star	*negma*
Europe	*uroba*	Stone	*hagar*
Hill	*tel*	The sun	*esh-shams*
Island	*gezireh*	Town	*medeena*
Lake	*birka*	Valley	*waddy*
Land	*attian*	Village	*belad*
Moon	*āmar*	The world	*ed-dunya*

HOUSEHOLD

Basin	*tisht*	Key	*mooftah*
Bath	*hammam*	Kitchen	*matbakh*
Bed	*sereer*	Kitchen range	*fūrn*
Bell	*garras*	Lamp	*lamba, fanūs*
Blanket	*battaneea*	Lock	*kalūn*
Candle	*shama'*	Mattress	*murtaba*
Candlestick	*shama' dan*	Mirror	*mirra-ya*
Carpet	*bussat, sigardeh*	Mosquito net	*namūseea*
Chair	*kūrsy*	Pillow	*makhada*
Clock	*sa'ah*	Pillow-case	*kees-el-makhada*
Closet	*bayt el addab*	Roof	*sa-af*
Cupboard	*dūlāb*	Sheet	*melai-yah*
Curtain	*setara*	Soap	*saboon*
Door	*bab*	Staircase	*sillim*
Drawer	*dorg*	Table	*tarabayza*
Filter	*filtr*	,, dining	*soofra*
Floor	*ardee-ya*	Towel	*fūtah hammam*
Garden	*genayna*	Wall	*hayta*
House	*bayt*	Window	*shebbak*, plu. *shebabeek*
Jug	*abreek*		

MEALS, FOOD, &c.

Apple	*toofāh*	Beer	*beera*
Apricot	*mish-mish*	Bottle	*gazaz*
Banana	*mōz*	Bread	*aysh*
Beans	*fūl*	Breakfast	*fatūr*
Beef	*lahm ba'ary*	Butler	*suffrāgy*

APPENDIX I

MEALS, FOOD, &c.—*continued.*

Butter	*zibda*	Meat	*Lahma*
Cabbage	*currūmb*	Melon (water)	*shammam, battikh*
Carrot	*gazar*	Milk	*laban*
Cheese	*gibna*	Mustard	*mūstarda*
Chicken	*farkha*	Mutton	*lahma dāny*
Cigarettes	*sagā-yer*	Napkin	*fūta*
Coffee	*'ah-wa*	Nuts	*būndu'*
Cork	*filla*	Oil	*zayt*
Corkscrew	*bareema*	Olive	*zaytūn*
Cucumber	*kheeār*	Onion	*bassel*
Cup	*fingan*, plu. *anageen*	Orange	*borto'ān*
Dates	*ballah*	Pear	*kommetra*
Decanter	*'oollah*	Peas	*bissilla*
Dinner	*a'asha*	Pepper	*fil-fil*
Drinks	*mushrūbat*	Plate	*sahn*, plu. *suhūn*
Eggs	*bayd*	Pork	*lihm khanzeer*
Figs	*teen*	Potatoes	*batātis*
Fish	*samuk*	Rice	*rūz*
Flour	*da'eek*	Salt	*malh*
Food	*akel*	Sauce	*salsa*
Fork	*shoka*	Soup	*shorba*
Fruit	*frūta*	Spinach	*sabanikh*
Glass (tumbler)	*cubbai-ya*	Spoon	*ma'allaga*
Grapes	*'enab*	Strawberries	*frowla*
Jam	*merrubba*	Sugar	*sūkker*
Kidney	*kelouy*	Sweet (pudding)	*hel-ū*
Knife	*sekeena*	Table-cloth	*ghata es-soofra*
Lamb	*kharūf*	Tea	*shai*
Lemon	*limūn*	Tomatoe	*tomātim*
Lemonade	*limonāda*	Veal	*lahma agāly*
Lettuce	*khass*	Vegetables	*khodarat*
Liver	*kibda*	Vinegar	*khall*
Luncheon	*ghadda*	Wine	*nebeet*
Mandarine	*Yūsef-effendi*		

MANKIND, RELATIONS

Boy	*walad*	Man	*rāgel*, plu. *rigala*
Bride	*arūssa*	Mother	*umm*
Brother	*akh*	People	*nas*
Daughter	*bint*	Sister	*ukht*
Family	*'īla*	Son	*ibn*
Father	*abb*	Widow	*azaba*
Girl	*bint*	Wife	*zōgah*
Husband	*zōg*	Woman	*sitt*

PARTS OF THE BODY

Arm	*dira'a*	Hair	*sha'ar*
Back	*dahr*	Hand	*eed*
Blood	*dam*	Head	*ras*
Body	*gism*	Heart	*'alb*
Bone	*adm*	Leg	*sak*
Brain	*mookh*	Mouth	*fom*
Ears	*widān*	Nose	*manakheer*
Eyes	*ayn*	Skin	*gild*
Face	*wish*	Stomach	*batn*
Finger	*soba'a*	Teeth	*sinān*
Foot	*rigel*		

APPENDIX I

CLOTHES, &c.

Boots	*gizam*	Rug	*battaneea*
Brush	*fursha*	Scissors	*ma'ass*
Button	*zorār*	Shawl	*shal*
Clothes	*hedūm*	Shirt	*'amees*
Coat	*sitra'a*	Slippers	*shibshib*
Collar	*ya'ah*	Socks	*shorabat*
Drawers	*libbas*	Sponge	*suffinga*
Gloves	*aldiwān*	Stick	*assay-ya*
Great-coat	*balto*	Stud	*zorār*
Handkerchief	*mandeel*	Suit of clothes	*badla*
Hat	*bornayta*	Thread	*kheit*
Needle	*ibra*	Tie	*bombagh*
Pin	*dubbūs*	Trousers	*bantalūn*
Pocket	*gayb*	Waistcoat	*seederv*
Razor	*moos*		

PROFESSIONS, TRADES, &c.

Carpenter	*naggar*	Messenger	*sai-ee*
Clerk	*kātib*	Officer	*zābet*
Coachman	*arbaggy*	Policeman	*shaweesh*
Consul	*'onsul*	Porter	*shayyal*
Cook	*tabbākh*	Postman	*bostaggy*
Doctor	*hakeem*	Servant	*haddam*, plu. *haddameen*
Donkey boy	*hammār*		
Doorkeeper	*bowab*	Soldier	*askerry*
Engineer	*muhandez*	Tailor	*khayyat, tarzy*
Gardener	*ganayny*	Washerman	*ghassāl*
Groom	*syse*	Watchman	*ghafeer*
Guide / Interpreter	*terrgomān*		

ANIMALS, &c.

Ant	*naml*	Goose	*wizz*
Bird	*tayr*	Hawk	*sakr*
Buffalo	*gammūs*	Hornet	*dabbūr*
Calf	*egle*	Horse	*hussan*, plu. *khail*
Cat	*'ottah*	Kite	*hedayya*
Camel	*gamal*	Mosquito	*namūs*
Chicken	*fahkha*	Mule	*bagl*
Cow	*ba'ara*	Pig	*khanzeer*
Crow	*ghūrāb*	Pigeon	*hamam*
Dog	*kalb*	Quail	*simmān*
Donkey	*homār*	Rabbit or hare	*arnab*
Duck	*batt*	Rat or mouse	*far*
Flea	*barghūt*, plu. *baragheet*	Scorpion	*a'raba*
		Sheep	*kharūf*
Fly	*dubbāna*, plu. *dubbān*	Snake	*teabān*
		Snipe	*bekasseen*
Gazelle	*gazala*	Turkey	*dik rūmy*
Goat	*gidye*		

APPENDIX I

METALS

Brass	*nahass asfar*	Lead	*rūsass*
Copper	*nahass ahmar*	Silver	*fudda*
Gold	*dahab*	Steel	*sūlb*
Iron	*hadeed*	Tin	*suffee-eh*

COLOURS

Black	*iswid*	Green	*akhdar*
Blue	*azra'*	Red	*ahmar*
Brown	*asmar*	White	*abiad*
Colour	*lōn*	Yellow	*asfar*

NUMERALS, DATES, &c.

1 *wāhid*	10 *'ashara*	19 *tissa'tashar*	60 *sitteen*
2 *etnayn*	11 *hedashar*	20 *eshreen*	70 *saba'een*
3 *talāta*	12 *etnashar*	21 *wāhid ou eshreen*	80 *tamaneen*
4 *arba'a*	13 *talatashar*		90 *tissa'een*
5 *khamsa*	14 *arba'tashar*	30 *talateen*	100 *meeya*
6 *sitta*	15 *khamstashar*	31 *wāhid ou talateen*	1000 *alf*
7 *saba'a*	16 *sittashar*		1st *el awal*
8 *tamania*	17 *saba'tashar*	40 *arba'een*	2nd *ettāny*
9 *tissa'a*	18 *tamantashar*	50 *khamseen*	3rd *ettālit*

Once	*marra*	Year	*sana*, plu. *seneen*
Twice	*marretain*	Month	*shahr*, plu. *ash-hur*
Three times	*telāt marrāt*	Week	*gūma'*
Half	*nuss*	Day	*yōm*, plu. *ai-yam*
Quarter	*rōbh*	Hour	*sa'ah*, plu. *sa'at*
Date	*tareekh*	Minute	*dagayg*
Sunday	*yom el hadd*	Morning	*sōbh*
Monday	*yom el etnayn*	Afternoon	*bā'd ed-dohr*
Tuesday	*yom et-talāt*	Night	*layl*
Wednesday	*yom el arba'*	To-day	*en-nahar-da*
Thursday	*yom el khamees*	Yesterday	*embareh*
Friday	*yom el gūma'*	To-morrow	*bookrah*
Saturday	*yom es-sapt*	Last week	*el gūma' elly fātet*
Summer	*sayf*	Next week	*el gūma' elly gai-ya*
Winter	*sheeta*		

NOUNS

Age	*omr*	Cartridge	*khartūsh*
Air	*houah*	Case	*elba*
Answer	*radd*	Certificate	*sha-hāda*
Antiquities	*anteeka*	Chain	*cateena*
Axe	*balta*	Change (money)	*fakka*
Bag	*shanta*	Cigarettes	*sagā-yer*
Ball	*korah*	Clerk	*kātib*
Basket	*sabat*	Cloth (stuff)	*'umāsh*
Bill	*hissāb*	Coal	*fahm*
Bird	*tayr*	Cotton	*'otn*
Blotting-paper	*warra' nashāf*	Cream	*ishta*
Book	*kitāb*	Day	*yōm*
Box	*sandūk*	Dust	*torāb*
Boot polish	*boy-a*	East	*shar'*
Bridge	*koobry*	Envelope	*zarf*

NOUNS—*continued.*

Face	*wish*
Feather	*reesh*
Ferry	*ma'adeeya*
Fire	*nar*
Flowers	*ward*
Fool	*magnūr*
Friend	*sahib*
God	*'allah*
Gentleman, Mr.	*khawāga*
Grass	*hasheesh*
Guide	*terrgomān*
Gun	*būndūkee-ya*
Hammer	*shakūsh*
Handle	*eed*
Ice	*talg*
Ink	*hibr*
Inkstand	*da-wai-yeh*
Interpreter	*mūtargim*
Judge	*'ady*
Lady	*sitt*
Leaf	*warra'a*
Leather	*gild*
Letter	*gou-ab*, plu. *gewabat*
Light	*nūr*
Line	*khatt*, plu. *khetūt*
Market	*sūk*
Master	*seed*
Matches	*kabreet*
Messenger	*sai-ee*
Middle	*woost*
Money	*fellūs*
Nail	*moosmar*
Name	*ism*
News	*khabber*
Newspaper	*goornāl*
Noise	*ghāgha*
North	*bahry*
Oar	*mu'dāf*
Officer	*zābet*
Order	*amr*
Page	*saheefa*
Paint	*boy-a*
Paper	*warra*
Parcel	*tard*
Peasant	*fellah*
Pen	*'alam*
Peneil	*'alam rusass*
Petition	*tallab*
Petroleum	*gāz*

Piastre	*'eersh*, plu. *'oorūsh*
Piastre, half	*tareefa*
Piece	*hitta*
Place	*mahal*
Postage stamp	*warra' bōsta*
Pound (money)	*guinee*
Pound (weight)	*rutl*
Price	*taman*
Question	*sū-āl*
Rain	*matar*
Receipt	*wassl*
Reward	*baksheesh*
Rope	*habl*, plu. *hibāl*
Saddle	*sarg*
Sail	*alla'a*
School	*madrassa*
Screw	*alla'ōz*
Servant	*khaddam*, plu. *khaddameen*
Side	*barr*
Skin	*gild*
Smell	*reeha*
Smoke	*dokhān*
Soldier	*askerry*, plu. *asārker*
South	*'ibly*
Stable	*establ*
Star	*negma*, plu. *noogūm*
String	*dūbara*
The sun	*esh-shems*
Temple	*birba*
Thief	*harāmy*
Thing	*hāga*, plu. *hagāt*
Time	*sa'ah*
Tobacco	*dokhān*
Tomb	*torba*
Tree	*shagara*, plu. *ashgār*
Wage	*oogra, maheeya*
Watch	*sa'ah*
Water	*moyya*
Weather	*hou-ah*
Weight	*wazn*
West	*gharb*
Wheel	*'agola*
Whip	*kūrbag*
Wind	*reeh*
Wire	*silk*
Wood	*khashab*
Word	*kalma*, plu. *kalemat*
Work	*shooghl*

ADJECTIVES

All	*kull*
Angry	*zālān*
Bad	*battāl*
Better	*ah-san*
Big	*kebeer*
Boiled	*maslu*
Broker.	*maksūr*
Busy	*mashghūl*
Cheap	*rakhees*
Cold	*bārid*

APPENDIX I

ADJECTIVES—*continued.*

Dead	*ma-yit*	More	*aktar*
Deep	*ghoweet*	Narrow	*da-ya'*
Difficult	*sāb*	New	*gedeed*
Dirty	*wissekh*	Nice	*kwa-yees*
Drunk	*sakrān*	Old	*'adeem, agūz* (age)
Dry	*nāshif*	Open	*maftūh*
Easy	*khafeef*	Other	*tāny*
Empty	*fādy*	Perfect	*tam-ām*
English	*ingleesy*	Plenty	*ze-adda*
Every	*kull*	Polite	*mu-addab*
Except	*illa*	Poor	*fa'eer*
Expensive	*ghāly*	Pretty	*gameel*
Fat	*simeen, takheen*	Private	*khosūsy*
Fine	*kwa-yees*	Public	*umūmy*
Free	*fādy*	Quiet	*hādy*
French	*fransowy*	Ready	*hāder*
Fresh	*tāza*	Rich	*ghāny*
Full	*maliyan*	Right	*ta-yib*
German	*almāny*	Round	*medowar*
Good	*tā-yib*	Safe	*ameen*
Greek	*rūmy*	Same	*zay-bādu*
Happy	*sa-yeed*	Sharp (cute)	*sharter*
Hard	*gāmed*	Sharp (edged)	*masnūn*
Heavy	*ta'eel*	Shut	*ma'fūl*
High	*'āly*	Smooth	*na-yem*
Honest	*shareef*	Soft	*taree*
Hungry	*ga'an*	Square	*mir-abba'*
Ill	*a-ee-yan*	Strong	*'ow-wy*
Important	*mohem*	Tall	*'āly, toweel*
Italian	*taliāny*	Thick	*takheen*
Large	*kebeer*	Thin	*rofai-ya*
Last	*ākher*	Thirsty	*atshān*
Lazy	*kaslān*	Tired	*tābān*
Light	*khafeef*	Wet	*mablūl*
Long	*toweel*	Whole	*kullu*
Low	*wā-tee*	Wide	*wasseh*
Many	*keteer*	Wrong	*ghaltān*

ADVERBS, &c.

After	*bā'd*	Late	*wakhry*
Afterwards	*bā'dayn*	Much	*keteer*
Alone	*wahedu*	Near	*oorā-yeb*
Always	*temelly*	Nearly	*ta'reeban*
At once	*dilwā't*	Never	*abadan*
Before	*'abl*	Only	*buss*
Behind	*warra*	Opposite	*'oodām*
Between	*bayn*	Outside	*burra*
Direct	*alla tūl*	Perhaps	*yimkin*
Downstairs	*taht*	Punctually	*musbūt*
Early	*badry*	Quickly	*bil agel*
Enough	*buss*	Since	*min*
Far	*ba-yeed*	Still	*lissa*
Front	*'ooddām*	There	*henak*
Here	*hena*	Upstairs	*fō'*
Inside	*gū-wa*	Very	*keteer, 'ow-wy*

APPENDIX I

VERBS

Unless otherwise stated, the imperative of the verb is given.

Agree, I	*a'abil*
Allow, I shall	*assarah*
(I shall not . .)	*massarahsh*
Ask	*essal*
Beat	*edrub*
(do not .	*ma-tedrubsh*
Begin	*ebtiddy*
Broke, I	*kasert*
Buy	*eshterry*
Can you ?	*ti'der*
Call	*endah*
Care, take	*hāsseb, hally bāllak*
Come (*imp.*)	*ta'āla*
(I come)	*aggy*
(I came)	*gayt*
(he came)	*gā*
Cut	*e'ta'a*
Dress, I	*albis*
Drink, I	*ashrub*
Drive	*arkeb*
Eat, I	*'ākal*
(he ate)	*akul*
Fear, I	*kha-yeef*
(do not .)	*ma-takhafsh*
Fetch	*geeb, hat*
Fill	*emlah*
Finish	*ekh-las*
Forgot, I	*nesseet*
(do not . . .)	*ma-tin-sash*
Give me	*eddeeny*
(I gave)	*eddayt*
Go	*rūh*
(I am going)	*arōh*
(going)	*rā-ya*
(gone)	*rā*
Hear, I	*asma'a*
Help	*sā-id*
Hire, I wish to	*awz a'agga*
Hold	*imsik*
Insulted me, He	*shatum-ni*
Know, I don't	*moosh-'ārraf*
(do you . . . ?)	*ta'ārraf*
Learn	*ta'āllim*
(I am . . . ing)	*be-tāllim*
Leave (let remain)	*seeb*
Like, I	*a-heb*
(do you . . . ?)	*te-heb*
Listen	*esma'a*
Look for	*dowar alla*
Look at	*shūf*
Make	*'amel*
Mean, I	*yani*
(what do you . . .?)	*yani ay*
Mend	*sallah*
Necessary, It is (must)	*lāzim*
Obey	*tā-weh*
Open	*efta*
Ordered, I	*'oolt*
Pack	*sattef*
Pay, I shall	*ha-edfa*
(I have paid)	*daffāt*
Play, I	*a-la'ab*
Pour out	*farragh*
Prepare	*huddar*
Put	*hōtt*
(past)	*hutt*
Read	*e'ra*
(past)	*a'rayt*
Receive	*estilim*
(past)	*wassalny*
Reply	*rudd*
(past)	*ruddayt*
Return	*erga*
(I shall)	*harga*
Ride	*erkeb*
(I wish to)	*owz-arkeb*
Row	*addif*
Run	*egry*
Say	*ool*
(I said)	*oo'lt*
See, I	*ashūf*
(I saw)	*shooft*
Seize	*imsik*
(he seized)	*messek*
Sell me	*bee'ely*
(he sold)	*ba'eh*
Show me	*warreeny*
Shut	*i'fil*
Sit down please	*et fadl, o'od*
Sleep, I	*anam*
(past)	*nemt*
Smoke, I	*ashreb dokhān*
Sorry, I am	*ma'alaysh*
Speak	*kallem*
(I spoke)	*kallemt*
Start, I	*esāfar*
(past)	*safert*
Stole, he	*sara'*
Swim, do you ?	*ta'āruf te'oom*
Take	*khod*
(I took)	*khut*
Talk, don't	*eskūt*
(he is . . . ing)	*yatkalem*
Teach	*'allim*
Tell me	*ool-ly*
Think, I	*azūn*
(do you ?)	*tezūn*
Tidy up	*ratteb*
Tie up	*erbūt*
Truth, speak the	*etkallem dōghry*
Understand, I don't	*moosh fahem*
(do you . . . ?)	*fehemt*

VERBS—*continued.*

Use	*estame*
Wait (for me)	*estanna*
(I waited)	*estannayt*
Wake me	*saheeny*
Walk	*imshi*
(I . . .)	*amshi*
Want, I	*owz*
(do you . . . ?)	*owz*
Was, I	*kūnt*
(he was)	*kan*
Wash	*eghshil*
Wear	*eibes*
(I wear)	*albis*
Work	*cshtaghel*
Write	*akteb*
(I wrote)	*katabt*

MISCELLANEOUS

And	*weh*
At	*fee*
(at the)	*f'il*
By	*be* or *b'*
For	*alla-shan*
From	*min*
He	*hū-wa*
His	. . . *u*, as a termination to a noun
I	*ana*
In	*fee*
(in the)	*f'il*
It	*hū-wa*
Me	. . . *y*, or . . . *ny*, as a termination
Mine	*bita'i*
My	. . . *y*, as a termination
No	*la'*
Nobody	*ma-feesh had*
Not. The negative is formed by the word *moosh* before the verb, or, better, *ma-* or *m-* before the verb, and *-ish* or *-sh* after. Thus, "I saw" = *ana shooft*, and "I did not see" = *ana ma-shooft ish.* "I make" = *ana 'amel*, "I don't make" = *ana m-amel·sh*	
Not yet	*lissa*
On	*ala*
Over	*fo'*
Please	*min fadlak*
She	*hee-ya*
Than	*min*
Thanks	*katter kheerak*
The. The article is "el," but it become "er," "et," "es," "esh," or "ez," before "r," "t," "s," "sh," or "z"	
They	*hom*
To	*leh*, or *l'*
What ?	*ay*
When ?	*aymta*
Whence	*min ayn*
Where ?	*fayn*
Which, who	*elly*
Who ?	*meen*
Whose ?	*bita'ameen*
Why ?	*lay, alla-shan-ay*
With	*and, wee-ya*
Without	*min gheer*
Under	*taht*
Until	*lehad*
Yes	*ai-wa*
Yet	*lissa*
You	*enta*
Your	. . . *k*, or . . *ak*, a a termination.
Yours	*bita'ak*

Good morning, or good day	*nahārak sa-yeed*
Good night	*lel-tak sa-yeeda*, or *sa-yeeda*
To-morrow morning	*bookra es-sōbh*
What is the time, please ?	*es-sa'ah kam, min fadlak*
Call me at (six) o'clock	*saheeny es-sa'ah (sitta)*
I wish to start at . . . o'clock	*awz esāfer fee sa'ah . . .*
Meet me at the (hotel) at . . . o'clock	*abeelny fil (locunda) fee sa'ah . .*
Have dinner ready at eight o'clock punctually	*hadder ela'asha fee sa'ah tamania tamam*
Ring the bell	*edrab el garras*
What is your name ?	*ismak ay*
How old are you ?	*omrak kam senna*
It does not matter	*ma'alaysh*
What is the matter ?	*khabber ay*

MISCELLANEOUS—*continued.*

Hold your tongue	*eskūt*
How much is this ?	*kam da*
Will you give me some . . . please	*eddeeny shu-wa-ya . . min fadlak*
I shall only pay (ten) piastres	*ana adfa buss (ashara) 'oorūsh*
Can you give me change ?	*'andak fakka*
I am much obliged to you	*kattar kheerak keteer*
Do not beat your horses	*ma-tedrubsh khaylak*
What is your number	*nimrettak ay*
I shall report you to the police	*rā-yeh aballagh anak lel bōlice*
Go away ! I shan't give you anything	*Imshi, ma-deelaksh hāga*
When is there a train to (Cairo) ?	*amyta fee 'att: e le (masr)*
When does the train start ?	*aymta yesāfar el 'attre*
How far is it to . . . ?	*'add ay ba-yeed le . . .*
Will you show me the way to . . . please ?	*warreeny es-sikka le . . ., min fadlak*
How much do you charge per day ?	*el oogra kam fil yōm*
This donkey is no good ; get me another	*el homār da moosh kwa-yes, hat ghayro*

APPENDIX II

HOTELS, CONSULAR AGENTS, BANKS, &c.

HOTELS

CAIRO

THE SAVOY. SHARIA KASR-EL-NIL. Telephone No. 125, Cairo.

Open in winter only (from about December 20 to April 10). 250 rooms. Private sitting-rooms and suites. Bedrooms with toilet and bath attached. Electric light and lift. Hairdresser's shop in the hotel.

Restaurant—American Bar—Billiards.

The hotel has a garden and tennis-court.

TARIFF.—Single bedrooms, from pt. 50 to pt. 120 per day.
Double ,, ,, 100 ,, 200 ,,
Sitting-rooms ,, 200 ,, 500 ,,
Breakfast . . . . pt. 12
Luncheon (*table d'hôte*). . . . . . ,, 30
,, in restaurant . . . . . ,, 40
Dinner (*table d'hôte*) . . . . . . ,, 40
,, in restaurant . . . . . . ,, 50 to 75

The hotel has a fine ballroom, as well as rooms for private dinners and receptions. A small dance is given every Saturday.

SHEPHEARD'S. SHARIA KAMEL. (Five minutes from the station.) Telegraphic address: "Shepheard's, Cairo." Telephone Nos. 12 and 900.

Open all the year round. 350 rooms—500 beds. Private sitting-rooms and suites of apartments. Electric light and lifts. Hairdresser in the hotel. Railway booking-office in the building.

Restaurant—Grill Room—American Bar—Billiards.

The hotel has a garden and tennis-court.

TARIFF.—Single bedroom, from pt. 40 per day.
Double ,, ,, 80 ,,
Sitting-room ,, 80 ,,
Bedroom, with bath and toilet, pt. 120 per day.
Private suites by arrangement.
Breakfast . . . . pt. 10
Luncheon (*table d'hôte*) . . . . . . ,, 20
,, in restaurant . . . . . ,, 25
Dinner (*table d'hôte*) . . . . . . ,, 30
,, in restaurant . . . . . ,, 40
Meals *en pension* for not less than a week . ,, 50 per day

The hotel has two ballrooms and also private rooms for receptions. A small dance is given every Monday in winter. A band plays on the terrace every afternoon.

CONTINENTAL. THE OPERA SQUARE. Telephone No. 75.

Open all the year round. 400 rooms, 500 beds.

Restaurant—Grill Room—Billiards.

Hairdresser in the hotel. Electric light and lifts. Garden and tennis-court.

TARIFF.—Single bedroom, from pt. 30 to pt. 100 per day.
Double ,, ,, 60 ,, 150 ,,
Sitting-room ,, 100 ,, 450 ,,
Bedroom, with bath and toilet, by arrangement.
Private suites of apartments by arrangement.

Breakfast	pt. 10
Luncheon (*table d'hôte*)	,, 25
,, in restaurant	,, 30
Dinner (*table d'hôte*)	,, 30
,, in restaurant	,, 40

Meals *en pension* (for not less than one week)
From pt. 40 to pt. 65 per day.
Private rooms for receptions are provided.

GHEZIREH PALACE. ON THE ISLAND OF GHEZIREH (about two miles from Cairo).

Telegraphic address: "Palace—Cairo." Telephone, No. 217.
200 rooms—300 beds.

The hotel is situated in a large and beautiful garden on the banks of the Nile. A steam ferry runs every ten minutes to Cairo. Motor omnibuses and carriages are always waiting to convey visitors to and from Cairo. Hotel opens in winter (from about December 15 to April 20).

TARIFF.—Single bedroom, from pt. 40 per day.
Double ,, ,, 80 ,,
Sitting-room ,, 80 ,,
Bedroom, with bath and toilet, from pt. 120 per day.
Private suites of apartments by arrangement.

Breakfast	pt. 10
Luncheon (*table d'hôte*)	,, 20
,, in restaurant	,, 25
Dinner (*table d'hôte*)	,, 30
,, in restaurant	,, 40
Meals *en pension* (for not less than one week)	,, 50 per day.

American Bar—Three Billiard Tables.

Electric light and lifts. Hairdresser always in attendance. Telegraph office in the gardens.

The hotel is three minutes' walk from the "Sporting Club," where there are tennis-courts, polo-grounds, a twelve-hole golf course, croquet grounds, squash racquet-courts, and a racecourse.

Splendid ballroom and reception-rooms. Small dances are given every Thursday. A band plays on the terrace every afternoon and during dinner.

HOTEL D'ANGLETERRE. SHARIA MAGHRABY. Telephone No. 299.

Opens in the winter season (December to April). 100 rooms. Private suites and sitting-rooms. Electric light and lift.

TARIFF.—Single bedroom, from pt. 30 to pt. 60 per day.
Double ,, ,, 60 ,, 100 ,,
Sitting-room ,, 60 ,, 250 ,,
Private suites by arrangement.

Breakfast	pt. 10
Luncheon	,, 20
Dinner	,, 30

Meals *en pension*, by arrangement.

MENA HOUSE. AT THE PYRAMIDS. Telephone No. 1555. Telegraphi address: "Mena, Cairo."

Electric tram service from Cairo in forty minutes.
200 rooms.

Restaurant—American Bar—Two Billiard Tables.

Electric light and lift. Three tennis-courts. Nine-hole golf course Chemist's shop. Hairdresser in attendance. Swimming-bath.

There is a church in the grounds and a resident chaplain and doctor. Telegraph office on the premises.

TARIFF.—Single bedroom, from pt. 35 per day.
Double „ „ 70 „
Sitting-room „ 60 „
Private suites of apartments by arrangement.
Breakfast, from pt. 10 to pt. 15 per day.
Luncheon (*table d'hôte*) . . . . pt. 20
„ in restaurant . . . „ 25
Dinner (*table d'hôte*) . . . . „ 30
„ in restaurant . . . . „ 40
Meals *en pension* for not less than a week . „ 50 per day.

The hotel has two ballrooms where small dances are given from time to time. In the grounds is a racecourse where gymkhanas are held.

SEMIRAMIS. KASR-EL-DOUBARA. Telephone No. 1890. Telegraphic address: "Semiramis, Cairo."
280 rooms. Situated on the banks of the Nile.
Restaurant—Grill Room—American Bar—Billiards.

Roof garden. Garden and tennis-court. Electric light and lifts. Ballrooms. Hairdresser in attendance.

TARIFF.—Single bedroom, from pt. 40 per day.
Double „ „ 80 „
Sitting-room „ 100 „
Bedroom with bath „ 120 „
Private suites by arrangement.
Breakfast . . . . pt. 10
Lunch (*table d'hôte*) . . „ 20
„ in restaurant . . „ 30
Dinner (*table d'hôte*) . . „ 30
„ in restaurant . . „ 40

NATIONAL. SHARIA SULIMAN PASHA. Telephone No. 1543.
Open from December 1 to April 30. 200 rooms.
Restaurant—Grill Room—American Bar—Billiards.
Electric light. Hydraulic lift. Hairdresser.

TARIFF.—Single bedroom, from pt. 20 to pt. 60 per day.
Double „ 40 „ 100 „
Sitting-room „ 40 „ 80 „
Breakfast . . . . pt. 6
Luncheon . . . . pt. 20 to 25
Dinner . . . . „ 25 „ 30
Meals *en pension* . . „ 40 „ 60

EDEN PALACE. OPPOSITE THE ESBEKIEH GARDENS. Telephone No. 341.
Open all the year round. 200 beds.

TARIFF.—Single bedroom from pt. 20 to pt. 30 per day
Double „ . „ 40 „ 50 „
Sitting-room . „ 30 „ 50 „
Meals *en tension*. „ 40 „ 65 „
Breakfast . . . . pt. 6
Luncheon . . . . „ 16
Dinner . . . . . „ 20

BRISTOL. NEAR THE ESBEKIEK GARDENS. Telephone No. 530.
Open all the year round. 140 beds.

TARIFF.—Single bedroom . from pt. 20 per day
Double „ . „ 40 „
Sitting-room . „ 60 „
Pension . . . . . from pt. 300 per week
Breakfast . . . . pt. 10
Luncheon . . . . . . pt 16 to pt. 20
Dinner . . „ 20 „ 25

METROPOLE. Ismailia Quarter. Telephone No. 184.
Open all the year round. 90 beds.

Tariff.—Single bedroom	from pt. 25 per day
Double „	„ 50 „
Pension	„ 50 „
Breakfast	pt. 6
Luncheon	„ 15
Dinner	„ 20

IMPERIAL. Rond-Point, Kasr-el-Nil.
Open all the year round. 60 rooms.

Tariff.—Single bedroom	from pt. 40 per day
Double „	„ 60 „
Pension, by arrangement	„ 40
Breakfast	pt. 5
Luncheon	„ 16
Dinner	„ 20

NEW KHEDIVIAL. Sharia Kamel. Telephone No. 157?
Open all the year round. 110 beds.

Tariff.—Single bedroom	from pt. 20 to pt. 30 per day
Double „	„ 40 „ 50 „
Sitting-room	„ 30 „ 50 „
Pension	from pt. 350 per week
Breakfast	pt. 6
Luncheon	„ 16
Dinner	„ 20

PENSIONS

PENSION SIMA. Sharia Magraby. (Near Turf Club.)
Inclusive terms, from pt. 300 per week. Electric light. Garden. Private suites of apartments. Open all the year round.

CARLTON HOUSE. Kasr-el-Nil. Telephone Nc. 1602.
Open all the year round.

Pension . . . . . . from pt. 50 per day

ROSSMORE HOUSE. 11 Sharia-el-Madabegh.
Open all the year round. Inclusive terms, from pt. 40 to pt. 60 per day.

ANGLO-AMERICAN.
Open all the year round.

Single room	from LE10 to LE12 per month
Double rooms	„ „ 16 „ „ 18 „
Sitting-rooms	„ „ 20 per month

HELOUAN

RAND HOTEL. Three minutes from the station. Telephone No. 28 Helouan.
Open during the winter season. 150 rooms.

Tariff.—Single bedroom	from pt. 30 to pt. 80 per day
Double „	„ 60 „ 150 „
Sitting-room	„ 80 „ 300 „

Room with bath attached, by arrangement.
Private suites by arrangement.

Breakfast	pt. 10
Luncheon	„ 25
Dinner	„ 30

The hotel has a garden and tennis-court. Electric light and lift.

Billiards—American Bar.

There is a fine ballroom where small dances are held from time to time. Under the management of the Grand Hotel is the Helouan Golf Course, the largest and best in Egypt; it consists of eighteen holes, and has a professional in charge.

HOTEL DES BAINS. Near the Baths. Telephone No. 22 Helouan.
Open in winter only. 60 rooms. Moderate terms.

Tennis and Golf—Billiards.

TARIFF.—Single bedroom .	from pt. 30 to pt. 40 per day	
Double ,, .	,, 60 ,, 80 ,,	
Sitting-room	,, 60 ,, 120 ,,	
Breakfast		pt. 8
Luncheon		,, 20
Dinner		,, 25

TEWFIK PALACE HOTEL. Open in winter.
The hotel was built for a palace by the late Khedive Tewfik Pasha. Terms on application.

HOTEL-SANATORIUM EL-HAYAT. Telephone No. 44 Helouan.
Open from October to May. 200 rooms.

TARIFF.—Single bedroom	from pt. 40 per day
Double ,, .	,, 60 ,,
Sitting-room . .	,, 80 ,,
Bedroom with bath .	,, 120 ,,
Pension . . .	,, 60 ,,

HOTEL HELTZEL. Telephone No. 41 Helouan.
Open all the year round. 60 beds.

TARIFF.—Single bedroom	from pt. 20 per day
Double ,, ...	,, 40 ,,
Breakfast	pt. 5
Luncheon	,, 15
Dinner	,, 16

WINTER HOTEL. Telephone No. 60 Helouan.
Open from October to May. 40 beds.

TARIFF.—Single bedroom	from pt. 50 per day
Double ,, .	,, 100 ,,
Sitting-room	, 50 ,,
Breakfast	pt. 5
Luncheon	pt. 15
Dinner	pt. 20
Full *pension*	from pt. 50 per day

HOTEL-PENSION ANTONIO. Telephone No. 56 Helouan.
Full *pension* from pt. 40 per day.

ZEITOUN (near Cairo)

GRAND HOTEL ZEITOUN. Open all the year round. Fine garden.
Inclusive terms, from pt. 40 per day.

ALEXANDRIA

SAVOY PALACE. Telephone Nos. 1845 and 1928 Alexandria.
Open all the year round. 150 rooms. Electric light and lift.

Restaurant—Billiards—Gardens.

TARIFF.—Single bedroom	from pt. 30	to pt. 60	per day
Double ,,	,, 50	,, 90	,,
Sitting-room	,, 60	,, 80	,,
Bedroom with bath attached	,, 40	,, 60	,,
Private suites	,, 150	,, 300	,,
Breakfast			pt. 10
Luncheon (*table d'hôte*)			,, 20
,, in restaurant			,, 25
Dinner (*table d'hôte*)			,, 30
,, in restaurant			,, 35
Pension	from pt. 50 per day		

A band plays twice daily.

KHEDIVIAL HOTEL. Telephone No. 267 Alexandria.

Open all the year round. 140 rooms. Electric light and lift.

TARIFF.—Single bedroom	from pt. 40	per day
Double ,,	,, 60	,,
Sitting-room	, 100	
Bedroom with bath	, 80	,,
Private suites	, 300	,,
Breakfast		pt. 10
Luncheon (*table d'hôte*)		,, 20
,, in restaurant		,, 25
Dinner (*table d'hôte*)		,, 30
,, in restaurant		,, 40
Meals *en pension*	from pt. 50 per day	

GRAND HOTEL (NEAR THE BOURSE). Telephone No. 372 Alexandria.

Open all the year round. 70 rooms.

TARIFF.—Single bedrooms	from pt. 25	per day
Double ,,	,, 50	,,
Breakfast		pt. 6
Luncheon	from	,, 20
Dinner	,,	,, 20

WINDSOR HOTEL. Facing the sea. Telephone No. 796 Alexandria.

Open all the year round. 75 rooms.

TARIFF.—Single bedroom	from pt. 20	per day
Double ,,	,, 35	,,
Sitting-room	50	,,
Pension	50	,,
Breakfast		pt. 8
Luncheon		,, 15
Dinner		,, 20

RAMLEH

GRAND CASINO SAN STEFANO. RAMLEH. Telephone No. 15 Ramleh.

Open all the year round. 200 rooms. Electric light and lift. Sea bathing. Lawn tennis. Billiards. Band twice daily. Frequent concerts.

TARIFF.—Single bedroom	from pt. 40	per day
Double ,,	,, 80	,,
Sitting-room	80	,,
Rooms with bath	80	,,
Breakfast		pt. 8
Luncheon		,, 25
Dinner		,, 30

HOTEL BEAU-RIVAGE. RAMLEH. Telephone No. 186.

Open all the year round. 40 rooms. Gardens. Sea bathing. Tennis-court.

TARIFF.—Single bedroom . . . . from pt. 50 per day
Double ,, ... ,, 100 ,,
Sitting-room . . . . . ,, 60 ,,
Suites of apartments by arrangement.
Breakfast . . . . pt. 10
Luncheon . . . . from ,, 20
Dinner . . . . ,, ,, 25

CARLTON. BULKELEY, RAMLEH Telephone No. 173.
Open all the year round. 44 rooms. Inclusive terms from pt. 50 per day.

NEW VICTORIA HOTEL. RAMLEH. Telephone No. 370.
Open all the year round. 60 rooms.
TARIFF.—Single bedroom . . . . from pt. 50 per day
Double ,, ... ,, 100 ,,
Sitting-room . . . . . , 50 ,,
Private suites . . . . . ,, 250 ,,
Breakfast . . . . pt. 18
Luncheon . . . . ,, 20
Dinner . . . . ,, 25
Meals *en pension* from pt. 40 per day

VILLA MARGHERITA. RAMLEH. Telephone No. 23 Ramleh
Open all the year round. 30 rooms.
TARIFF.—Single bedroom . . . . from pt. 20 per day
Double ,, . ,, 40 ,,
Sitting-room . ,, 20 ,,
Breakfast . . . . pt. 5
Luncheon . . . . ,, 15
Dinner . . . . ,, 20
Full *pension* . . . . from pt. 50 per day

HOTEL PLAISANCE. RAMLEH. Telephone No. 54.
Open all the year round. *Pension* from pt. 40 per day.

PORT SAID

SAVOY HOTEL. FACING THE SEA. Telephone No. 102 Port Said.
Open all the year round.
TARIFF.—Single bedroom . . . . from pt. 27 per day
Double ,, ... ,, 54 ,,
Sitting-room . . . . . ,, 100 ,,
Private suites and bedrooms with baths attached by arrangement
Breakfast . . . . pt. 10
Luncheon . . . . ,, 20
Dinner . . . . ,, 25
Pension . . . . from pt. 65 per day

EASTERN EXCHANGE HOTEL. Telephone No. 34 Port Said.
Open all the year round. 100 rooms.

CONTINENTAL HOTEL. Telephone No. 49 Port Said.
Open all the year round.
TARIFF.—Single bedroom . . . . from pt. 20 per day
Double ,, ... ,, 40 ,,
Sitting-room . . . . . ,, 20 ,,
Breakfast . . . . pt. 10
Luncheon . . . . ,, 20
Dinner . ,, 25

ISMAILIA

HOTEL DES VOYAGEURS. NEAR THE STATION. Open all the year round.

TARIFF.—Single bedroom . . . . from pt. 10 per day
Double " . " 20 "
Breakfast . . . . pt. 5
Luncheon . . . . " 10
Dinner . . . . " 10

SUEZ

HOTEL BACHET. SUEZ DOCKS. Telephone No. 7 Suez.
Open all the year round.

TARIFF.—Single bedroom . from pt. 20 per day
Double " . . . " 35 "
Breakfast . . . . pt. 10
Luncheon . . . . " 15
Dinner . . . . " 17

HOTEL BEL-AIR. Telephone No. 11 Suez. Open all the year round.

TARIFF.—Single bedroom . from pt. 12 per day
Double " . . . . . " 24 "
Breakfast . . . . pt. 8
Luncheon . . . . " 12
Dinner . . . . " 12
Pension . . . . . from pt. 35 per day

FAYOUM

GRAND KAROUN HOTEL. MEDINET-EL-FAYOUM (near the station).
Full *pension*, including services of dragoman, from pt. 50 per day.

HOTEL MOERIS, ON LAKE KAROUN. *Via* Abchaway station, Egyptian State Railways.

Full *pension*, from pt. 80 per day. Hire of sailing-boats, per day pt. 80; half-day, pt. 50. Guns for hire, pt. 10 per day. Cartridges on sale. Fare from the station to the hotel by carriage, pt. 20., including baggage.

NOTE.—This hotel is open in winter only; it is under the management of the Grand Karoun Hotel, Fayoum. Notice should be given beforehand by intending visitors, so that a carriage may meet the train at Abchaway station.

ASSIOUT

NEW HOTEL. NEAR THE STATION.

LUXOR

THE WINTER PALACE. CLOSE TO THE RIVER.

Open in winter only. Electric light and lift. Private suites of apartments. Gardens. Restaurant.

The hotel was opened in 1907 only, and the arrangements are of the most modern and luxurious description.

TARIFF.—Single bedroom . from pt. 40 per day
Double " . . . . . . " 70 "
Sitting-room . . . . . " 100 "
Bedroom with bath and toilet attached, from pt. 60 per day.
Private suites of apartments by arrangement.
Breakfast . . . . . . pt. 15
Luncheon (*table d'hôte*) . . . . . . " 20
" in restaurant . . . . . . " 25
Dinner (*table d'hôte*) . . . . " 30
" in restaurant . . . . " 40
Meals *en pension* . . . from pt. 50 per day

Specially reduced terms in November, December and after March 15.

APPENDIX II

THE LUXOR HOTEL. Near the River.

Open all the year round. Fine gardens. English church in the grounds. Tennis-court. Electric light.

Tariff.—Single bedroom . . . . from pt. 30 per day
Double ,, . ,, 50 ,,
Sitting-room . ,, 80 ,,
Breakfast . . . . pt. 15
Luncheon . . . . . ,, 20
Dinner . . . . ,, 25
Full *pension* . . . . from pt. 80 per day

Specially reduced rates in November and December and after March 15.

Other hotels at Luxor are the "Karnak," "Savoy," "Grand," and Grande Pension de Famille."

ASSOUAN

CATARACT HOTEL. Situated above the Nile (near the station).

Open in winter only. Electric light and lift. Gardens and tennis-courts.

Tariff.—Single bedroom . . . . from pt. 40 per day
Double ,, ... ,, 70 ,,
Sitting-room . . . . . ,, 100 ,,
Bedroom with bath and toilet attached, by arrangement.
Private suites of appartments by arrangement.
Breakfast . . . . pt. 15
Luncheon (*table d'hôte*) . . . . . ,, 20
,, in restaurant . . . . . ,, 25
Dinner (*table d'hôte*) . . . . . . ,, 30
,, in restaurant . . . . . . ,, 40
Meals *en pension* . . . from pt. 50 per day

Specially reduced terms in November, December, and after March 15.

SAVOY HOTEL. On Elephantine Island.

Open in winter only. Splendid gardens. Tennis-courts. Electric light and lift.

Tariff.—Single bedroom . . . . from pt. 40 per day
Double ,, ... ,, 70 ,,
Sitting-room . . . . . ,, 100 ,,
Bedrooms with bath and toilet attached, by arrangement.
Private suites of apartments by arrangement.
Breakfast . . . . . pt. 15
Luncheon (*table d'hôte*). . . . . . ,, 20
,, in restaurant . . . . . ,, 25
Dinner (*table d'hôte*) . . . . . . ,, 30
,, in restaurant . . . . . . ,, 40
Meals *en pension* . . . from pt. 50 per day

Specially reduced rates in November and December and after March 15.

GRAND HOTEL. Facing the River.

Open all the year round. Electric light.

Tariff.—Single bedroom . . . . from pt. 30 per day
Double ,, . ,, 50 ,,
Sitting-room . ,, 80 ,,
Breakfast . . . . pt. 15
Luncheon . . . . ,, 20
Dinner . . . . . ,, 25
Full *pension* from pt. 80 per day

APPENDIX II

CLUBS

CAIRO

Name.	*Address.*	*Secretary.*
Turf Club.	Sharia El-Maghraby.	H. Aspinall.
Khedivial Sporting Club.	Ghezireh.	K. H. Marsham, Esq.
Khedivial Club.	22 Chareh El-Manakh.	Alexander Tinkel.
Cercle Artistique.	Sharia El-Madabegh.	Mons. H. Lamba.
Automobile Club.	Ghezireh Palace.	Alexander Comanos.

ALEXANDRIA

Union Club.	6 Rue Ancienne Bourse.	H. M. Dodwell.
Cercle Khedivial.	2 Rue Cherif Pacha.	Albert Cumbo.
Mohammed Aly Club.	Rue Rosette.	N. G. Sabbagh.
Alexandria Sporting Club.	Ibrahimieh, Ramleh.	A. S. Preston.
British Club.	15 Rue Gare de Ramleh.	A. R. Purvis.
Khedivial Yacht Club.	Ras-el-Tin.	Alexander Grafton.
Club San Stefano.	San Stefano, Ramleh.	

KHEDIVIAL SPORTING CLUB, GHEZIREH

Secretary: Keith Marsham, Esq.

This club is formed for race meetings, gymkhanas, and athletic sports, as well as for the games of cricket, lawn tennis, golf, polo, racquets, hockey, croquet, and football.

Membership is restricted to applicants elected by the committee, on the proposal of two members.

Subscriptions are as under:

Life member . .	£30 sterling
Resident members, married.	pt. 500 per annum.
,, unmarried	,, 360 ,, ,,
Country members	,, 200 ,, ,,

Temporary members (*i.e.*, visitors and others) require to be introduced by a member of the club, and pay the following subscriptions:

Playing Members

Whole season . . .	pt. 500	Two weeks	pt. 150
One month	,, 250	One week	,, 100

Non-Playing Members

On band-days (Tuesdays and Thursdays), pt. 25 per day; other days, pt. 15. Visitors to Cairo wishing to join the club as temporary members should apply to the Secretary.

CHURCHES

CAIRO

Church of England.—All Saints Church, Bonlac Street. Sunday services, 8.30 A.M., 10.30 A.M., and 6 P.M.

Church of Scotland.—St. Andrew's Church, close to headquarters of the Army of Occupation. Sunday services, 10.30 A.M. and 6 P.M.

Roman Catholic Church.—Saint Joseph, Emad-el-Din Street (Ismailieh). Mass at 7, 8, 9, 10, and 11 A.M.

Jesuits' Church, Faggalah and Abbas Streets.

German Lutheran.—19 El-Maghraby Street (Ismailieh).

ALEXANDRIA

Church of England.—St. Mark's Church, Mohammed Aly Square. Sunday services, 8 A.M. and 6.15 P.M.

All Saints Church, Bulkeley, Ramleh. Sunday services, 8.30 A.M. and 6.30 P.M.

Church of Scotland.—St. Andrew's Church (Presbyterian), near post office. Sunday services, 10.30 A.M. and 6 P.M.

Roman Catholic Church, St. Catherine's Church, St. Catherine Square. Jesuit Church, Abd-el-Monein Street.

APPENDIX II

BANKS

CAIRO

National Bank of Egypt, Kasr-el-Nil Street.
The Bank of Egypt, Kasr-el-Nil Street.
The Anglo-Egyptian Bank, Kasr-el-Nil Street.
The Crédit Lyonnais, El-Bosta Street.
The Imperial Ottoman Bank, El-Manakh Street.
The Agricultural Bank of Egypt, No. 6 Zervudaki Street.
Deutsche Orient Bank A.G., No. 4 Midan Suarés.
The Crédit Foncier Egyptien, El-Manakh Street.

ALEXANDRIA

The National Bank of Egypt, Stamboul Street.
The Bank of Egypt, Tewfik Pasha Street.
The Anglo-Egyptian Bank, Cherif Pacha Street.
The Crédit Lyonnais, Cherif Pacha Street.
The Imperial Ottoman Bank, Mohammed Aly Street.
The Agricultural Bank of Egypt, 17 Mohammed Aly Street.

DIPLOMATIC AND CONSULAR AGENTS

GREAT BRITAIN

Agent and Consul-General.—Sir Eldon Gorst, K.C.B., Kasr-el-Doubara, Cairo.
Consul.—A. D. Alban, Standard Life Buildings, Soliman Pacha Street, Cairo.
Consuls-General.—E. B. Gould, I.S.O., Alexandria; D. A. Cameron, Port Said
Consul.—V. A. Laferla, Suez.

UNITED STATES OF AMERICA

Agent and Consul-General.—Lewis Morris Iddings, Kaser-el-Doubara.
Consul.—John Griffen, Shawarby Pacha Street, Cairo.
Agents.—E. Alexander Powell, Alexandria; H. Broadbent, Port Said; F. T Peake, Suez; Georges Wissa Bey, Assiout.

APPENDIX III

MISCELLANEOUS INFORMATION

EGYPTIAN MONEY

THE monetary system of Egypt rests, since 1885, on a single gold standard, with subsidiary silver, nickel, and copper coins. The unit is the Egyptian pound, worth approximately £1 0*s*. 6*d*. in English money. The Egyptian pound is divided into 100 piastres and the piastre into 10 milliemes.

Practically the only gold coin in circulation is the English sovereign, which is worth 97½ piastres and passes everywhere. There are a few Egyptian and Turkish 100-piastre and 50-piastre pieces and French napoleons in circulation, but these are seldom met with.

The National Bank of Egypt issues notes of the value of LE100, LE50 LE10, LE5, LE1 and 50 piastres. The following Egyptian coins are in circulation :

Silver

Pt. 20 (worth about 4*s*. 2*d*. or 1 dollar or 5 francs).
Pt. 10 (worth about 2*s*. 1*d*. or 50 cents or 2·50 francs).
Pt. 5 (worth about 1*s*. or 25 cents or 1·25 francs).
Pt. 2 (worth about 5*d*. or 10 cents or 50 c.).
Pt. 1 or 10 milliemes (worth about 2½*d*. or 5 cents or 25 c.).

Nickel

Pt. 1 or 10 milliemes (worth about 2½*d*. or 5 cents or 25 c.).
Pt. ½ or 5 milliemes (worth about 1¼*d*.).
2 milliemes (worth about ½*d*.).
1 millieme (worth about ¼*d*.).

N.B.—Pt. stands for "piastre tarif," and is the ordinary method of writing "piastre."

WEIGHTS AND MEASURES

The metric system is generally used in Egypt, though English units are frequently met with and also certain Egyptian units. Of the latter the following are the most likely to be useful :

The Pik (24 kirats) = 22·83 in. or 0·585 metre.
The Feddan, used in land measurement = 4200 sq. metres (roughly one acre).
The Rotl is almost equal to 1 pound (weight).
The Okah or Oke = 2¾ lb.
The Kantar = 100 rotls or 36 okes (roughly 100 lb.).
The metrical and English equivalents are approximately :

1 kilometre	=	0·621 mile or 1094 yds. (8 kilometres = 5 miles very nearly).		
1 mile	=	1609 metres.		
1 metre	=	3 ft. 3⅜ in.		
1 yard	=	91½ centimetres.		
1 foot	=	30½ ,,		
1 inch	=	2½ centimetres.		
1 kilogram	=	2¼ lb. (2·205 lb.		
1 pound	=	454 grammes.		
1 metrical ton	=	1000 kilograms	=	2205 lb.
1 English ,,	=	2240 lb.	=	1016 kilograms.
1 sq. metre	=	1·196 sq. yd., about 10¾ sq. ft.		
1 acre	=	4047 sq. metres	=	4840 sq. yd.
1 cubic metre	=	1·308 cub. yd.	=	35·32 cub. ft.—about 220 gallons.

(1 cubic metre of fresh water weighs practically 1 ton, 2207 lb.)

APPENDIX III

POSTAL INFORMATION

Postal Rates

Within Egypt

	Pt.	Mm.
Letters, local, for 30 grammes (1 oz.) or fraction		3
To other towns in Egypt, for 30 grammes (1 oz.) or fraction		5
Newspapers		1
Postcards		2
Parcels, not exceeding 1 kilogram (2¼ lb.)	3	
,, ,, 3 ,, (6½ ,,)	4	—
,, ,, 5 ,, (11 ,,)	5	—

Foreign

	Pt.	Mm.
Letters to Great Britain, Italy, India, Canada, South Africa, Australia, and most other British possessions, for 20 grammes (⅔ oz.) or fraction		5
Other countries in the Postal Union		—
Postcards		4
Newspapers, &c., for 50 grammes (1⅔ oz.) or fraction	—	2
Parcels to Great Britain :		
Via Gibraltar, not exceeding 1 kilogram (2¼ lb.)	6	—
,, ,, ,, 3 ,, (6½ ,,)	9	—
,, ,, ,, 5 ,, (11 ,,)	12	
Via France or Italy, not exceeding 5 kilograms (11 lb.)	15	

N.B.—All parcels must be accompanied by a despatch note and a customs declaration properly filled in : these can be obtained free at the post offices.

Registration of Letters

	Pt.	Mm.
Inland service	—	5
Foreign ,,	1	—

Money Orders, &c.

	Pt.	Mm.
Inland service (up to LE100), for each LE or fraction		[illegible]
,, minimum charge for each order		—
Sudan service, for each LE or fraction	—	5
,, minimum charge	1	

British Postal Orders are issued payable in Great Britain or British possessions of values from 6*d.* to 21*s.*

	Pt.	Mm.
Foreign Money Orders, for each LE or fraction up to LE4	1	
,, ,, for each LE2 or fraction above LE4	1	[illegible]

Mails to Europe

British (*via* Brindisi), in winter	Sunday
German (*via* Naples)	Wednesday
Italian	Thursday
French (*via* Marseilles)	Friday
Austrian (*via* Brindisi)	Saturday

Mails from Europe

Italian	Sunday
German	Monday
Austrian	,,
French	Tuesday
British	Wednesday

APPENDIX III

TELEGRAPHIC INFORMATION

Egyptian Service

	Pt.	Mm.
The rates for telegrams within Egypt are, for every two words or fraction	—	5
Minimum charge for each message	2	
Telegrams marked "URGENT" take precedence above all other private telegrams, and are charged triple rates, *i.e.*, for every two words	1	5

Delivery of telegrams is free within 2 kilometres of the receiving office. For longer distances a charge is made which must be paid in advance.

	Pt.	Mm.
More than 2 and less than 4 kilometres	2	5
,, 4 ,, 8 ,,	5	
,, 8 ,, 12 ,,	10	—

Telegrams are not delivered to a greater distance than 12 kilometres from the receiving office.

A receipt should be asked for by the sender of every telegram.

The sender of a telegram must sign his name, though not necessarily for transmission.

In non-coded telegrams words of more than fifteen letters (except in the case of the name of the town of destination) and numbers of more than five figures are charged as two words.

In code telegrams words of more than ten letters are charged as two.

Telegraph Offices.—Telegrams can be despatched from all the principal towns in Egypt and from nearly all railway stations. At the larger places messages in European languages (Latin characters), as well as in Arabic, are taken. At the other offices only Arabic messages can be transmitted.

Sudan Telegraph Service

	Between Egypt and the Sudan.	Sudan (Interior).
Urgent telegrams, for every 2 words or fraction	4 Pt.	2½ Pt.
Minimum charge	16 ,,	10 ,,
Ordinary telegrams, for every 2 words or fraction	1½ ,,	1 ,,
Minimum charge	6 ,,	4 ,,
Deferred telegrams, for every 4 words or fraction	1½ ,,	1 ,,
Minimum charge	3 ,,	2 ,,

Delivery of deferred telegrams is made not less than 48 hours after despatch.

Foreign Service. *Via* Eastern Telegraph Co.

Rates per word from Cairo, Alexandria, Suez, and Port Said to:

	Pt.	Mm.
Aden	7	7
Argentine Republic	24	8
Australia—Australia proper	16	6
,, New Zealand	18	2
,, Tasmania	17	8
Austria-Hungary } Belgium }	4	8
Canada	9	6
China—Hong-Kong, Shanghai, Amoy, and Foochow	21	4
,, Canton and Macao	22	3
Denmark }		
France }		
Germany }		
Gibraltar }		
Great Britain and Ireland }		
Greece }		
Holland }		
India—India and Burmah	9	2

APPENDIX III

	Pt.	Mm.
India—Ceylon	9	6
Italy	4	8
Japan	29	
Malta Norway	4	8
Persia (*via* Rhodes)	9	0
,, (*via* Bombay)	15	0
Portugal Russia in Europe	4	8
,, in Asia	6	2
South Africa—Cape Colony, Natal, Orange River Colony, and Transvaal	16	8
,, Southern Rhodesia	17	6
,, Northern Rhodesia and British Central Africa	18	8
Spain	4	8
Straits Settlements	16	0
Suakin	3	5
Sweden Switzerland Turkey in Europe	4	8
,, Asia	6	7
United States of America—New York City	9	6
,, New York (State), districts of Columbia and Pennsylvania	10	4
Illinois, Indiana, Ohio, Michigan, and Georgia	10	8
,, California and Washington (State)	12	1

Rates to other places will be given on application to the offices of the Eastern Telegraph Co. in Cairo, Alexandria, Suez, and Port Said.

TELEPHONES

Telephone systems have been established at Cairo, Alexandria, Port Said, Suez, and Helouan. In addition to these, trunk telephones are in operation between Cairo and Alexandria, and Tantah, Cairo, Alexandria.

Trunk Telephone Rates:	Pt.
Ordinary: every 3 minutes or fraction	5
Urgent: every 3 minutes or fraction	15

Public call offices have been established at the following places:

ALEXANDRIA.—Central Office, St. Mark's Buildings.
Bourse Khedivial.
El Moayad Newspaper Office.
Egyptian Bar.
Walker and Meimarachi, Ltd.

RAMLEH.—Central Office, Halt No. 2.
Casino San Stefano.

CAIRO.—Central Office, Opera Square.
Bourse Khedivial.
Sault's, confectioners.
Continental Hotel.
New Bar.
Obelisk Bar.
St. James's Bar.

HELOUAN.—Central Office.

ZEITOUN.—Central Office.

TANTAH.—Central Office.

CUSTOMS

☛ An 8 per cent. *ad valorem* duty is charged on all goods imported into the country, except in the case of coal, timber, cattle, fresh meat, &c., on which the charge is 4 per cent.

The duty on manufactured tobacco is pt. 25 per kilo from Turkey and pt. 27 from all other countries. Cigars are charged pt. 25 per kilo.

An export duty of 1 per cent. is charged on all products of Egypt and the Sudan.

A duty is charged on all antiquities exported, which is assessed by the Antiquities Department. Without a permit from the above Department no antiquities can be exported.

There are bonded warehouses at Alexandria, Port Said, Suez and Cairo, and consignments (except inflammables and bulk cargoes) can be sent to Cairo in bond and cleared there.

The personal effects of visitors to Egypt are not charged for unless new, except in the case of such articles as guns, bicycles, motor-cars, saddles, &c. &c.

People settling in Egypt for the first time are entitled to import their personal effects, furniture, &c., free of duty, provided these are not new.

INFORMATION FOR MOTORISTS

Importation of Cars

Great care should be exercised in packing cars for delivery to Egypt. To avoid breakage, all fittings, such as lamps, &c., should be separately packed. A rebate is given on cars which have been used previous to their importation into the country; this rebate varies in proportion to the length of time they have been in use.

Motor Licences

Any individual bringing a motor-car into Egypt must obtain a licence, together with enamel number, from the Governorat of Cairo or Alexandria, at a cost of pt. 53. It is essential for the owner to bring the car to the Governorat for inspection, or to supply the following details: Make and colour of car; horse-power; number of people the car will hold, including driver; name, residence. and nationality of owner.

Garages

The Auto-Cabs Co., Ltd., Boulac Street, Cairo

Telegrams: "Auto." Telephone No. 2042.

Garage charges

For storing and cleaning private cars, per month	pt. 250
Petrol, per case of 40 litres	,, 65

Chauffeurs cannot be engaged without car.

For hire of motor-cabs, four places including place beside the driver, the prices are:

For 1 hour or less, by day or night . .	pt. 30
Above 1 hour, every 15 minutes	,, 5
Every 15 minutes waiting	,, 5
For 10 hours by day or night within City circle . .	,, 200
,, ,, ,, outside ,, .	,, 300

These cars can also be hired by distance.

Grand Garage du Caire, Maarouf Street, Boulac, Cairo

Telegrams: "Grangara." Telephone No. 1573.

Motor-Car Tariff

Morning	pt. 150
Afternoon	,, 250
Whole night	,, 250
By time	Varying according to time hired
Chaufteur without car, per day	pt. 50
Petrol, per 4-gallon tin	,, 32

Electric and petrol cars hired and sold, and all repairs executed.

APPENDIX III

GARAGE EGYPTIEN GALLIA (EUGENE NAHMAN ET CIE)

Rue Young, Alexandria. Telephone No. 291 Alexandria.
Artin Bey Street (off Bab-el-Hadid Street, Cairo). Telephone No. 538 Cairo.
Telegrams : " Edison."

Electric motor-cars hired and sold.

Electric motor-cars stored, cleaned, charged and repaired, not including chauffeur, per month LE20.

Hire of electric *coupés* and landaulets, for about six months' engagement LE60 per month.

Charging of electric motor-cars, pt. 4 per kilowatt-hour.

INTRODUCTION OF FIREARMS AND AMMUNITION INTO EGYPT

Persons desiring to bring rifles, shot-guns, or firearms into Egypt can do so without a permit on condition that they are for their own private use, and are not new.

If the firearms are new, though private, application for permits must be made in writing to :

The Director of Artillery,
The Citadel, Cairo.

All arms will be subject to the usual Customs charges, *i.e.*, 8 per cent. on their value.

All persons desiring to import ammunition in considerable quantities for their own use must first obtain a permit from the Ministry of the Interior Cairo.

The permission necessary for the transport of this ammunition by railway is accorded by the Governor of the port.

The Egyptian railways do not carry ammunition by passenger trains, but passengers may take, in their private luggage, small quantities of safety cartridges free of charge.

QUAIL SHOOTING

A licence is required for shooting quail in Giza Mudiria. It is obtainable from Messrs. Cook and Son, the Turf Club, and the principal hotels, and must be renewed in February each year. Price, LE1.

The localities in which quail-shooting is authorised are specified on each licence.

ANTIQUITIES DEPARTMENT

The Department is under the superintendence of the Director-General of Antiquities, the Museum of Egyptology, Cairo. Chief Inspectors of Antiquities are stationed at :

Luxor	for Upper Egypt.
Assiout	for Middle Egypt.
Sakkara	for Ghizeh Moudirieh.
Mansourah	for Lower Egypt.

Tickets to visit antiquities are issued :	Price.
(1) For Sakkara (obtainable from the Museum in Cairo, from Messrs. T. Cook and Son, or from the Reis of Antiquities at Sakkara)	pt. 5
(2) To ascend or enter the Pyramids of Ghizeh (obtainable from Ghizeh Moudirieh and at the Pyramids) .	,, 10
(3) For the whole of Egypt (including Sakkara but not Ghizeh), obtainable from the Museum in Cairo, Messrs. T. Cook and Son, and the Inspector of Antiquities at Luxor .	,, 120

Application to excavate during the next winter should be made to the Director-General of Antiquities before June.

APPENDIX III

BANK AND GOVERNMENT HOLIDAYS

Accession of H.H. the Khedive	January 8
Qurban Bairam (five days)	January
Mulid-el-Nebi	April 25
Shem-el-Nassim	May 6
Birthday of H.H. the Khedive	July 12
Cutting of the Khalig	August
Ramadan Bairam (four days)	November
Holy Carpet	variable
Departure of the Mahmal	variable
Return of the Mahmal	variable

FULL MOONS, 1907–8

1907.—November 20, December 19.

1908.—January 18, February 17, March 18, April 16, May 16, June 14, July 13, August 12, September 10, October 9, November 8, December 7.

TABLE OF DISTANCES IN KILOMETRES BETWEEN CAIRO AND PRINCIPAL TOWNS BY RAIL AND RIVER

	From Kasr-el-Nil Bridge.	From Cairo Station.		From Kasr-el-Nil Bridge.	From Cairo Station.
Kasr-el-Nil	—	—	Sohag	497	477
Hawamdieh	17	28	Akhmim	505	-
Bedreshein	24	33	Guirgueh	538	502
Ayat	50	59	Baliana	555	518
Wasta	85	92	Farshout	590	545
Beni-Souef	120	124	Nag-Hamadi	600	553
Bibeh	140	146	Deshena	632	578
Maghagha	175	180	Kena	662	608
Minieh	245	247	Luxor	726	671
Abou-Kerkas	268	267	Armant	740	691
Roda	285	285	Esneh	784	728
Manfalout	354	347	Edfou	835	777
Assiout	396	375	Kom Ombo	902	836
Tahta	459	435	Assouan	945	884

APPENDIX IV

TIME-TABLES

EGYPTIAN STATE RAILWAYS

CAIRO—ALEXANDRIA

		A.M.	A.M.	NOON		P.M.	P.M.	P.M.	P.M.
				Luncheon-car Express.				Dining-car Express.	Sleeping-car, Cairo to Alexandria, until further notice
CAIRO	dep.	7.30	9.30	12. 0	—	4. 0	4.50	6.35	11.30
Choubra	,,	—	—	—	—	—	—	—	11.43
Calioub	,,	—	—	—	—	—	—	—	11.59
									A.M.
Kaha	,,	—	—	—			—	—	12.17
Toukh	,,	—	—	—	—	—	—	—	12.31
Sandanhour	,,	—	—	—	—	—	—	—	—
Benha	,,	8.15	10.15	12.42	—	4.45	—	7.20	12.55
Kouesna	,,	—	—	—	—	—	—	—	1.17
Birket-el-Sab	,,	—	—	—	—	5.13	—	—	1.36
Defrah	,,	—	—	—	—	—	—	—	1.54
TANTAH	arr.	8.55	10.55	1.18	P.M.	5.30	6. 3	8. 0	2. 5
TANTAH	dep.	8.59	10.59	1.22	2.15	5.34	6. 7	8. 4	2.13
Choubra-Namleh	,,	—	—	—	—	—	—	—	2·25
Kafr-el-Zayat	,,	9.17	11.17	—	2.33	5.52	—	8.22	2.45
Tewfikieh	,,	—	—	—	—	—	—	—	2.57
Teh-el-Baroud	,,	9.35	—	—	2.51	6.10	—	—	3.17
Saft-el-Melouk	,,	—		—	—	—	—	—	3.32
Denchal	,,		—	—	—	—	—	—	3.43
Damanhour	,,	10. 1	11.56	—	3.17	6.36	—	9. 1	4. 3
Sahali	,,	—		—	—	—	—	—	—
Abou-Hommous	,,	—		—	—	—	—	—	4.28
Dessounès	,,	—		—	—		—	—	4.40
Mâmal-Guezaz	,,	—		—	—		—	—	4.52
Kafr-el-Daouar	,,	—		—	3.52		—	—	5. 5
El-Beda	,,	—		—	—		—	—	5.17
Ezbet-Khourched	,,	—	—	—	—		—	—	5.28
Mâllaha	,,	—		—	—	—	—	—	—
		P.M.							
Sidi-Gaber	,,	10.51	12.46	2.57	4.16	7.26	7.41	9.51	5.45
Hadra	,,	—	—	—	—	—	—	—	5.53
ALEXANDRIA	arr.	11. 0	12.55	3. 5	4.25	7.35	7.50	10. 0	6. 0

The principal trains only are shown.
Times between 6 P.M. and 6 A.M. are indicated by a heavy line.

ALEXANDRIA—CAIRO

					Luncheon-car Express.			Dining-car Express.	Sleeping-car, Alexandria—Cairo until further notice.
		A.M.	A.M.	A.M.	NOON	P.M.	P.M.	P.M.	P.M.
ALEXANDRIA	dep.	7. 0	9. 0	10.30	12. 0	3.40	4.25	6. 0	11.30
Hadra	,,	—	—	—	—	—	—	—	11.40
Sidi-Gaber	,,	7.10	9.10	10.40	12.10	3.50	4.34	6.10	11.48
Mallaha		—	—	—	—	—	—	—	—
									A.M.
Ezbet-Khourched	,,	—	—	—	—	—	—	—	12. 3
El-Beda	..	—	—	—	—	—	—	—	12.14
Kafr-el-Daouar	,,	—	—	11. 2	—	4.11	—	—	12.28
Mâmal-Guezaz	,,	—	—	—	—	—	—	—	12.39
Dessounès	,,	—	—	—	—	—	—	—	12.51
Abou-Hommous	,,	—	—	—	—	—	—	—	1. 5
Sahali	,,	—	—	—	—	—	—	—	—
Damanhour	,,	7.58	9.58	11.40	—	4.44	—	6.58	1.32
Denchal	..	—	—	—	—	—	—	—	1.48
Saft-el-Melouk	,,	—	—	—	—	—	—	—	1.59
				P.M.					
Teh-el-Baroud	,,	8.22	—	12. 5	—	5. 8	—	—	2.17
Tewfikieh	..	—	—	—	—	—	—	—	2.34
Kafr-el-Zayat	,,	8.40	10.35	12.24	—	5.26	—	7.35	2.49
Choubra-Namleh	,,	9. 6	1—	—	—	—	—	—	3. 6
TANTAH	arr.	.5	0.51	12.40	1.43	5.42	6. 7	7.51	3.16
	dep.	.	0.55	—	1.47	5.46	6.11	7.55	3.24
Defrah	..	—	—		—	—	—	—	3.37
Birket-el-Sab		—	—		—	—	—	—	3.57
Kouesna		—	—		—	—	—	—	4.14
Benha	,,	9.44	11.39		2.26	6.29	—	8.39	4.42
Sandanhour		—	—		—	—	—	—	—
Toukh		—	—		—	—	—	—	5. 1
Kaha		—	—		—		—	—	5.14
Calioub		—	—		—		—	—	5.34
Choubra	,,	—	—		—	—	—	—	5.49
CAIRO	arr.	10.25	12.20		3. 5	7.10	7.25	9.20	6. 0

ISMAILIA—SUEZ DOCKS

			P.M.	P.M.
ISMAILIA		dep.	2.15	9.45
Néfiché		,,	2.25	9.55
Fayed		,,	3. 1	10.31
Génété		,,	3.26	10.56
SUEZ	Rue Colmar	arr.	4. 3	11.33
	,,	dep.	4.13	11.43
	Terre-plein	,,	4.19	11.49
	Docks	arr.	4.20	11.50

SUEZ DOCKS—ISMAILIA

			A.M.	P.M. Through Carriage to Cairo Saturdays.
SUEZ	Docks	dep.	7.30	5.40
	Terre-plein	,,	7.32	5.42
	Rue Colmar	arr.	7.37	5.47
		dep.	7.50	6. 0
Génété		,,	8.31	6.41
Fayed		,,	8.56	7. 6
Néfiché		,,	9.30	7.40
ISMAILIA		arr.	9.38	7.48

The principal trains only are shown.
Times between 6 P.M. and 6 A.M. are indicated by a heavy line.

CAIRO—PORT SAID, *via* BENHA

Station		A.M.	A.M.	A.M. (Luncheon-car, Cairo—Port Said. Through Carriage to Suez on Wednesdays.)	P.M.	P.M. (Dining-car, Cairo—Port Said.)
CAIRO	*dep.*	7. 0		11. 0		6.15
BENHA	*arr.*	7.41		11.41		6.56
	dep.	7.46	10.40	11.46	5.10	7. 1
Cheblanga	,,	—	10.53	—	5.24	—
Mit-Yazid	,,	—	11. 3	—	5.35	—
Minet-el-Gamh	,,	8.10	11.10	—	5.42	7.25
Godaiedah	,,	—	11.18	—	5.50	—
Zancaloun	,,	—	11.28	—	6. 1	—
ZAGAZIG	*arr.*	8.31	11.37	12.26	6.10	7.46
	dep.	8.35	11.42	12.31	6.18	7.52
Abou-Akhdar	,,	8.46	11.54	—	6.31	
Abou-Hammad	,,	8.58	12.10	—	6.47	
Tel-el-Kebir	,,	9.14	12.27	—	7. 7	
Kassassine	,,	9.30	12.46	—	7. 6	
Mahsamah	,,	9.40	12.58	—	7.28	8.55
Abou-Soueir	,,	9.52	1.12	—	7.[illegible]2	—
Néfiché	,,	10. 9	1.28	—	8. 8	—
ISMAILIA	*arr.*	10.16	1.35	1.59	8.15	9.26
	dep.	10.24		2. 9		9.36
El-Ferdan	,,	10.40		—		—
Ballah		10.53		—		—
Kantarah		11. 8		—		10.11
Le Cap	,,	11.21		—		
Tineh	,,	11.34		—		—
Ras-el-Eich	,,	11.47		—		—
PORT SAID	*arr.*	12. 5		3.30		11. 0

PORT SAID—CAIRO, *via* BENHA

Station		A.M.	A.M.	P.M. (Luncheon-car, Port Said—Cairo.)	P.M.	P.M. (Dining-car, Port Said—Cairo.)
PORT SAID	*dep.*		8.10	12.30		6.45
Ras-el-Eich	,,		8.29	—		—
Tineh	,,		8.42	—		—
Le Cap	..		8.55	—		—
Kantarah			9.11	—		
Ballah	,,		9.23	—		
El Ferdan	,,		9.36	—		—
ISMAILIA	*arr.*		9.51	1.51		8. 6
	dep.	6.20	9.59	2. 1	3. 0	8.17
Néfiché	,,	6.28	10. 7	—	3. 9	—
Abou-Soucir	,,	6.44	10.21	—	3.25	—
Mahsamah	,,	6.58	10.34	—	3.39	8.52
Kassassine	,,	7.10	10.45	—	3.51	—
Tel-el-Kebir	,,	7.31	11. 5		4.12	—
Abou-Hammad	,,	7.50	11.19	—	4.28	
Abou-Akhdar	,,	8. 4	11.31	—	4.43	
ZAGAZIG	*arr.*	8.15	11.41	3.28	4.54	9.50
	dep.	8.21	11.47	3.33	5. 0	9.55
Zancaloun	,,	8.31	—	—	5.10	
Godaiedah	,,	8.42	—		5.21	
Minet-Gamh	,,	8.51	12. 9		5.31	10.17
Mit-Yazid	,,	8.57	—		5.37	
Cheblanga	,,	9. 8	—		5.48	
BENHA	*arr.*	9.20	12.32	4.13	6. 0	10.40
	dep.		12.44	4.19		10.44
CAIRO	*arr.*		1.25	5. 0		11.25

The principal trains only are shown.
Times between 6 P.M. and 6 A.M. are indicated by a heavy line.

CAIRO—LUXOR

			A.M.	A.M.	A.M.	P.M.	P.M.	P.M.	P.M.	P.M.	P.M.
CAIRO . .	dep.		7. 0	8.30	9.30	2.30	5.15	*6.30	6.45	8. 0	9.30
Embabeh . .	,,		7.11	—	9.40	2.41	—	—	6.55	—	—
Boulac-Dacrour .	,,		7.22	—	9.51	2.52	—	—	7. 6	—	—
G[illegible]h . . .	,,		7.30	—	9.59	3. 1	—	—	7.14	—	—
Abou-el-Nomros .	,,		7.39	—	10. 8	3. 9	—	—	—	—	—
Tammouh . .	,,		7.47	—	10.16	3.16	—	—	—	—	—
Hawamdieh . .	,,		7.57	—	10.26	3.25	—	—	7.33	—	—
Bedreshein . .	,,		8. 6	—	10.35	3.34	—	—	7.41	—	—
Mazghouna . .	,,		8.24	—	10.53	3.51	—	—	7.58	—	—
Balideh . .	,,		8.35	—	11. 4	4. 1	—	—	—	—	—
Ayat . . .	,,		8.47	—	11.16	4.12	—	—	8.17	—	—
Matanieh . .	,,		8.57	—	11.25	4.21	—	—	8.25	—	—
Kafr-Ammar . .	,,		9.10	—	11.38	4.33	—	—	8.37	—	—
[illegible]h . .	,,		9.25	—	11.52	4.46	—	—	8.50	—	—
					P.M.						
WASTA . .	arr.	A.M.	9.36	9.51	12. 3	4.56	6.36	8. 0	9. 0	9.21	10.51
	dep.	6.40	10.18	9.59	12. 9	5. 1	6.43	8. 8		9.25	10.55
Beni-Hodeir . .	,,	6.55	10.33	—	12.24	5.15	—	—		—	—
Achemant . .	,,	7. 6	10.45	—	12.36	5.25	—	—		—	—
Bouche . . .	,,	7.17	10.57	—	12.48	5.36	—	—		—	—
Beni-Souef . .	,,	7.35	11.14	10.41	1. 7	5.52	7.25	8.53		10. 7	11.37
Tezment . .	,,	7.45	—	—	—	6.10	—	—		—	—
Tansa . .	,,	7.56	11.32	—	1.25	6.19	—	—		—	—
B[illegible]h . .	,,	8.17	11.48	—	1.44	6.34	7.59	—		—	—
			P.M.								
Fachen . .	,,	8.37	12. 9	—	2. 5	6.54	8.19	—		—	—
Fant . . .	,,	8.50	12.23	—	2.19	7. 8	—	—		—	—
											A.M.
Maghaghah . .	,,	9. 9	12.44	11.50	2.38	7.27	8.48	10. 1		11.16	12.46
[illegible]-Wak . .	,,	9.21	12.57	—	2.51	7.40	—	—		—	—
Moaddah . .	,,	9.30	1. 7	—	3. 1	7.50	—	—		—	—
Beni-Mazar . .	,,	9.38	1.16	—	3.11	8. 0	9. 8	—		—	—
f[illegible]y . .	,,	9.55	1.33	—	3.28	8.17	9.22	—		—	—
Kolossana . .	,,	10. 8	1.46	—	3.42	8.31	—	—		—	—
								sleeping-cars. First class only.		Wednesdays, and Saturdays, until November 29.]	

Station										Train de Luxe. Dining- and	Dining- and Sleeping-cars on Mondays,	
Sadut	,,		10.18	1.56		—	353	8.42	9.40	—	—	—
Etsa	,,		10.31	2.10		—	4. 7	8.56	—	—	—	—
El Borgayah	,,	A.M.	10.43	2.22		—	4.20	9. 8	—	—	—	—
MINIEH	arr.	—	165	2.34		P.M. 12.50	4.32	9.20	10. 5	*11. 1	M. 12.16	1.46
	dep.	5.30	11. 3	2.42		12.57	4.42			11. 9	12.24	1.53
Mis	,,	5.48	11.20	3. 1		—	5. 0			—	—	—
Abou-Kerkas	,,	6. 2	11.34	3.14		1.24	5.15			—	—	—
Eml.	,,	6.13	11.45	3.27		—	5.26			A.M.		
Rah		6.33	M. 12. 4	3.47		1.50	5.46			—	—	—
Mwi		6.47	12.16	3.59		2. 2	5.59			—	1.30	3. 1
Dair-Moes		7. 3	12.31	4.15		—	6.15			—	—	—
Deirout	,	7.20	12.48	1.32		2.31	6.33			1. 1	1.58	3.30
Nazali-Ganoub	,	7.39	1. 9	4.51		—	6.52			—	—	—
Beni-Korra	,	7.55	1.22	5. 4		—	7. 5			—	—	—
Manfalout	,,	8.13	1.53	5.22		3.12	7.23			—	—	4.12
Bei- Hin	,,	8.31	2.11	5.40		—	7.41			—	—	—
ASSIOUT	arr.	8.50	2.30	5.59		3.45	8. 0			2.13	3. 6	4.45
	dep.	8.56	235	6. 5		3.52				2.18	3.12	5.20
Ma	,,	9.14	2.53	6.23		—				—	—	5.37
Abou-Tig	,,	9.29	3. 8	6.38		4.20				—	—	5.51
Sedfa	,,	9.45	3.24	6.54		4.35				—	—	6. 6
Tima	,,	10. 1	3.40	7.10		4.51				3.10	4. 4	6.21
Mta	,,	10.17	3.50	7.20		—				—	—	6.31
Tahta	,,	10.33	4. 7	7.36		5.14				—	4.25	6.46
Mha	,,	10.51	25	7.54		—					—	7. 5
Chandaoui	,,	11. 4	4.42	8. 7		—				—	—	7.19
SOHAG	arr.	11.16	4.55	8.20	P.M.	5.51				4. 5	5. 1	7.32
	dep.	11.21			3. 0	5.59				4.11	5. 6	7.40
Hah	,,	11.31			3.12	—				—	—	7.52
Menchah	,,	11.44			3.27	—				—	—	8. 6
Assirat	,,	11.58			3.44	—				—	—	8.21

* This tain will run on ys, ys, and Saturdays, commencing December 2. Later on in the season it will run ly; the date will be notified at. A ss ar is provided for passengers' ts only.

N.—Times between 6 P.M. and 6 A.M. are indicated by a heavy line

CAIRO—LUXOR—*continued.*

		P.M.	P.M.	P.M.	A.M. (*Train de Luxe.* Dining- and Sleeping-cars. First class only.)	M. (Dining- and Sleeping cars, on Mondays, Wednesdays and Saturdays, until November 29.)	A.M.
Guergueh .	*dep.*	12.14	4. 1	6.45	*4.56	5.51	8.38
Bardis .	,,	12.26	4.14	—	—	—	8.52
Baliana . .	,,	12.37	4.27	7.14	5.16	6.11	9. 6
Abou-Choucha .	,,	12.51	4.39	—	—	—	9.22
A- diet . .	,,	1. 4	4.51	—	—	—	9.52
Jonction de Kharga	,,	—	4.58	7.41	—	6.37	10. 0
Frout . .	,,	1.20	5. 8	—	—	—	10.12
Nag-Hamadi . .	,,	1.30	5.22	8. 3	6. 1	6.58	10.27
Dabbeh . .	*arr.*		5.34	—	—	—	10.39
Faou . . .	*dep.*		5.50	—	—	—	10.56
Dech na . .	,,		6. 3	8.48	6.34	7.31	11.9
Samata . . .	,,		6.14	—	—	—	11.21
Aoulad-Amr . .	,,		6.25	—	—	—	11.33
Kneh . . .	,,		6.50	9.28	7.14	8.13	11.58
							P.M.
Kift . . .	,,		7.18	—		8.38	12.24
Kous . . .	,,		7.35	10. 5	—	8.52	12.41
Khizam . .	,,		7.57	—	—	9.12	1. 2
LUXOR . . .	*arr.*		8.15	10.40	8.35	9.30	1.20

* This train will run on Mondays, Wednesdays, and Saturdays (from Ciro), commencing Dcember 2. Later on in the season it will run ally; the date will be notified ler. A second-class ar is provided for passengers' sts only.

NOTE.—Times be wen 6 M. and 6 A.M. are i did by a aly line.

LUXOR—CAIRO

		A.M.				A.M.	A.M.	M.		P.M.	P.M.	P.M.
LUXOR	dep.	5.45						7. 0		3. 0	5.30	*6.30
Khizam	,,	6. 4						—		3.19	—	—
Kous	,,	6.27						7.36		3.41	6. 8	—
Kift	,,	6.41						—		3.55	6.21	—
Keneh	,,	7.10						8.14		4.23	6.48	7.47
Aoulad-Amr	,,	7.30						—		4.43	—	—
Samata	,,	7.41						—		4.54	—	—
Dechena	,,	7.54						8.52		5. 7	7.27	8.25
Faou	,,	8. 4						—		5.17	—	—
Dabbeh	,,	8.21						—	P.M.	5.35	—	—
Nag-Hamadi	,,	8.35						9.26	2.10	5.49	8. 2	8.59
Farchout	,,	8.48						—	2.22	6. 2	—	—
Jonction de Kharga	,,	8.58						9.44	—	6.12	8.21	—
Abou-Tichet	,,	9. 6						—	2.37	6.20	—	—
Abou-Choucha	,,	9.20						—	2.51	6.34	—	—
Baliana	,,	9.35						10.12	3. 5	6.49	8.47	9.41
Bardis	,,	9.46							3.16	7. 2	—	—
Guergueh	,,	10. 2						10.35	3.31	7.18	9.10	10.4
Assirat	,,	10.17						—	3.45	7.33	—	—
Menchah	,,	10.32						—	3.59	7.48	—	—
Balasfourah	,,	10.45						—	4.12	8. 2	—	—
SOHAG	ar.	10.55				A.M.	A.M.	11.16	4.21	8.12	9.51	10.45
	dep.					6.35	9.15	1123	4.26	8.21	9.57	10.51
Chandaouil	,,					6.50	9.29	—	4.40	8.34	—	—
Maragha	,,					7. 4	9.43	—	4.53	8.46	—	—
								M.				
Tahta	,,					7.23	10. 1	12. 1	5.15	9. 3	—	—
[illegible]ta	,,					7.39	10.16	—	5.30	9.17	—	—
Tema	,,					7.52	10.30	12.24	5.42	9.29	10.56	11.50
Sedfa	,,					8. 6	10.46	—	5.55	9.41	—	—
											Dining- and Sleeping-cars on Tuesdays, Thursdays, and Sundays until November 28.	*Train de Luxe.* Dining- and Sleeping-cars. First class only.

* This train will run on Tuesdays, Thursdays, and Sundays, commencing on D[illegible]er 1. Later on in the season it will run [illegible]; this will be notified [illegible]er. A [illegible]ss [illegible]ar is [illegible]d for passengers' servants only.

NOTE.—Times bet[illegible]en 6 [illegible]M. and 6 A.M. are i[illegible]d by a [illegible]y line.

LUXOR—CAIRO—(c inted)

			M.	A.M.	A.M.	A.M.	A.M.	P.M.	P.M.	P.M.		
Abou-Tig . . .	dep.					8.22	11. 3	—	6.10	9.56	—	—
Mîa . . .	,,					8.37	11.19	—	6.24	10. 9	—	—
Assiout . . .	arr.					8. 54	11.36	1.13	6.40	10.25	11.45	A.M. *12.39
	dep.				7. 0	8.59	11.46	1.19	6.45	10.50	11.52	12.44
Beni-H ssin . . .	,,				7.20	9._0	P.M. 12. 7	—	7. 5	—	—	—
Manfalout . . .	,,				7.39	9.40	12.28	—	7.25	11.25	—	—
Beni-Korra . . .	,,				7.54	9.56	12.45	—	7.41	—	—	—
Nazali-Ganoub . .	,,				8.7	10. 9	1. 7	—	7.53	—	—	—
Deirout . . .	,,				8.28	10.30	1.28	2.32	8.14	A.M. 12. 6	A.M. 1. 4	2. 0
Dair-Moës . . .	,,				8.43	10.45	1.43	—	8.28	—	—	—
Mallawi . . .	,,				9. 0	11. 2	2. 3	2.59	8.44	12.34	1.29	—
R dah . . .	,,				9.14	11.16	2.17	—	8.58	—	—	—
Etlidem . . .	,,				9.31	.47	2.34	—	9.15	—	—	—
Abou-Kerkas . . .	,,				9.43	11.58	2.46	—	9.26	—	—	—
Mansafis . . .	,,				9.57	P.M. 12.12	3. 0	—	9.39	—	—	—
M ɪᴇʜ . . .	arr.				10.13	12.28	3.16	3.58	9.55	1.31	2.28	3.34
	dep.		5. 0	6.25	10.23	2.20	4.20	4. 7		1.39	2.37	3.42
El Borgayah . . .	,,		5.13	—	10.37	2.34	4.34	—		—	—	—
Etsa . . .	,,		5.26	—	10.50	2.47	4.47	—		—	—	—
Samallout . . .	,,		5.40	—	11. 5	3. 2	5. 2	—		—	—	—
Kolossana . . .	,,		5.50	—	11.16	3.13	5.12	—		—	—	—
Matay . . .	,,		6. 5	—	11.31	3.28	5.27	—		—	—	—
Beni-Mazar . . .	,,		6.20	—	11.47	3.44	5.43	—		—	—	—
Mah . . .	,,		6.29	—	11.56	3.53	5.52	—		—	—	—
Aba-el-Wakf . . .	,,		6.39	—	P.M. 12. 6	4. 3	6. 2	—		—	—	—
Maghaghah . . .	,,		6.54	7.29	12.42	4.18	6.17	5.11		2.43	3.41	4.46
Fant . . .	,,		7.11	—	12.59	4.35	6.34	—		—	—	—
Fachen . . .	,,		7.27	7.57	1.15	4.51	6.52	—		—	—	—
Bibeh . . .	,,		8.31	8.16	1.40	5.11	7.11	—		—	—	—

Thursdays, and Sundays until November 28.

Sleeping-cars. First class only.

Tansa . . .	,,		8.44	—	1.55	5.26*	7.25	—		—	—	—
Tezment . . .	,,		8.53	—	—	—	7.35	—		—	—	—
Beni-Souef . . .	,,		9. 5	8.48	2.16	5.51	7.48	6.20		3.52	4.51	5.55
Bouche . . .	,,		9.17	—	2.30	6. 4	8. 1	—		—	—	—
Achemant . . .	,,		9.27	—	2.42	6.16	8.12	—		—	—	—
Beni-[illegible]ir . . .	,,		9.36	—	2.53	6.26	8.23	—		—	—	—
WASTA . . .	arr.	A.M.	9.48	9.26	3. 6	6.39	8.35	7.10		4.30	5.29	6.33
	dep.	6.55	9.57	930	3.12	7.28		7.14		4.34	5.34	6.38
Rekkah . . .	,,	7. 8	10.10	—	3.25	7.40		—		—	—	—
Kafr-Ammar . . .	,,	7.23	10.25	—	3.40	7.54		—		—	—	—
Matanieh . . .	,,	7.36	10.38	—	3.53	8. 7		—		—	—	—
[illegible]at . . .	,,	7.46	10.49	10. 0	4. 3	8.17		—		—	—	—
Balideh . . .	,,	7.58	11. 1	—	4.15	8.28		—		—	—	—
Mazghouna . . .	,,	8.12	11.15	—	4.29	8.42		—		—	—	—
Bedreshein . . .	,,	8.29	11.32	—	4.46	8.58		—		—	—	—
Hawamdieh . . .	,,	8.39	11.42	10.31	4.56	9. 8		—		—	—	—
Tammouh . . .	,,	8.47	11.51	—	5. 4	9.16		—		—	—	—
			P.M.									
A[illegible]u-e[illegible]nos . . .	,,	8.56	12. 0	—	5.12	9.24		—		—	—	—
Gizeh . . .	,,	9. 7	12.11	—	5.22	9.34		—		—	—	—
Boulac-Dacrour . . .	,,	9.15	12.20	—	5.30	9.41		—		—	—	—
Embabeh . . .	,,	9.26	12.31	—	5.41	9.51		—		—	—	—
CAIRO . . .	arr.	9.35	12.40	11. 5	5.50	10. 0		8.45		6. 5	7. 5	8. 0

Dining- and Sleeping-cars on Tuesdays,

Train de Luxe. Dining and

* This train will run on Tuesdays, Thursdays, and Sundays (from Luxor), commencing on D[illegible]er 1. [illegible] on in the season it will run daily; this will be notified [illegible]r. A second-class [illegible]r is provided for passengers' servants on y.

NOTE.—[illegible]es [illegible]en 6 P.M. and 6 A.M. are i[illegible]d by a heavy line.

LUXOR—ASSOUAN

						A.M.	A.M.	P.M.
LUXOR	*dep.*					6.20	10.30	2.4[illegible]
Armant	,,					7. 7	11. 7	3.3
Chagab						7.26	11.21	3.5
Maalla						7.39	—	4.
Matâna						8. 8	11.51	4.3
							P.M.	
Esneh						8.45	12.1[illegible]	5.14
Sabaieh						9.2[illegible]	12.4	[illegible]
Mahamid					A.M.	9.4	1.	
Edfou					6. 0	10.4	1.4	
Sirrag					6.34	11.1	2.1	
Silwa					7. 7	1.5	2.3	
						P.M.		
Kagoug					7.26	12.3[illegible]	2.50	
Kom Ombo					9.25	1.2	[illegible]	
Daraw					9.48	1.4		
Khattara					10.51	2.4		
Guezireh	,,				11.[illegible]	3.		
Junction	,,				11.	3.2	—	
ASSOUAN—Town	*arr.*				11.	3.3	5. 0	
		A.M.	A.M.	A.M.	P.M.			
	dep.	7. 0	9. 0	10.4[illegible]	2.1[illegible]	4. 0	5.10	
Junction	,,	7. 8	9. 8	10.5	2.1	4. 8	5.23	
SHALLAL	*arr.*	7.25	9.25	1.1	2.3	4.2	5.40	

Luncheon-car, Luxor—Shellal.

FAYOUM LINES

		A.M.	A.M.	P.M.	P.M.	
WASTA	*dep.*	6.55	10.20	3.25	7.20	5
El Rous	,,	7.13	10.38	3.42	7.38	M. 52
Siala	,,	7.29	10.54	3.56	7.54	1 6
Edwa	,,	7.40	11. 5	4. 5	8. 5	1 P. 15
FAYOUM	*arr.*	7.51	11.16	4.15	8.16	10.25
	dep.	8. 0	11.41		8.39	
			P.M.			
Senaro	,,	8.17	12.8		9. 5	
Abchaway	,,	8.32	12.35		9.30	
ABOUXAH	*arr.*	8.40	12.45		9.40	

		A.M.	A.M.	P.	P.M.	P.M.
FAYOUM	*dep.*	8.30	11.50	4.[illegible]	8.50	10.35
			P.M.			
Biahmo	,,	8.49	12. 9	4.40	9. 9	10.54
SENNOURES	*arr.*	9. 0	12.20	4.50	9.20	11. 5

Times between 6 P.M. and 6 A.M. are indicated by a heavy line.

ASSOUAN—LUXOR

				A.M.	A.M.	A.M.	NOON	P.M.	P.M.
SHALLAL	*dep.*			8. 0	9.40	10. 5	12. 0	2.50	6. 0
Junction	,,			8.18	—	10.25	12.18	3. 8	6.18
ASSOUAN—Town . .	*arr.*		A.M.	8.25	10. 3	10.32	12.25	3.15	6.25
	dep.		5.50		10.15		1.45		
Junction	,,		6.10		—		2. 5		
Guezireh			6.20		10.27		2 15		
Khattara			6.48		10.49		2.43		
Daraw			7.44		11.34		3.46		
Kom Ombo			8.10		11.49		4.10		
					P.M.				
Kagoug			8.55		12.25		4 55		
Silwa			9.16		12.41		5.16		
Sirrag		A.M.	9.47		1 5		5.47		
Edfou	,,	5.45	10.28		1 38		6.18		
Mahamid	,,	6.30	11.13		2.14				
Sabaïeh	,,	6.54	11.37		2.32				
			P.M.						
Esneh	,,	7.37	12.25		3. 4				
Matâna	,,	8. 6	12.51		3.24				
Maalla	,,	8.34	1.19		—				
Chagab	,,	8.47	1.32		3.54				
Armant.	,,	9. 8	1.53		4.11				
LUXOR	*arr.*	9.50	2.35		4.45				

ncheon-car, "Shalall—Luxor.

FAYOUM LINES

			A.M.	A.M.		P.M.
ABOUXAH . .	*dep.*		6.20	10. 0		3.40
Abchaway . .	,,		6.44	10.11		4. 4
Senaro . . .	,,		7.14	10.26		4.34
FAYOUM . .	*arr.*	A.M.	7.34	10.40	P.M.	4.54
	dep.	5.40	8.18	10.50	1.50	5.34
Edwa	,,	5.51	8.32	11. 7	2. 5	5.47
Siala	,,	6. 0	8.43	11.18	2.17	5.58
El Rous. .	,,	6.14	8.58	11.33	2.33	6.13
WASTA . . .	*arr.*	6.30	9.15	11.50	2.50	6.30

		A.M.	A.M.	P.M.	P.M.	P.M.
SENNOURES .	*dep.*	7. 0	9.30	1. 0	5. 0	9.40
Biahmo . .	,,	7.15	9.45	1.15	5.11	9.55
FAYOUM . .	*arr.*	7.30	10. 0	1.30	5.25	10.10

Times between 6 P.M. and 6 A.M. are indicated by a heavy line.

CAIRO—MANSOURAH, *via* ZAGAZIG

		A.M.	A.M.	A.M.	P.M.	P.M.	
CAIRO	*dep.*	5.45	7.45	11.25	2.40	5.40	
Calioub	,,	6.11	8.12	11.50	3. 5	6. 5	
Bilbeis	,,	7.28	9.19	1. 0	4.18	7.18	
ZAGAZIG	*arr.*	7.55	9.44	1.27	4.45	7.42	
	dep.		9.54	1.49	5. 0	7.55	
Abou-Kebir . .	,,		10.30	2.26	5.38	8.30	
MANSOURAH . .	*arr.*		11.50	3.45	7.10	9.55	

ABOU-KEBIR—SALHIEH

		A.M.	A.M.	P.M.	P.M.	P.M.	P.M.
ABOU-KEBIR . .	*dep.*	7.45	11.20	2.50	4.15	5.50	8.45
Facous . .	,,	8.11	11.46	3.15	4.40	6.15	9.28
SALHIEH . . .	*arr.*	8.55	12.30		5.20		10.20

TANTAH—MANSOURAH—DAMIETTA

		A.M.	A.M.	A.M.	P.M.	P.M.	P.M.
TANTAH .	*dep.*	5.30	9.15	11.15	2. 5	6.15	8.15
Mehallet-Roh . . .	,,	5.54	9.36	11.34	2.25	6.36	8.35
MANSOURAH . .	*arr.*	7. 4	10.45	12.34	3.25	7.40	9.35
	dep.	7.16		12.38		7.45	
Cherbine Junc.	,,	7.53		1.12		8.20	
Farascour . . .	,,	8.48		2. 0		9. 8	
DAMIETTA . .	*arr.*	9.15		2.30		9.35	

TANTAH—DAMANHOUR, *via* DESSOUK

		A.M.			A.M.	P.M.	P.M
TANTAH	*dep.*	5. 0			11.50	3.20	6.
Mehallet-Roh Junc. .	,,	5.20	A.M.		12.14	3.44	6.2
Kalline Junc. . .	,,	6.13	8.20	A.M.	1.11	4.42	7.2[illegible]
Dessouk	,,	6.46	8.54	11. 0	1.44	5.15	7.56
DAMANHOUR . .	*arr.*	7.20	9.30	11.35	2.20	5.50	8 30

CHERBINE—KALLINE

		A.M.	P.M.				
CHERBINE JUNC. .	*dep.*	9. 5	3.45				
KALLINE JUNC. . .	*arr.*	12.10	6.50				

Only the principal trains and stations are mentioned.

MANSOURAH—CAIRO, *via* ZAGAZIG

		A.M.	A.M.	A.M.	P.M.	P.M.
MANSOURAH . .	*dep.*		6. 0	9.30	1. 0	4.15
Abou-Kebir . . .	,,		7.32	11. 3	2.29	5.39
ZAGAZIG . . .	*arr.*		8. 4	11.32	3. 0	6.10
	dep.	6. 0	8.45	11.50	3.45	6.20
Bilbeis . . .	,,	6.31	9.16	12.21	4.16	6.47
Calioub . . .	,,	7.39	10.29	1.34	5.29	7.59
CAIRO . . .	*arr.*	8. 0	10.50	1.55	5.50	8.20

SALHIEH—ABOU-KEBIR

		A.M.	A.M.	P.M.	P.M.	P.M.	P.M.
SALHIEH . . .	*dep.*	5. 0	9. 5	12.50	4.45	5.40	7.30
Facous . . .	,,	6. 0	9.49	1.38	5.10	6.28	7.55
ABOU-KEBIR . .	*arr.*	6.32	10.10	2. 0		6.50	

DAMIETTA—MANSOURAH—TANTAH

		A.M.	A.M.	A.M.	P.M.	P.M.	P.M.
DAMIETTA . .	*dep.*		7.10		2. 5	4.10	
Farascour . . .	,,		7.46		2.40	4.46	
Cherbine Junc. . .	,,		8.29		3.22	5.29	
MANSOURAH . .	*arr.*		9. 1		3.53	6. 1	
	dep.	7.10	9. 6	11.55	3.58	6. 6	8. 5
Mehallet-Roh . .	,,	8.16	10.13	12.55	4.59	7.13	10.29
TANTAH . . .	*arr.*	8.35	10.30	1.12	5.15	7.30	11. 0

DAMANHOUR—TANTAH, *via* DESSOUK

		A.M.	A.M.	NOON	P.M.	P.M.	P M.
DAMANHOUR . .	*dep.*	8.10	10.15	12. 0	2.35	6.10	15
Dessouk . . .	,,	8.52	10.50	12.37	3.11	6.47	55
Kalline Junc. . .	,,	9.27		1.10	3.45	7.21	10:25
Mehallet-Roh Junc. .	,,	10.23		2. 1	4.41	8.16	
TANTAH . . .	*arr.*	10.43		2.20	5. 0	8.35	

KALLINE—CHERBINE

		A.M.	P.M.
KALLINE JUNC. .	*dep.*	9.35	1.45
CHERBINE JUNC. .	*arr.*	12.40	4.55

Only the principal trains and stations are mentioned.

TANTAH—ACHEMOUN LINE

TANTAH—ACHEMOUN

		A.M.	A.M.	P.M.	P.M.
TANTAH	*dep.*	5.45	11.30	2.40	6.30
Chebine-el-Kom . . .	,,	6.33	12.22	3.25	7.21
Menouf	,,	7. 6	12.59	3.57	7.55
ACHEMOUN . . .	*arr.*	7.50	1.45	4.40	8.40

ACHEMOUN—TANTAH

		A.M.	A.M.	P.M.	P.M.
ACHEMOUN . . .	*dep.*	6.15	8.30	3. 5	5. 0
Menouf	,,	7. 4	9.17	3.55	5.46
Chebine-el-Kom . . .	,,	7.37	9.52	4.30	6.20
TANTAH	*arr.*	8.20	10.35	5.15	7. 5

NOTE.—Only the principal stations are mentioned.

TANTAH—ZIFTEH

		A.M.	A.M.	A.M.	P.M.
TANTAH	*dep.*	5.15	9.15	11.50	6. 0
MEHALLET-ROH . . .	*arr.*	5.34	*9.36	*12.14	*6.23
	dep.	5.39	9.40	12.20	6.40
ZIFTEH	*arr.*	6.40	10.45	1.25	7.45

ZIFTEH—TANTAH

		A.M.	A.M.	P.M.	P.M.
ZIFTEH	*dep.*	6.55	11. 0	3.25	8. 0
MEHALLET-ROH . . .	*arr.*	*7.55	*12. 0	*4.30	9. 5
	dep.	8.16	12.55	4.41	9.10
TANTAH	*arr.*	8.35	1.12	5. 0	9.30

* Change trains at Melhallet-Roh Junction.

CAIRO—BARRAGE

		A.M.	A.M.	A.M.	P.M.	P.M.	P.M.	P.M.
CAIRO . . .	*dep.*	6.15	8.40	10.45	1.15	3.40	5.25	7.55
Calioub . . .	,,	6.38	8.58	11. 8	1.38	3.58	5.43	8.23
BARRAGE . . .	*arr.*	6.50	9.10	11.20	1.50	4.10	5.55	8.35

BARRAGE—CAIRO

		A.M.	A.M.	P.M.	P.M.	P.M.	P.M.	P M
BARRAGE. . .	*dep.*	7. 5	9.35	12. 5	2.50	4.40	6.20	[illegible]
Calioub . . .	,,	7.19	9.48	12.19	3. 3	4.54	6.34	[illegible]
CAIRO . . .	*arr.*	7.40	10. 5	12.40	3.20	5.15	6.55	10.[illegible]

Principal trains and stations only are mentioned.

CAIRO (PONT LIMOUN)—MATARIEH—MARG

Cairo, *dep.*				
5. 0 A.M.	9.30 A.M.	3. 0 P.M.	7.30 P.M.	Marg, *dep.*—Every half-hour from 5.40 A.M. until 11.10 P.M.; also at 12.40 and 2.10 A.M.
5.30 ,,	10. 0 ,,	3.30 ,,	†*7.45 ,,	Matarieh, *dep.* — Every half-hour from 5.49 A.M. till 11.19 P.M.; also at *7.34, *8.9, *8.39 A.M., *2.9, *5.9, *5.39, *7.39, *8.9, 11.45 P.M., and 12.49, 1.15, 2.19 A.M.
6. 0 ,,	10.30 ,,	4. 0 ,,	8. 0 ,,	
6.30 ,,	11. 0 ,,	4.30 ,,	8.30 ,,	
†*6.45 ,,	11.30 ,,	†*4.45 ,,	9. 0 ,,	
7. 0 ,,	12. 0 NOON	5. 0 ,,	9.30 ,,	
7.30 ,,	12.30 P.M.	†*5.15 ,,	10. 0 ,,	
†*7.45 ,,	1. 0 ,,	5.30 ,,	10.30 ,,	
8. 0 ,,	†*1.15 ,,	6. 0 ,,	†11. 0 ,,	
†*8.15 ,,	1.30 ,,	6.30 ,,	12. 0 MN.	
8.30 ,,	2. 0 ,,	7. 0 ,,	†12.45 A.M.	
9. 0 ,,	2.30 ,,	†*7.15 ,,	1.30 ,,	

* Express trains. † Matarieh only.

Time occupied by journey from—

Pont Limoun to Matarieh, 15 minutes by express.
21 minutes by slow train.

Pont Limoun to Marg, 29 minutes.

RUE COLMAR SUEZ DOCKS

Rue Colmar, *dep.*		
5.18 A.M.	11.18 A.M.	5.33 P.M.
5.48 ,,	11.48 ,,	6.18 ,,
6.18 ,,	12.48 P.M.	6.48 ,,
6.48 ,,	1.33 ,,	7.18 ,,
7.18 ,,	2. 3 ,,	7.48 ,,
8.18 ,,	2.33 ,,	8.18 ,,
8.48 ,,	3. 3 ,,	8.48 ,,
9.18 ,,	3.33 ,,	9.33 ,,
9.48 ,,	4.13 ,,	10.33 ,,
10.18 ,,	4.33 ,,	11.43 ,,
10.48 ,,	5. 3 ,,	

SUEZ DOCKS—RUE COLMAR

Docks, *dep.*		
5.30 A.M.	11. 0 A.M.	5.40 P.M.
6. 0 ,,	11.30 ,,	6. 0 ,,
6.30 ,,	12.15 P.M,	6.3 ,,
7. 0 ,,	1.15 ,,	7. ,,
7.30 ,,	1.45 ,,	7 3 ,,
8. 0 ,,	2.15 ,,	8. ,,
8.30 ,,	2.45 ,,	8.30 ,,
9. 0 ,,	3.15 ,,	9. ,,
9.30 ,,	3.45 ,,	10. ,,
10. 0 ,,	4.45 ,,	11. ,,
10.30 ,,	5.15 ,,	

Time occupied by journey, 6 minutes

EGYPTIAN STATE RAILWAYS

ALEXANDRIA—EDFINA

		*		*	*	*	*		*	*	*
			A.M					P.M			
Alexandria .	dep.	A.M.	7 30	A.M.	A.M.	P.M	P.M.	3.20	P.M.	P.M.	M.
Sidi-Gaber Junc.	,,	6 0	7.44	9.10	10.50	12.25	[illegible]. 0	3.34	4.10	6.10	50
Ramleh . .	,,	6 11	7.58	9.21	11. 1	12.36	2.11	3.48	4.21	6.21	1
Aboukir . .	,,	6.37	—	9.47	11.27	1. 2	2.37	4.24	4.47	6.47	[illegible].27
Edkou . .	,,		9. 6					5.20			
Rosetta . .	,,		9.48					6 0			
Edfina . . .	arr.		10.30					6.40			

Trains marked thus * start from the Alexandria-Ramleh Railway Co.'s station at Sidi-Gaber, not from the E.S.R. station.

EDFINA—ALEXANDRIA

			A.M.						P.M.		
Edfina	dep.		5.10						3. 0		
Rosetta	,,		6. 4						3.53		
Edkou	,,	A.M.	6.42	A.M.	A.M.	P.M.	P.M.	P.M.	4.33	P.M.	P.M.
Aboukir	,,	6.40	7.55	10. 0	11.35	1.10	2.45	55	—	7. 0	8.35
Ramleh	,,	7. 7	8.22	10.27	12. 2	1.37	3.12	4 22	5.44	7.27	9. 2
Sidi-Gaber Junc. .	,,	7.17	8.35	10.37	12.12	1.47	3.22	5.32	6. 2	7.37	9.12
Alexandria . .	arr.		8.45						3.15		

FAYOUM LIGHT RAILWAY CO.'S TIME-TABLES

FAYOUM—TAMIEH

		A.M.	P.M.
Fayoum .	dep.	10.40	3.40
Sennourés	..	—	5.20
Tamieh .	arr.	12.20	6.15

TAMIEH—FAYOUM

		A.M.	P.M.
Tamieh .	dep.	6.15	12.50
Sennourés	,,	7.15	—
Fayoum	arr.	8.40	2.30

FAYOUM—LAHUN

		A.M.	P.M.
Fayoum .	dep.	6. 5	2.40
Hawara .	,,	6.39	3.15
Lahun .	arr.	7.20	3.55

LAHUN—FAYOUM

		A.M.	P.M.
Lahun .	dep.	7.40	4.10
Hawara .	,,	8.24	4.51
Fayoum	arr.	8.55	5.20

FAYOUM—GHARAK

		A.M.	A.M.	P.M.
Fayoum .	dep.	6. 0	9. 0	3.45
Gharak .	arr.	8. 5	11. 5	5.45

GHARAK—FAYOUM

		A.M.	P.M.	P.M.
Gharak .	dep.	6. 0	1. 0	3.45
Fayoum .	arr.	8. 5	3. 5	5.45

FAYOUM—NAZLEH-WADI

		A.M.	P.M.
Fayoum . .	dep.	8.45	4. 0
Nazleh-Wadi	arr.	10.40	5.55

NAZLEH-WADI—FAYOUM

		A.M.	P.M
Nazleh-Wadi	dep.	6. 0	1.20
Fayoum .	arr.	7.55	3.15

Principal trains and stations only are mentioned

APPENDIX IV

EGYPTIAN DELTA LIGHT RAILWAY CO.

HELOUAN BRANCH

WINTER TIME-TABLE

STATIONS.		A.M.	A.M.	A.M.	A.M. Exp.	A.M.	A.M. Exp.	A.M. Exp.	A.M.	P.M. Exp.
CAIRO (Bab-el-Louk)	*dep.*	6.50	7.30	8. 0	9.15	9.30	10.15	11.15	11.30	12.15
Saida Zenab . .	,,	6.54	7.34	8. 4	—	9.34	—	—	11.34	—
Fin-el-Khalig .	,,	—	7.37	—	—	9.37	—	—	11.37	—
Saint Georges. .	,,	6.59	7.40	—	—	9.40	—	—	11.40	—
Sahel-el-Ebli .	,,	7. 4	7.45	—	—	9.45	—	—	11.45	—
Meadi . . .	,,	7.10	7.50	8.16	—	9.50	—	—	11.50	12.29
TOURAH . .	*arr.*	7.14	7.53	8.20	9.32	9.53	10.32	11.32	11.53	12.33
	dep.	7.17		8.22	9.34		10.34	11.34		12.34
Massarah . .	,,	7.27		8.32	—		10.44	—		—
HELOUAN . .	*arr.*	7.35		8.40	9.50		10.52	11.50		12.50

STATIONS.		P.M. Exp.	P.M.	P.M.	P.M. Exp.	P.M. Rpde.	P.M.	P.M. Exp.	P.M. Exp.	P.M.
CAIRO (Bab-el-Louk)	*dep.*	1.15	1.30	2.15	3.15	*3.30	3.35	4.15	5.15	5.30
Saida Zenab . .	,,	—	1.34	—	—	—	3.39	—	—	5.34
Fin-el-Khalig .	,,	—	1.37	—	—	—	3.42	—	—	5.37
Saint Georges. .	,,	—	1.40	2.22	—	—	3.45	—	—	5.40
Sahel-el-Ebli .	,,	—	1.45	—	—	—	3.50	—	—	5.45
Meadi . . .	,,	—	1.50	2.33	—	-	3.55	—	—	5.50
TOURAH . .	*arr.*	1.32	1.53	2.37	3.32	—	3.58	4.32	5.32	5.53
	dep.	1.34		2.38	3.34	—		4.34	5.34	
Massarah .	,,	1.44		2.48	—	—		4.44	—	
HELOUAN . .	*arr.*	1.50		2.56	3.50	4. 0		4.52	5.50	

STATIONS.		P.M. Exp.	P.M. Rpd.	P.M. Exp.	P.M.	P.M. Exp.	P.M. Exp.	P.M.	P.M.	A.M.
CAIRO (Bab-el-Louk)	*dep.*	6.20	6.45	7.30	7.35	8.30	9.40	10.40	11.40	1.30
Saida Zenab . .	,,	—	—	—	7.39	—	—	10.44	11.44	—
Fin-el-Khalig .		—	—	—	—	—	—	—	—	—
Saint Georges. .		—	—	—	7.44	—	—	10.49	11.49	1.38
Sahel-el-Ebli .		—	—	—	—	—	—	—	—	—
Meadi . . .	,,	—	—	—	7.53	—	—	10.59	11.59	—
									A.M.	
TOURAH . .	*arr.*	6.37	—	7.47	7.55	8.47	9.57	11. 3	12. 3	1.50
	dep.	6.39	—	7.49		8.49	9.58	11. 5	12. 4	1.51
Massarah .	,,	6.49	—	—		8.59	—	11.15	—	—
HELOUAN . .	*arr.*	6.57	7.15	8. 5		9.17	10.14	11.23	12.20	2. 7

* Sundays only.

APPENDIX IV

EGYPTIAN DELTA LIGHT RAILWAY CO.

HELOUAN BRANCH

Winter Time-table—(*continued*)

Stations.		A.M.	A.M.	A.M. Rpde.	A.M. Exp.	A.M.	A.M. Exp.	A.M. Exp.	A.M.
Helouan . . .	*dep.*	6. 0	7. 0	7.45	8. 0		9.10	10.10	
Massarah . . .	,,	6.10	—	—	8.10		—	10.20	
Tourah . . .	*arr.*	6.18	7.16	—	8.18	—	9.26	10.28	—
	dep.	6.20	7.18	—	8.20	8.40	9.28	10.30	10.40
Meadi . . .	,,	6.25	7.23	—		8.44	—	—	10.44
Sahel-el-Ebli . .	,,	—	7.29	—		8.49	—	—	10.49
Saint Georges . .	,,	—	7.34	—	—	8.54	—	—	10.54
Fin-el-Khalig . .	,,	—	—	—		8.57	—	—	10.57
Saida Zenab . .	,,	—	7.39	—	—	9. 0	—	—	11. 0
Cairo (Bab-el-Louk) .	*arr.*	6.39	7.42	8.15	8.37	9. 3	9.45	10.47	11. 3

Stations.		A.M. Exp.	P.M. Exp.	P.M.	P.M.	P.M. Exp.	P.M.	P.M. Exp.	P.M. Exp.	P.M.
Helouan . .	*dep.*	11.10	12.10		1.10	2.10		3.10	4.10	-
Massarah . .	,,	—	12.20		—	—		3.20	—	
Tourah . .	*arr.*	11.26	12.28	—	1.26	2.26	—	3.28	4.26	—
	dep.	11.28	12.30	12.40	1.28	2.28	2.40	3.30	4.28	4.40
Meadi . .	,,	—	—	12.44	1.33	—	2.44	—	—	4.44
Sahel-el-Ebli .	,,	—	—	12.49	—	—	2.49	—	—	4.49
Saint Georges .	,,	—	—	12.54	1.44	—	2.54	—	—	4.54
Fin-el-Khalig .	,,	—	—	12.57	—	—	2.57	—	—	4.57
Saida Zenab .		—	—	1. 0	1.49	—	3. 0	—	—	5. 0
Cairo (Bab-el-Louk)	*arr.*	11.45	12.47	1. 3	1.52	2.45	3. 3	3.47	4.45	5. 3

Stations.		P.M. Exp.	P.M. Rpde.	P.M. Exp.	P.M.	P.M. Exp.	P.M. Exp.	P.M.	P.M. Exp.	P.M.	A.M. Exp.
Helouan .	*dep.*	5.10	*6. 0	6.20		7.30	8.15		9.30	10.30	12.45
Massarah .	,,	5.20	—	—		7.40	—		—	10.40	—
Tourah .	*arr.*	5.28	—	6.36	—	7.48	8.31	—	9.46	10.48	1. 1
	dep.	5.30	—	6.38	6.45	7.50	8.33	8.40	9.48	10.50	1. 2
Meadi . .	,,	—	—	—	6.49	—	—	8.44	—	10.55	—
Sahel-el-Ebli .	,,	—	—	—	6.54	—	—	—	—	—	—
Saint Georges.	,,	—	—	-	6.59	—		8.53	—	11. 5	—
Fin-el-Khalig	,,	—	—	-	7. 2	—		—	—	—	—
Saida Zenab .	,,	—	—	—	7. 5	—	—	8.58	—	11.10	—
Cairo (Bab-el-Louk) .	*arr.*	5.47	6.30	6.55	7. 8	8. 7	8.50	9. 1	10. 5	11.13	1.19

* Sundays only.

APPENDIX IV

SUDAN GOVERNMENT RAILWAYS

WINTER TIME-TABLE

KHARTOUM—HALFA

		Express. Dining and Sleeping Cars.	Boat Express. Dining and Sleep'g Cars.
		P.M.	P.M.
KHARTOUM N.	*dep.*	9.15*b*	9.15*e*
Kadaru .	,,	—	—
Gubba .	,,	—	—
Wad Ramleh	,,	10.30	10.30
Gebel Gerri .	,,	—	—
		A.M.	A.M.
Wad Ben Naga	,,	12.45*c*	12.45*f*
Shendi .	,,	2. 0	2. 0
Taragma .	,,	—	—
Kabushia .	,,	—	—
Om Ali .	,,	—	—
Mutmir .	,,	3.50	3.50
Aliab .	.	—	—
Zeidab .	,,	4.55	4.55
El Damar .	,,	5.30	5.30
ATBARA .	*arr.*	5.50	5.50*x*
			P.M.
Port Sudan	,,	7.25*d*	8.15
Suakin .	,,	11. 0*d*	8.30
		P.M.	P.M.
ABOU HAMED	*dep.*	12.30*g*	12.30
		A.M.	
KAREIMA	*arr.*	11.45*d*	—
		P.M.	P.M.
HALFA . .	,,	10.15*g*	10.15

		Express. Dining and Sleeping Cars.	Boat Express. Dining and Sleep'g Cars.	Intermediate Express.
		P.M.	P.M.	P.M.
HALFA .	*dep.*	3. 0*b*	—	3. 0
		A.M.		
Kareima .	,,	10.35	—	A.M.
Abou Hamed	,,	1.50*c*		1.50
Suakin .	,,	9.35*b*	4. 0*h*	—
Port Sudan	,,	10. 0	8. 0	—
			A.M.	A.M.
Atbara .		9. 0*c*	11.30*i*	8.10
El Damar .	,,	9.25	11.55	—
			P.M.	
Zeidab .	,,	9.57	12.27	1st, 2nd, and 3rd class only.
Aliab .	,,	—	—	
Mutmir .	,,	11. 8	1.38	
Om Ali .	,,	—	—0	
Kabushia .	,,	—	—	
Taragma .	,,	P.M.	—	
Shendi .	,,	1. 5	3.35	
Wad Ben Naga	,,	2.10	4.4	
Gebel Gerri .	,,	—	—	
Wad Ramleh	,,	4.25	6.55	
Gubba .	,,	—	—	—
Kadaru .	,,	—	—	P.M.
KHARTOUM N.	*arr.*	5.30	8. 0	7. 5

b Sundays, Thursdays. *c* Mondays, Fridays. *d* Tuesdays, Saturdays. *e* Tuesdays. *f* Wednesdays. *g* Mondays, Wednesdays, Fridays. *h* Fridays. *i* Saturdays. *x* Through coach for Halfa to be detached.

APPENDIX IV

SUDAN GOVERNMENT RAILWAYS

SUAKIN—ATBARA—KHARTOUM NORTH—HALFA

	Boat Express.	Mixed.
	P.M.	P.M.
Suakin { Graham's Pt. *dep.*	4. 0*g*	9.35*d*
Suakin { Shata ,,	4.15	9.50
Handub . ,,	4.50	10.25
Sallom Junc. . ,,	6.10	11.20
Port Sudan . *arr.*	7.20	—
Port Sudan *dep.*	8. 0*a*	10.0
Asotriba . ,,	—	10.50
Sallom Junc. *arr.*	9.10	11.40
Sallom Junc. . *dep.*	9.20	11.55
		P.M.
Obo . .	—	1.20
Kamobsana ,,	11. 5	2.35
Erba	—	3.50
	A.M.	
Gebeit . ,,	1. 0*b*	5.10
Summit . . ,,	2. 0	6.25
Barameyu	—	7. 0
Erheib	—	7.35
Thamiam ,,	3.40	8.15
Einha	—	9. 0
Shideib .	—	9.45
Talgwareb ,,	5.30	10.20
		A.M.
Atbara Junc. *arr.*	11. 0	4.50*c*
	P.M.	P.M.
Khartoum N. . ,,	8. 0	5.30
Abu Hamed . ,,	—	12.15
		A.M.
Kareima . ,,	4.45	4.45*f*
		P.M.
Halfa .	—	10.15*c*

	Boat Express.	Mixed.
	P.M.	P.M.
Halfa . . *dep.*	—	3. 0*d*
	.	A.M.
Kareima . ,,	—	10.35*d*
Abu Hamed . ,,	—	1.50*e*
	P.M.	P.M.
Khartoum N. ,,	9.15*h*	9.15*d*
	A.M.	A.M.
Atbara Junc. ,,	7.15*i*	9.50*e*
	P.M.	P.M.
Talgwareb . ,,	1.28	7. 0
Shideib .	—	7.45
Einha . .	—	8.55
Thamiam . ,,	3.15	10.30
Erheib . .	—	11.40
		A.M.
Barameyu . ,,	—	12.45*f*
Summit. .	—	2. 0
Gebeit . . ,,	5.20	3.10
Erba . .	—	3.50
Kamobsana . ,,	—	4.45
Obo . . ,,	. .	5.25
Sallom Junc. *arr.*	7. 0	5.55
Sallom Junc. *dep.*	7.10	6.15
Asotriba . ,,	. .	6.55
Port Sudan *arr.*	8.15	7.25
Sallom Junc. *dep.*	7.10	9.40
Handub . ,,	7.50	10.20
Suakin { Shata ,,	8.25	10.55
Suakin { Graham's Pt. . *arr.*	8.30	11. 0

a Fridays. *b* Saturdays. *c* Sundays. *d* Thursdays, Sundays. *e* Fridays, Mondays. *f* Saturdays, Tuesdays. *g* Fridays, Saturdays, Mondays, Tuesdays. *h* Tuesdays. *i* Wednesdays.

APPENDIX IV

SUDAN GOVERNMENT RAILWAYS

ABU HAMED—ATBARA—KHARTOUM NORTH—PORT SUDAN

		Express	Mixed.
		P.M.	
HALFA .	*dep.*	3. 0*	-
Halfa Camp	,,	3.12*	
No. 6 Station	,,	9.40*	
		A.M.	
ABU HAMED .	*arr.*	1.35**b*	—
KAREIMA	*dep.*	10.35*a*	—
			P.M.
Abu Hamed	,,	1.50*	1. 0*d*
Dagash		-	2.10
Abu Dis		-	3.30
Shereik .	,,	3.12*	5.40
Abu Sillem	,,	5.25*	8. 0
Abidia .	,,	6.25*	9.40
Berber .	,,	7.10*	10.50
Damalli .	,,	7.40*	11.35
			A.M.
ATBARA JUNC.	*arr.*	8. 0*	12.20*f*
		P.M.	P.M.
Khartoum N. .	,,	5.30	7. 5*e*
		A.M.	
PORT SUDAN .	,,	7.25*c*	

		Express	Mixed.
		A.M.	A.M.
PORT SUDAN .	*dep.*	10. 0*a*	
		P M.	
Khartoum N.	,,	9.15	7. 0*g*
		A.M.	P.M.
Atbara Junc. .	,,	†6.15*b*	7. 0*f*
Damalli.	,,	†6.40	7.45
Berber .	,,	†7. 5	8.40
Abidia .	,,	†7.50	9.45
Abu Sillem	,,	†9.57	11.55
			A.M.
Shereik	,,	†10.5	1.40*h*
Abu Dis .	..	—	3.10
Dagash	,,		4.25
		P.M.	
ABU HAMED .	*arr.*	†12.15	5.25
		A.M.	
Kareima	,,	4.45*b*	
		P.M.	
ABU HAMED .	*dep.*	†12.30	
No. 6 station .	,,	† 5. 0	
Halfa Camp .	,,	†10. 3	
HALFA .	*arr.*	†10.15	

a Sundays, Thursdays. *b* Mondays, Fridays. *c* Tuesdays, Saturdays. *d* Mondays, Wednesdays, Fridays, Saturdays. *e* Daily from Atbara. *f* Tuesdays, Thursdays, Saturdays, Sundays. *g* Daily to Atbara. *h* Mondays, Wednesdays, Fridays, Sundays. * Intermediate Express—Tuesdays to Atbara Junction. † Intermediate Express—Wednesdays to Halfa.

LOCAL TRAINS—PORT SUDAN—SUAKIN

		Mixed.	Mixed.
		A.M.	P.M.
PORT SUDAN .	*dep.*	8. 0*a*	5.30*b*
Asotriba .	,,	8.45	6.15
Sallom Junc.	,,	9.40	7.10
Handub .	..	10.20	7.50
Shata . .	,,	10.55	8.25
GRAHAM'S PT. .	*arr.*	11. 0	8.30

a Saturdays, Sundays, Mondays, Tuesdays, Fridays.
b Wednesdays, Thursdays.

		Mixed.	Mixed.
		A.M.	P.M.
GRAHAM'S PT.	*dep.*	9.35*a*	3.35*b*
Shata	,,	9.50	3.50
Handub	,,	10.35	4.25
Sallom Junc.	,,	11.40	5.30
		P.M.	
Asotriba .	,,	12.15	6.15
PORT SUDAN .	*arr.*	12.45	6.40

a Sundays, Wednesdays, Thursdays.
b Fridays, Saturdays, Mondays, Tuesdays.

Passengers for boat express to change at Port Sudan.

APPENDIX IV

SUDAN GOVERNMENT RAILWAYS

KAREIMA—ATBARA—KHARTOUM NORTH—PORT SUDAN

		Mixed.			Mixed.
		A.M.			A.M.
KAREIMA	*dep.*	10.35*a*	PORT SUDAN	*dep.*	10. 0*a*
		P.M.			P.M.
Kassingar		12.15	Khartoum North	,,	9.15*a*
Amraho .	,,	1.35			A.M.
Abu Haraz	,,	3. 0	Atbara Junction	,,	6.15*b*
Abu Gharban	,,	4.15			P.M.
Dakfili .	,,	5.35	Halfa . .	,,	3. 0*a*
El Kab .	,,	6.40	Abu Hamed . .	,,	4. 5*b*
Keheili .	,,	8. 0	No. 10 Junction .	,,	5.20
Mehaiza .	,,	9.35	Mehaiza . .		6.25
No. 10 Junction	,,	10.40	Keheili . . .	,,	7.40
ABU HAMED .	*arr.*	11.45	El Kab . . .	,,	9. 0
Halfa . .	,,	10.15*b*	Dakfili . . .		10.20
		A.M.	Abu Gharban		11.40
Atbara Junction	,,	8. 0*b*			A.M.
		P.M.	Abu Haraz .		12.50*c*
Khartoum North	,,	5.39*b*	Amraho. . .	,,	2.15
		A.M.	Kassingar .	,,	3.45
PORT SUDAN .	,,	7.25*c*	KAREIMA . .	*arr.*	4.45

a Sundays, Thursdays. *b* Mondays, Fridays. *c* Tuesdays, Saturdays.

EGYPTIAN STATE RAILWAYS

RAILWAY FARES AND BAGGAGE RATES

	1st class.	2nd class.	Baggage per 10 kilograms.
	Pt.	Pt.	Milliemes.
Cairo to			
Abchaway	67½	34	25.0
Alexandria	87½	43½	32.16
Assiout	132½	66	46.37
Assouan	258½	129	57.09
Ayat	29	14½	11.16
Baliana	168	84	50.6
Barrage Single	6	4	5.2
Return	8½	5½	
Bedrechein	16½	8½	6.46
Benha	23	11½	8.98
Bilbeis	28½	14½	11.0
Damanhour	66½	33	24.57
Damietta	85½	43	31.52
Facous	52½	26½	19.67
Fayoum (Medinet)	59½	30	22.12
Ismailia	70	35	25.88
Kena	190½	95½	52.22
Luxor	206	103	53.33
Mansourah	63½	32	23.56
Minieh	99½	49½	36.48
Port Said	95	47½	34.97
Rosetta	105	52½	38.41
Salhieh	60½	30½	22.55
Shellal	261	130½	57.29
Sidi-Gaber	86	43	31.62
Suez (docks)	98	49	36.05
(town)	96½	48½	35.51
Tantah	41½	21	15·69
Tel-el-Kebir	50½	25	18.81
Zagazig	37	18½	14.07
Alexandria to			
Aboukir Single	5½	4½	5.02
Return	8½	7	
Assouan	307½	154	60.62
Cairo	87½	43½	32.16
Edfina	34	17	12.94
Luxor	255	127½	56.86
Rosetta	34½	17½	13.1
Tantah	56½	28	20.97

	1st class.	2nd class.	Baggage per 10 kilograms.
	Pt.	Pt.	Milliemes.
Port Said to			
Assouan	318	195	61.38
Cairo	95	47½	34.97
Ismailia	37½	19	14.24
Luxor	264½	132½	57.54
Suez (town)	75	37½	27.65
Suez (town) to			
Cairo	96½	48½	35.51
Ismailia	44½	22	16.67
Port Said	75	37	27.65
Fayoum (Medinet) to			
Abou Kerkas	89	44½	32.81
Abouxah	12	6	5.02
Abchaway	10	5	4.3
Assiout	118½	59½	42.93
Assouan	247½	124	56.12
Cairo	59½	30	22.12
Dair-Moës	100½	50½	36.88
Luxor	192½	96½	52.36
Sennourès	6	3	2.86
Shellál to			
Alexandria	310	155	60.82
Assouan	5	2½	2.86
Cairo	261	130½	57.29
Luxor	91½	45½	33.57
Port Said	320½	160	61.56
Suez	320½	160½	61.58
Assiout to			
Abou Kerkas	52	26	19.38
Assouan	164	82	50.29
Baliana	65	32½	24.14
Cairo	132½	66	46.37
Dair-Moës	35	17½	13.26
Fayoum (Medinet)	118½	59½	42.93
Kena	95	47½	34.97
Luxor	111½	56	40.84
Sohag	44	22	16.5

EGYPTIAN STATE RAILWAYS

RAILWAY FARES—(*continued*)

	1st class.	2nd class.	Baggage per 10 kilograms.		1st class.	2nd class.	Baggage per 10 kilograms.
	Pt.	Pt.	Milliemes.		Pt.	Pt.	Milliemes.
Baliana to				**Luxor to**			
Assiout	65	32½	24.14	Cairo	206	103	53.33
Assouan	128	64	45.45	Esneh	28½	14½	11.0
Cairo	168	84	50.6	Edfou	50½	25	18.81
Luxor	68½	34½	25.38	Fayoum (Medinet)	192½	96½	52.36
Kena	43½	22	16.34	Kena	30½	15	11.64
				Kom Ombo	73	36½	27.02
Kena to				Port Said	264½	132½	57.54
Assiout	95	47½	34.97	Shellal	91½	45½	33.57
Assouan	105½	52½	38.59				
Baliana	43½	22	16.34	**Assouan to**			
Cairo	190½	95½	52.22	Alexandria	307½	154	60.62
Luxor	30½	15	11.64	Cairo	258½	129	57.09
				Edfou	48½	24½	19.82
Luxor to				Esneh	68	34	25.25
Alexandria	255	127½	56.86	Kom Omoo	24½	12½	9.52
Assiout	111½	56	40.84	Luxor	87½	44	32.27
Assouan	87½	44	32.27	Port Said	318	195	61.38
Baliana	68½	34½	25.38	Shellal	6	3	2.86

Children.—Children under four years of age are carried free of charge. From four to ten years of age, at half rate. Only in the latter case are they entitled to a seat.

MATARIEH LINE FARES

Between any stations.

1st class, single	3 pt.	..	Return	4½ pt.
2nd ,,	2 ,,	..	,,	3 ,,

SLEEPING-CAR SUPPLEMENTS

From Cairo to Luxor	100 pt.	*vice versa*	100 pt.
,, ,, Sohag	90 ,,	,,	75 ,,
,, ,, Assiout	70 ,,	,,	70 ,,
,, ,, Alexandria	30 ,,	,,	30 ,,
,, Assiout to Luxor	35 ,,	,,	55 ,,

LUNCHEON- AND DINING-CAR TARIFF

Breakfast (with meat)	10 pt.
Luncheon	20 ,,
Dinner	25 ,,

RESERVED COMPARTMENTS

Applications for reserved compartments must be addressed to the departure station at least twenty-four hours in advance. Compartments thus applied for will be reserved, when circumstances permit, against payment of the price of five tickets for a first-class compartment, and six tickets for a second class compartment. These fares must be paid at the departure station.

SALOONS

Saloons can be attached to all trains provided they are disengaged. As long notice as possible should be given beforehand to the station-master of the departure station, or to the Traffic Manager E.S.R. Cairo, who will furnish all particulars.

SALOONS BETWEEN LUXOR AND ASSOUAN

Saloons, with or without sleeping-berths, may be hired between Luxor and Assouan by parties not exceeding six persons. The price is LE3 in addition to the ordinary first-class fares.

Application for these should be made to the General Superintendent at Luxor twenty-four hours in advance.

SPECIAL TRAINS

Applications for special trains must be addressed to the departure station at least five hours in advance. The letter must state the destination, number of passengers, class of carriages, number and description of animals to be transported, and approximate weight of the luggage.

The price of a special train is calculated upon the number of passengers, plus 20 per cent. of the ordinary fares. Animals and luggage are charged for at the ordinary coaching rates.

The minimum charge for the train is fixed at 200 milliemes per kilometre, with a minimum total charge of LE5 (five Egyptian pounds).

Demurrage rates will be charged in accordance with the tariff.

TRANSPORT OF BAGGAGE

Transport charges must be paid on all luggage excepting that taken in the compartments.

Luggage must not be placed in the corridors of the carriages.

Passengers may leave their luggage at the principal stations against receipt, at the rate of 5 milliemes per parcel, and per twenty-four hours or portion of twenty-four hours.

If the luggage is left at the arrival station, the transport receipt for same must be given up with the parcels.

Luggage may also be sent by goods train, at the same rates, and under the same conditions as those established for the transport of goods. For rates apply to "The Goods Manager," E.S.R., Cairo, and all station-masters.

CAB FARES

CAIRO

By distance.

	Pt.
If hired and discharged within the City circle, 4 kilometres (about 2½ miles) radius from Opera Square ;	
For 1 kilometre, or part	3
For each extra kilometre, or part	2
If hired within and discharged without, an additional 2 piastres must be paid for every kilometre or part of kilometre outside the circle.	
If hired by distance, for each wait of 15 minutes . .	2

By time.

If hired by time (driver to be notified).

	Pt.
For 1 hour or less, by day or night	8
Above 1 hour: every 15 minutes or less	2
For 12 hours, by day or night	60

Special fares.	Single. Pt.	Return after waiting		Pt.
Polo ground		1	hour	15
Ghezireh Hotel		1	,,	15
Grand Stand (race days)	15	3	,,	30
Ghizeh Zoological Gardens	10	2	,,	20
Pyramids	40	3	,,	60
Foom-el-Khalig	8	1	,,	15
Old Cairo	10	1	,,	18
Abbassieh Barracks	8	1	,,	15
Koobeh-les-Bains	12	1	,,	20
Heliopolis and Virgin's Tree	25	2	,,	40
Citadel	8	1	,,	15
Tombs of Khalifs	10	3	,,	30
Rod-el-Farag	8	2	,,	20
Shoobra Palace	10	½	,,	15

Extra payments.

Whether hired by distance or time:	Pt.
For each package carried outside	1
If more than 3 persons carried, each extra person	1

ALEXANDRIA

Town tariff.	One-horse Cab. Pt.	Two-horse Cab. Pt.
A drive not exceeding 10 minutes	2	3
,, ,, ,, 20 ,,	2½	4
,, ,, ,, 30 ,,	3	5

Beyond 30 minutes, 2 pt. for every quarter of an hour for a two-horse cab, and 1½ pt. for a one-horse cab.

Fractions of a quarter of an hour count as a quarter of an hour.

From 11 P.M. to 6 A.M. the above fares are increased by ½ pt. for a one-horse cab and 1 pt. for a two-horse cab, for every ½-hour or fraction.

Special tariff from the interior to the exterior of the town, and vice versa:

	One-horse	Two-horse
Drive to Hadra, No. 3 Palace, Lombroso, Ibrahimieh Casino	5	8
Going and returning, with half-hour waiting	8	12
Drive to Ibrahimieh, Sidi-Gaber, Wardian, Abattior	7	10
Going and returning, with one hour waiting	10	15
Drive to Bulkeley (Station), Antoniadis, Nouzha Gardens	8	12
Going and returning, with one hour waiting	14	20
Drive to Fleming, Souk, Bacos	10	14
Going and returning, with 1 hour waiting	15	22
Drive to San Stefano, Hotel Beau-Rivage, Ramleh (Government Railway), Hagar Nawatieh, Mex:		
Going only (San Stefano excluded)	14	18
Going only (to San Stefano)	12	16
Going and returning, with 1½ hour waiting	20	30

By night the above fares will be increased in the same way as for the town tariff.

APPENDIX IV

RAMLEH AND SIDI-GABER

The town tariff applies to Ramleh district when cabs are taken and dismissed within the perimeter of the said district, *i.e.*, between Abou-Nawatir, Hotel Beau-Rivage, Gabrial Station. The same for Ibrahimieh district included between Collines de Hadra, Ramleh Road, Cleopatra Baths and the sea.

	Pt.	Pt.
From Sidi-Gaber Station to Bacos, Souk, Rosetta Road and Greek Church (Zizinia)	6	8
Beyond that limit, *i.e.*, from Sidi-Gaber to San Stefano, Beau-Rivage, &c.	8	10

NILE FERRIES, CAIRO

Ghezireh Hotel.*
English Bridge and Ghezireh.
Kasr-el-Nil and Foom-el-Khalig.
Roda I. and Old Cairo.*
Ghezireh and Qatr-el-Nabi Wakr.
El Khabiri, Tura and Sheikh Etman.
Eshra and Quasr Bint-el-Barudi.
Bein-el-Qusura.

Fares: First class, 1 pt., on steam ferry. Ordinary fare, ½ pt.

CAIRO DONKEY FARES

	Pt.
For a short ride in town	2
For a short ride by the hour . . .	3
For a short ride by the day . . .	10 to 15
For a whole day outside town . . .	20

Besides the above fares the donkey-boy will expect a little *bakshish*, the amount of which will depend upon how long he has been engaged. A piastre or two will be sufficient.

PORT OF ALEXANDRIA

Tariff for Passenger-boat Hire

	Day Service. Pt.	Night Service. Pt.
For one or two passengers from the Landing-places or Quays to:		
Any ship in the Careening Basin or at the Arsenal Wharf .	2	3
Any ship in the Inner Harbour	3	4½
Any ship or place on shore in the Outer Harbour as far as Buheirah Beacon and end of Breakwater, or *vice versa* .	5	8
Any ship outside the Passes or Port Adjami, or *vice versa* .	10	15
By the hour with two men:		
For the first hour	8	10
For each additional hour	6	8
By the hour with four men:		
For the first hour	9	12
For each additional hour	6	8

Extra Charges

Each trunk or portmanteau	1	1
Each small package not carried in the hand . .	½	½

* Steam Ferry.

APPENDIX IV

STEAMSHIP INFORMATION

The dates of sailing and fares, given below, are as accurate as possible, but cannot be guaranteed.

PENINSULAR AND ORIENTAL

London—Brindisi—Port Said—Cairo

(1st class only.) Approximate times:
Leave London, Friday night.
,, Brindisi, Sunday night.
Arrive Port Said, Wednesday morning.
,, Cairo, Wednesday 1.25 P.M. or 5 P.M.

Leave Cairo, Sunday 6.15 P.M.
,, Port Said, Sunday night.
Arrive London, Friday evening.

London (Tilbury Docks)—Marseilles—Port Said

Leaving London on Friday.
Leaving Marseilles on the following Friday morning about 10 A.M.
Arriving Port Said on Tuesday.

Port Said—Marseilles—London (Tilbury Docks)

Leaving Port Said on Monday after the arrival of the midday train.
Arriving Marseilles on Saturday.
Arriving London on Sunday.

	1st class.	2nd class
	£	£
Fares: between London and Port Said .	19 ..	13
between Marseilles, Port Said, and *vice versa*	13 ..	9

Overland P. & O. Express to Marseilles with sleeping-car, and Marseilles to Port Said, 1st class only, £23 16*s.* 2*d.*

ORIENT LINE

Sailings every other Friday, commencing November 1, 1907, from London Marseilles, Naples and Port Said.

For return sailings apply to the Company's Agent at Port Said.

	1st class.	2nd class.
	£	£
Fares: between Port Said and Marseilles	13	9
,, ,, ,, ,, London . .	19 ..	12
,, ,, ,, ,, Naples	9	7

BIBBY LINE

Liverpool—London—Marseilles—Port Said

Steamers leave Liverpool every other Thursday, commencing November 1907.

	1st class.
	£
Fares: between Port Said and Marseilles . . .	12
,, ,, ,, ,, London . . .	17

For return sailings apply to the Company's Agent at Port Said.

APPENDIX IV

ANCHOR LINE

Sailing between Liverpool, London, Marseilles, and Port Said every 10 days

		£
Fares : between Port Said and Marseilles	. .	9
„ „ „ „ London	. .	14
„ „ „ „ Liverpool	. .	14

For return sailings apply to the Company's Agent at Suez.

MOSS LINE

Liverpool—Malta—Alexandria

Leaving Liverpool every other Saturday, commencing November 2, 1907.
Return sailings from Alexandria about every 14 days.
For particulars apply to the Company's Agent at Alexandria.

	1st class.	2nd class.
	£	£
Fares : between Alexandria and Malta	5	3
„ „ „ Liverpool .	14	9

NORDDEUTSCHER LLOYD

Marseilles—Naples—Alexandria Service

By the steamers *Schleswig* and *Hohenzollern*, leaving Marseilles every Wednesday at 3 P.M., and Naples the following Friday at noon, arriving at Alexandria on Monday.

Return.—Leave Alexandria every Wednesday at 3 P.M., and Naples the following Saturday night, arriving Marseilles on Monday.

Fares : Marseilles and Alexandria and *vice versa*, 1st class from £13 ; 2nd class from £9.

Naples and Alexandria and *vice versa*, 1st class £11 ; 2nd class £8.

Southampton—Naples—Port Said Service

Steamers leave Southampton, Nov. 3, 12, 26 ; Dec. 1, 10, 24, 29 ; Jan. 7, 21, 26 ; Feb. 4, 18, 23 ; March 3, 17, 22, 31.

Steamers leave Naples, Nov. 7, 11, 21 ; Dec. 5, 9, 19 ; Jan. 2, 6, 16, 30 ; Feb. 3, 13, 27 ; March 2, 12, 26, 30 ; April 9.

Arrive Port Said, Nov. 11, 15, 25 ; Dec. 9, 13, 23 ; Jan. 6, 10, 20 ; Feb. 3, 7, 17 ; March 2, 6, 16, 30 ; April 3, 13.

Return.—Leave Port Said, Nov. 5, 14, 28 ; Dec. 3, 12, 26, 31 ; Jan. 9, 23, 28 ; Feb. 6, 20, 25 ; March 5, 9, 24 ; April 2, 16, 21, 30.

Leaves Naples, Nov. 9, 18 ; Dec. 2, 7, 16, 30 ; Jan. 4, 13, 27 ; Feb. 1, 10, 24, 29 ; March 9, 23, 28 ; April 6, 20, 25 ; May 4.

Arrive Southampton, Nov. 18, 27 ; Dec. 11, 16 25 ; Jan. 8, 13, 22 ; Feb. 5, 10 19 ; March 4, 9, 18 ; April 1, 6, 15, 29 ; May 4, 13.

	1st class.	2nd class.
	£	£
Fares : Port Said and Southampton or London	19	13
„ „ „ Naples	11 ..	8

Special

Leave New York, Jan. 18, Feb. 29.
Leave Naples, Jan. 29, March 11.
Arrive Alexandria, Jan. 31, March 13.

Leave Alexandria, Feb. 1, March 14.
Arrive Naples, Feb. 3, March 16.
Calling at Genoa.

APPENDIX IV

AUSTRIAN LLOYD S. N. COMPANY

Weekly Accelerated Service

Trieste—Brindisi—Alexandria

From Trieste on Thursdays at 11 A.M. From Brindisi on Fridays. Arrive Alexandria on Mondays.

Alexandria—Brindisi—Trieste

From Alexandria on Saturdays, at 4 P.M. Arrive Brindisi on Tuesdays, at 5 A.M. Arrive Trieste on Wednesdays, at 11 A.M.

		1st class.			2nd class.		
		£	*s.*	*d.*	£	*s.*	*d.*
Fares:	Trieste and Alexandria	13	6	7	9	0	10
	Brindisi and Alexandria	11	4	10	7	15	3

MESSAGERIES MARITIMES

Weekly Service

Marseilles—Alexandria

Leaving Marseilles on Thursdays. Arriving Alexandria on Tuesdays.

Alexandria—Marseilles

Leaving Alexandria on Fridays. Arriving Marseilles on Wednesdays.

Fares: 1st class, £12 9*s.* 7*d.*; 2nd class, £9 10*s.* 2*d.*

Sailings between Marseilles and Port Said and *vice versa,* about six times per month.

NAVIGAZIONE ITALIANA

Alexandria—Messina—Naples—Leghorn—Genoa

Leaving Alexandria every Thursday.
Arriving at Messina on Sundays.
,, ,, Naples on Mondays.
,, ,, Leghorn on Tuesdays.
,, ,, Genoa on Wednesdays.
Returning from Genoa on Saturdays.
,, ,, Leghorn on Mondays.
,, ,, Naples on Wednesdays
,, ,, Messina on Thursdays.
Arriving at Alexandria on Sundays.

		1st class.			2nd class.		
		£	*s.*	*d.*	£	*s.*	*d.*
Fares:	From Alexandria to Messina	8	16	0	6	0	0
	,, ,, ,, Naples	9	4	0	6	4	10
	,, ,, Leghorn	10	16	10	7	7	3
	,, ,, Genoa	11	7	6	7	14	10

P. HENDERSON & CO'S LINE OF STEAMERS

Liverpool—London—Port Said

Steamer leaves Liverpool every other Thursday, commencing November 14 1907. Arriving at Port Said thirteen days later.

Fares: From Port Said to London or Liverpool and *vice versa,* £12.

For return sailings apply to the Company's Agent at Port Said.

APPENDIX IV

PAPAYANI LINE (ELLERMAN LINES)

Sailing between Liverpool and Port Said and *vice versa* about every ten days.
Fares: Liverpool and Port Said, 1st class, £14.

KHEDIVIAL MAIL LINE

Alexandria—Piræus—Constantinople

Leaving Alexandria on Wednesdays. Arriving at Piræus on Fridays. Arriving Constantinople on Sundays.

Return.—Leave Constantinople on Tuesdays, and Piræus on Thursdays. Arriving at Alexandria on Saturdays.

	1st class.			2nd class.		
	£	s.	d.	£	s.	d.
Fares: Alexandria and Piræus . .	5	2	7	3	6	9
,, ,, Constantinople	8	4	1	5	2	7

RUSSIAN LINE

Alexandria—Piræus—Constantinople

Leaving Alexandria on Tuesdays. Arriving Piræus on Thursdays, and Constantinople on Fridays.

Return.—Leaving Constantinople on Tuesdays, and Piræus on Wednesdays. Arriving Alexandria on Fridays.

	1st class.				2nd class.		
	£	s.	d.		£	s.	d.
Fares: Alexandria and Piræus . .	5	4	0	..	3	12	0
,, ,, Constantinople	8	0	0	..	5	12	0

NILE STEAMER SERVICE

Cairo to Luxor, the First Cataract and Back

Cook's steamers will leave Cairo for a twenty days' tour on Nov. 12, 26; Dec. 3, 10, 17, 24, 31, 1907; Jan. 4, 7, 11, 14, 21, 28; Feb. 4, 11, 18, 25; March 3, 10, 1908. And leave Assiout for a fourteen days' tour on Jan. 8, 15, 22, 25, 29; Feb. 5, 8, 12, 19, 22, 26, and March 4, 1908.

HAMBURG AND ANGLO-AMERICAN NILE COMPANY

Tourist steamers leave Cairo at 10 A.M. every Friday, commencing Nov. 29, 1907; arrive at Assiout at 4 P.M. the following Monday; leave Assiout at noon on Tuesday; arrive at Luxor at 7 P.M. on Thursday: leave Luxor at 5 A.M. on Monday; arrive at Assouan at noon on Tuesday.

Return.—Leave Assouan every Thursday at noon, commencing Dec. 12, 1907; arrive at Luxor at noon on Friday; leave Luxor at 5 A.M. on Saturday; arrive at Assiout at 11 A.M. on Monday; leave Assiout at noon on Monday; arrive at Cairo at noon on Wednesday, except in the case of the first trip, which finishes the return journey at Luxor. Passengers will return to Cairo by rail.

Bi-weekly Express Steamers, between Luxor and Assouan, leave Luxor on Sundays and Wednesdays, and Assouan on Tuesdays and Fridays.

EXPRESS NILE STEAMERS COMPANY

Steamers leave Cairo every Saturday, commencing Dec. 14, 1907; arrive at Assiout on Tuesdays; leave Assiout on Wednesdays; arrive at Luxor on Fridays.

Return.—Leave Luxor every Sunday, commencing Dec. 22, 1907; arrive at Assiout on Tuesdays; leave Assiout Wednesdays; arrive at Cairo on Fridays.

Fares from £20.

INDEX

NOTE.—References in black figures are to time-tables.

INDEX

INDEX

INDEX

PRINTED BY BALLANTYNE AND CO. LIMITED
TAVISTOCK STREET, LONDON

CPSIA information can be obtained at www.ICGtesting.com
Printed in the USA
BVOW06s1844260816

460308BV00011B/74/P

9 781330 032039